Advance Praise for
Hungry Ghosts

"Hungry ghosts, with their misery of insatiable desires, are ever lurking in the shadows of the Buddhist world and, perhaps, in our own shadows. With his deft translations of their stories—at once funny, disturbing, and insightful—and his reflections on a broad range of narratives and visual art, Andy Rotman invites us to explore the teachings of hungry ghosts, especially on the destructive power of meanness and the transformative possibilities of charity and kindness."
—William Edelglass, director of studies at Barre Center for Buddhist Studies and associate professor at Emerson College

"In this delightful study of hungry ghost stories and imagery, Andy Rotman illuminates Buddhist psychological insights and social commentary on 'meanness' in ways that resonate with our own time. His vivid translations spring this ancient wisdom into life."
—Maria Heim, professor of religion, Amherst College, and author of *Voice of the Buddha: Buddhaghosa on the Immeasurable Words*

"Andy Rotman's elegant translations of the *Divyāvadāna* established him as the foremost English translator of Buddhist narrative literature. Here he turns his attention to the ten tales of *pretas*, or hungry ghosts, in the *Avadānaśataka*. Rotman's deeply insightful commentary and lucid, precise translations open these stories to the modern reader, revealing a profound exploration of what it is to be mean-spirited and of the consequences of being mean. This beautiful volume is a masterpiece of translation and commentary, a gift that is literary, historical, and most importantly, ethical."
—Jay Garfield, Doris Silbert Professor in the Humanities, Smith College, and the Harvard Divinity School

"It is a particular delight for me to see that another book with Rotman's excellent translations is now available to all those interested in the Buddhist intellectual world. As always philologically accurate and enjoyable to read, this book brings to life the messages of the old narratives about pretas who, eaten away by meanness in their human life, now lead an existence of continuous pain and perpetual hunger. At the same time, Rotman provides a most insightful discussion of the development of the hungry ghosts in both literary and visual sources and their importance even for modern Buddhism. This volume is undoubtedly a must-read for students of Buddhist thought and art."
—Monika Zin, Saxon Academy of Sciences and Humanities, Leipzig University, author of *Representations of the Parinirvāṇa Story Cycle in Kucha*

Hungry Ghosts

Andy Rotman

Wisdom

Wisdom Publications, Inc.
199 Elm Street
Somerville MA 02144 USA
wisdomexperience.org

Library of Congress Cataloging-in-Publication Data
Names: Rotman, Andy, 1966– author.
Title: Hungry ghosts / Andy Rotman.
Description: First edition. | Somerville: Wisdom Publications, 2021. |
Includes bibliographical references and index.
Identifiers: LCCN 2020046399 (print) | LCCN 2020046400 (ebook) |
ISBN 9781614297215 (paperback) | ISBN 9781614297352 (ebook)
Subjects: LCSH: Pretas (Buddhism) | Hell—Buddhism. | Kar-ma-pa (Sect) |
Good and evil—Religious aspects—Buddhism. | Sarvāstivādins—China—Tibet.
Classification: LCC BQ4520 .R68 2021 (print) | LCC BQ4520 (ebook) |
DDC 294.3/422—dc23
LC record available at https://lccn.loc.gov/2020046399
LC ebook record available at https://lccn.loc.gov/2020046400

ISBN 978-1-61429-721-5 ebook ISBN 978-1-61429-735-2

25 24 23 22 21
5 4 3 2 1

Cover design by Jess Morphew. Interior design by Gopa & Ted 2.
Typeset by Kristin Goble.
Cover image: "Flaming-Mouth Ghost King." Photograph courtesy of Osaka City Museum of Fine Arts. See plate 4 caption for details.

Printed on acid-free paper that meets the guidelines for permanence and durability of the Production Guidelines for Book Longevity of the Council on Library Resources.

Printed in the United States of America.

FSC www.fsc.org MIX Paper from responsible sources FSC® C005010

Please visit fscus.org.

To Sandy Huntington (1949–2020),
teacher, friend, and profound inspiration

Contents

Preface

HUNGRY GHOSTS ARE fascinating figures. At one level they are incredibly transparent—living testimonials, in body and word, to the dangers of meanness. And yet at another level they're inscrutable, for they also function as a kind of repository for Buddhist fears and anxieties about how we as humans can be led astray, and these change according to time and place. You too, hungry ghosts seem to say, can be led away from the dharma and end up in "the hell of your own meanness," echoing Charlotte Brontë's *Jane Eyre*.[1] So how do we circumvent this terrible fate? And what fears and anxieties are Buddhists addressing?

Unfortunately there is very little scholarship on hungry ghosts, and many of the primary texts are unavailable in translation. That's why I was so excited when Naomi Appleton and Karen Muldoon-Hules approached me with an intriguing proposition. They wanted to create a joint translation of the *Avadānaśataka* ("One Hundred Stories"), an early collection of Indian Buddhist narratives, with different scholars translating the various decades. They wanted to know if I would translate the ten stories on hungry ghosts. I immediately said yes.

Although the *Avadānaśataka* was translated into French by the inimitable Léon Feer and published in 1891, a new translation has long been on many wish lists. Feer crafted his translation directly from manuscripts. Between 1902 and 1909, however, Jacob Samuel Speyer, another early doyen of Buddhist studies, created a critical edition with an extensive apparatus that called into question a number of Feer's readings. The intervening century has also given rise to numerous scholarly works like databases, dictionaries, editions, translations, and studies that make a new translation all the more glaring in its absence.

I began working on the present volume just as I was finishing up *Divine Stories: Divyāvadāna, Part 2* (Wisdom Publications, 2017). At that time, in between rounds of reviews, rewrites, and copyedits, I wanted to keep my mind in the world of early Indian Buddhist narratives and on the intricacies of translation. Working on the present project allowed me to do so. What I didn't anticipate was how complicated, compelling, and insightful these stories would be.

After working on the translations of these stories intermittently for two years, I wrote a brief introduction to the decade, which I presented at the International Association of Buddhist Studies conference in Toronto in 2017 on a panel of those of us who had agreed to translate the *Avadānaśataka*: Naomi Appleton, Karen Muldoon-Hules, David Fiordalis, and Justin Fifield. After much discussion, we agreed to publish our portions of the work separately, even though the hope still remains that one day a complete and fully collaborative translation of the text can be published. Inspired by the conference and my cotranslators, I decided that I would vastly expand my introduction, polish my translation, and publish the work independently.

Acknowledgments

The current volume benefited enormously from the advice of friends and colleagues. My first thanks go to the members of Five College Buddhist Studies Faculty Seminar, especially Jay Garfield, Peter Gregory, Yanlong Guo, Jamie Hubbard, Maria Heim, Susanne Mrozik, Ruth Ozeki, Ben Bogin, and Sandy Huntington. In fall 2017, they responded to an early version of the introduction, and their comments were invaluable as I expanded it.

Thanks to a sabbatical from Smith College, I was able to work on the introduction throughout 2018, both in India and the United States. I spent the spring writing the first half of the introduction at various locations in India. In Goa, I was fortunate to have Ira Schepetin as a conversation partner and to have a wonderfully supportive community that included Rebecca Andrist, Mohan Baba, Martin Brading, Renee Garland, Helen Noakes, Niels and Stina Legêne, Hélène Salvadori, and Sophia Schepetin. In and around Khandwa, Sumiran Caprihan, Shaista Dhanda, and Eva Joosten offered me friendship and refuge. And in Banaras, Rabindra Goswami once again let me stay in his home, work in my favorite chair, and listen to him make his sitar sing. Thanks, too, to my ever-helpful friends in the city: Abhishek Agrawal, Shubha Goswami, Arun Himatsingka, Ramu Pandit, Hari Paudyal, Divyansh Shukla, Sebastian Schwecke, Rakesh Singh, and Virendra Singh.

I returned to the United States for the summer, and there I wrote the second half of the introduction, with an eye toward a kind of comparative ethics. Much of the writing was done at Northampton Coffee, for I found it helpful to be in the public sphere of a coffeehouse, with its spirit of camaraderie and debate, to ponder various forms of meanness and faith, both good and bad. Many thanks to the coffee shop's staff and patrons, especially Ernie Alleva, Lane Hall-Witt, Kevin Rosario, Amina Steinfels, and James Wilson. Thanks as well to Jonathan Stevens and Cheryl Maffei at Hungry Ghost Bread for their stellar baking and spirit of service.

In the fall, thanks to a Khyentse Foundation fellowship, I went back to India as visiting faculty in the Pali and Buddhist Studies Department at Savitribai Phule Pune University. There I presented parts of the book in the classroom and in public lectures and received very helpful feedback. My thanks to the department's students, staff, and faculty, especially Shrikant Bahulkar, Lata Deokar, Mahesh Deokar, Pradeep Gokhale, and Talat Praveen. And a special thanks to Gayatri Chatterjee for good food, company, and conversation.

Later that fall, once again in the United States, I presented portions of the book at the University of Chicago, at a memorial symposium for the much-missed Steven Collins, and at Cornell University, at a seminar for the South Asia and Buddhist Studies programs. Thanks to Dan Arnold, Whitney Cox, Wendy Doniger, Charles Hallisey, Matthew Kapstein, and Christian Wedemeyer; Tarinee Awasthi, Anne Blackburn, Bronwen Bledsoe, Daniel Boucher, Arnika Fuhrmann, Daniel Gold, Liyu Hua, Larry McCrea, and Sujata Singh.

A special thanks goes to Steven Collins, who advised me as a graduate student and whose insights and generosity have continued to inspire me. His comments about the evolution of hungry ghosts in the Pali tradition helped me recognize the idiosyncratic nature of many depictions of hungry ghosts in Buddhist materials, and how the realm of hungry ghosts could function as a kind of workshop for Buddhists to think through issues of human depravity. Professor Collins had a unique ability to combine philological, philosophical, and sociological observations into something that was somehow much more than the sum of its parts. I am lucky to have learned from him and thankful for all that he shared.

That year also saw the passing of my grandmother, Ida Rose Rotman, just shy of her 105th birthday. Ida was gratitude embodied, and her love and care offered a wonderful example of charity and its virtues. She was a teacher of the highest order, and I count myself blessed to have spent so much time in her presence.

In putting together this book, I was also fortunate to receive additional help and guidance: Peter Skilling reviewed the manuscript; Sara McClintock helped me with some puzzling passages in Tibetan; William Edelglass, Mitch Goldman, Elizabeth Huntington, Andrew Marlowe, Anne Mocko, Madhulika Reddy, Teodosii Ruskov, and Kate Schechter helped me see the humanity in hungry ghosts; William Elison (aka Akbar) and Christian Novetzke (aka Anthony) offered me brotherhood; and Emma offered me feline charms, asleep on my lap.

In compiling the images for this book, I benefited from the help of numerous institutions and individuals. For providing the images included in this volume, I want to thank Museum für Asiatische Kunst in Berlin; State Museum of Ethnology in Munich; Henry Ginsburg Fund and Fragile Palm Leaves Foundation in Bangkok; Rokudōchin-nō-ji in Kyoto; Osaka City Museum of Fine Arts; Shin Chion-in in Shiga Prefecture; Otsu City Museum of History; and yokai.com. And for advising me on hungry ghost imagery, many thanks to Naresh Bajracharya, Philip Bloom, Eric Huntington, Jinah Kim, Simona Lazzerini, Todd Lewis, Adeana McNicholl, Matthew Meyer, Takashi Midori, Andrew Nguy, Marylin Rhie, Lilla Russell-Smith, Peter Skilling, Donald Stadtner, Daniel Stevenson, Trent Walker, and Monika Zin. And a special thanks to Takashi Midori, who played a crucial role in helping me gain access to images from Japanese museums and temples.

I also want to thank everyone at Wisdom Publications for their consummate care and professionalism. Thanks to Daniel Aitken, publisher extraordinaire, and to Josh Bartok, Gopa Campbell, Laura Cunningham, Kat Davis, Ben Gleason, Kristin Goble, Alexandra Makkonen, Faith McClure, Kestrel Montague, Brianna Quick, L. S. Summer, and Pema Tsewang. And a special thanks to David Kittelstrom for being such an extraordinary editor and such a good friend.

And lastly I want to thank Janna White for her love and support, wisdom and compassion.

Introduction

Mātsarya and the Malignancy of Meanness

HUNGRY GHOSTS MAKE frequent and poignant appearances in early Buddhist literature and later Buddhist art, and there are diverse and telling accounts of their psychology and appearance that offer insight into the inner workings of Buddhist morality as well as ongoing anxieties about meanness and the dangers it poses to individuals, families, and communities. And yet there are surprisingly few academic studies of hungry ghosts, even though the topic, like many a hungry ghost in Buddhist stories and paintings, is hiding in plain sight. As William LaFleur suggests, hungry ghosts have been

> something of an embarrassment to modern Buddhists, including persons of the West who like their Buddhism rational and empirical; although these ghosts pop up all over the tradition, such persons dismiss them as external to "real" Buddhism, things that the popular mind dragged in during weak moments when the Buddhist philosophers—with their usual vigilance for maintaining the rational—were dozing.[2]

Regardless of the reason for this oversight, hungry ghosts deserve better, as do scholars and students of Buddhism. In what follows, in an effort to bring hungry ghosts out of hiding, I focus on one of the earliest collections of stories about hungry ghosts, the *Avadānaśataka*, or *One Hundred Stories*.

The *Avadānaśataka* is an anthology of narratives that, in its present Sanskrit recension, was likely compiled by a Buddhist monk from the Mūlasarvāstivādin community in northwest India[3] between the second and fourth centuries CE.[4] And considering that a number of the stories in the anthology have nearly word-for-word counterparts in the monastic legal code of the Mūlasarvāstivādins,[5] these stories may very well have functioned as a kind of law,[6] offering prescriptions for behavior for both monastics and laity.[7]

The text is divided into ten sections of ten tales each, with each "decade" having a different orientation: (1) predictions of becoming a buddha, (2 & 4) the Buddha's previous lives,[8] (3) predictions of becoming a solitary buddha, (5) hungry ghosts, (6) rebirth in heaven, (7) men from the Śākya clan who became arhats, (8) women who became arhats, (9) persons of irreproachable conduct, (10) the consequences of evil deeds.

This volume contains a translation of the fifth decade of stories, all of which concern hungry ghosts—more literally, "the departed" (*preta*), a term with an important Brahmanical backstory.[9] These hungry ghosts, along with animals and hell beings, constitute the miserable inhabitants of "the three realms of existence that no one desires."[10] The stories in this decade are an especially important record of early Buddhist thinking about hungry ghosts, as well as about ethics, eschatology, and ancestors, all the more so considering the dearth of extant representations of hungry ghosts in early Buddhist art.

More specifically, these stories recount the bad thoughts and actions various hungry ghosts cultivated as humans that led them to their current existence with its karmically customized miseries. In this way, the text offers a pathology of pretahood, and fundamental to this pathology is the cultivation and malignancy of what in Sanskrit is called *mātsarya*. In my translations of these stories I render the term as "meanness," relying on two senses of the term: it is an unwillingness to give or share—what might be termed "miserliness," "avariciousness," or "stinginess"—along with being unfair, unkind, and spiteful.

The Mechanics and Misery of Mātsarya

The stories in this volume explain the logic of mātsarya's development, the actions it engenders, the suffering it induces, and the ways it can be eradicated. All this is of the utmost importance, according to the text, for the karmic consequence of cultivating mātsarya is rebirth as a hungry ghost, and the result of engaging in the nefarious activities that mātsarya inspires is a unique set of torments. And one of those torments is elsewhere a wondrous attainment: the memory of past lives, although in this case it appears to be only the memory of those mātsarya-inspired activities from one's previous human life that caused the present hellish predicament.[11]

Consider this description from the story called "A Pot of Shit":

> The venerable Maudgalyāyana saw a hungry ghost who looked like a burned-out tree stump, naked and totally covered with hair, with a mouth like the eye of a needle and a stomach like a mountain.[12] She was ablaze, alight, aflame, a single fiery mass, a perpetual cremation. Tormented by thirst, she was racked with sensations that were searing, piercing, distressing, agonizing, and acute, and she was crying out in pain. She was foul smelling—really foul smelling. She looked like shit, and she was feeding on feces. And even those, she only procured with difficulty.

As the text goes on to explain:

> She runs around suffering,
> piles of shit everywhere,
> [wailing] "I drink and eat only shit!"

The venerable Maudgalyāyana then approaches the Buddha, who explains to him the deed that the hungry ghost performed in a previous life that led her to this present fate:

> Long ago, Maudgalyāyana, in the city of Vārāṇasī, there was a solitary buddha who had compassion for the poor and neglected and who stayed in remote areas. Afflicted with an illness, he entered Vārāṇasī for alms, since a doctor had prescribed for him [a diet] of wholesome food. He approached the home of a merchant.
>
> The merchant saw him and asked, "Noble one, do you need anything?"
>
> "Homemade nutritious food," he said.
>
> Then the merchant instructed his daughter-in-law: "Give wholesome food to the noble one."
>
> In his daughter-in-law there arose a feeling of mātsarya. "If I give him food today, he'll just come back again tomorrow." She retreated indoors, filled a bowl with shit, then covered it with food and proceeded to give it to the solitary buddha.
>
> Now the knowledge and insight of disciples and solitary buddhas does not operate unless they focus their attention. So the solitary buddha accepted the bowl, and only after accepting it did he realize how much it smelled. "She must have filled it with excrement," he thought. Then that great being dumped out his bowl to one side and departed.

The goal of the hungry ghost stories in the *Avadānaśataka* is pithily summarized at the end of nearly every story: "Work hard to rid yourself of mātsarya!"[13] And for good reason. To cultivate mātsarya is tantamount to securing for oneself a future rebirth as a hungry ghost.

Other texts likewise bear out this claim. For example, in the *Divyāvadāna* (*Divine Stories*)—another compilation of Buddhist narratives closely associated with the Mūlasarvāstivādins—a young boy arrives at a monastery and, seeing a wheel of existence inscribed in the entrance hall, asks the learned monk in charge for an explanation. When the boy asks, "And what deed did these [hungry ghosts] do to experience such suffering?" the monk explains, "Friend, they possessed mātsarya, they were close-fisted, and they clung to their possessions. From practicing, developing, and cultivating various mātsarya-inspired deeds, they now experience as a result such sufferings as hunger and thirst."[14]

But what exactly is mātsarya? As with the above example from the *Divyāvadāna*, the *Avadānaśataka* likewise pairs a form of mātsarya with some partial synonyms to create a cliché—in Sanskrit, *matsariṇī kuṭukuñcikā āgṛhītapariṣkārāḥ*. The term *kuṭukuñcikā* is etymologically ambiguous,[15] yet its meaning is reasonably clear: "close-fistedness" or "lacking generosity." The term *āgṛhītapariṣkārā* is more telling: it is "the holding close" or "clutching" (*āgṛhīta*) of one's "possessions" (*pariṣkārā*). These are descriptions of hoarders, those who don't share or practice charity. Nevertheless, hoarding on its own is not enough to explain why someone would shit in a monk's bowl.

Some help in making sense of mātsarya comes from various Pali materials, which likewise recognize *macchariya* (i.e., the Pali equivalent of *mātsarya*) as a kind of "avarice, stinginess, selfishness, envy . . . the main cause of rebirth in the Petaloka [i.e., realm of hungry ghosts]."[16] The great commentator Buddhaghosa, in particular, offers an intriguing account of the deep psychology of *macchariya* in his famous compendium, the *Visuddhimagga* (*Path of Purification*): "it is meanness [or, miserliness, avariciousness, etc.]. Its characteristic is concealing one's own prosperity, whether already attained or yet to be attained. Its function is not enduring the condition of sharing of that prosperity with others. Its manifestation is contraction, or its manifestation is close-fistedness. Its proximate cause is one's own prosperity. It should be seen as a condition of mental deformity."[17] Nevertheless, the Pali materials don't account for the spiteful "acting out" that we find in the *Avadānaśataka*.

Helpful as well is one story in this decade that doesn't concern mātsarya. "Sons" is something of an outlier in that it concerns *īrṣyā*—"jealousy" or "envy." Yet *mātsarya* and *īrṣyā*, and their Pali equivalents *macchariya* and *issā*, are often paired together, and they appear consecutively in some lists of the various "bonds to existence" (*saṃyojana*).[18] Not surprisingly, immediately before Buddhaghosa defines *macchariya* in the *Visuddhimagga*, he defines *issā*: "it is envying. It has the characteristic of being jealous of another's prosperity. Its function is to be dissatisfied with that [prosperity]. Its manifestation is an aversion from that [prosperity]. Its proximate cause is another's prosperity. It should be regarded as a bond to existence."[19]

For Buddhaghosa, the most immediate cause of *macchariya* is one's own "prosperity" (*sampatti*)—a kind of "success," "happiness," or "good fortune"—and the most immediate cause of *issā* is another's prosperity. So perhaps giving what one has gained to another, or contemplating such a prospect, or no longer receiving something because it is being given to another, could lead from one state to the other. In the clutches of these mental states, one seems to view the world as a brutal battleground for prosperity, whereby one's own gain is another's loss and another's gain is one's own loss. In "Sons," for example, a first wife who appears to be barren has been joined if not supplanted by a second wife who is now pregnant with the husband's first child, and when the first wife sees the second wife (not her!) being honored and cherished, she is filled with *īrṣyā*.[20] The honor and love she alone had once received is now being bestowed upon another, and she views this as a threat.

According to Buddhaghosa, *macchariya* manifests in a kind of "contraction" or "shrinking" (*saṅkocana*), "close-fistedness" or "tightness" (*kaṭukañcukatā*), and *issā* as a kind of "aversion" or "turning away" (*vimukhabhāva*). Buddhaghosa also goes on in the *Atthasālinī* to define *kaṭukañcukatā,* one of the closest synonyms of *macchariya*, in a telling manner: "A close-fisted person is one who, upon seeing a beggar, with bitterness contracts and draws in his mind."[21]

In defining each of these terms, Buddhaghosa focuses on forms of contraction or even retraction, a kind of drawing back or drawing in. But the hungry ghost stories in the *Avadānaśataka* feature the exact opposite: characters reaching out, acting out, and lashing out. In "Sons," for example, the first wife is so consumed with jealousy—in the Buddha's diagnosis, "jealous by nature"[22]—that she gives the second wife a drug that causes her to miscarry and then swears that she never did so.[23]

In trying to connect Buddhaghosa's explanations of these terms with the behavior of the characters in the *Avadānaśataka*, the image that comes to my mind is that of a cat on the hunt: first she contracts her body in a crouch, retracting her limbs as if compressing a coiled spring, and then she pushes off and leaps on her prey, trying to deliver a lethal blow. Retraction leads to extension; what at first appears to be a kind of closing down or shutting down is only a precursor to violent action.

Also helpful here is the repeated enumeration in Pali canonical sources and their commentaries of the five kinds of *macchariya*. One can possess *macchariya* with regard to residence (*āvāsa*), families (*kula*), material gain (*lābha*), reputation (*vaṇṇa*), and Buddhist doctrine (*dhamma*).[24] Once again Buddhaghosa's commentaries prove helpful. In the *Aṅguttara-nikāya* (*Numerical Discourses*), the Buddha explains that a nun who possesses the five kinds of *macchariya* "is deposited in hell as if brought there."[25] In his commentary, Buddhaghosa offers this explanation:

1. She is mean (in the sense of miserly) with her residence and cannot endure others living there.
2. She is mean with the families that support her and cannot endure others approaching them for support.
3. She is mean with material gain and cannot endure others acquiring it.
4. She is mean with her virtues (*guṇa* as a gloss for *vaṇṇa*) and cannot endure talk about the virtues of others.

5. She is mean with the dhamma and does not wish to share it with others.[26]

As with the previous discussion of *macchariya* and *issa*, here too we find a concern with both self and other: the nun's sense of "prosperity"—the term isn't used here but it would fit well—is challenged by the prospect (or worse, actuality) of another's prosperity. The thought of someone living in her residence or gaining the support of families that support her, or of her sharing what she has acquired or listening to accounts of other's virtues is basically unbearable—she simply "can't endure it" (*na sahati*). This is something like miserliness mixed with jealousy, reminiscent of what sometimes overcomes small children when they are required to share their toys.

Although the *Avadānaśataka* never lists the five kinds of mātsarya, it does make mention of one of them, demonstrating what seems to be an awareness of the categories. In the story called "Jāmbāla," a young boy loves latrines and putting shit in his mouth.[27] The Buddha explains that this is his karmic penance, for when he was a monk in a past life, he had "extreme mātsarya with regard to residence."[28] When he saw monks visiting the monastery, "he would lose his temper and become irritated, hostile, exasperated, and outraged,"[29] and when he saw them leave, he would be delighted and insult them nonetheless. Notice here that possessing mātsarya to an extreme degree—or perhaps, being possessed by mātsarya, for the monk clearly has little control over himself—leads him to "lose his temper" and "take offense" (*abhiṣajyate*) and then on to overwhelming anger. Simply seeing monks come to the monastery where he stays is enough to infuriate him, and the text offers a string of near synonyms to emphasize the point.[30] Then, as a result of his mātsarya, the monk commits an act of harsh speech against an arhat, suggesting that he smear his body with shit.

There seems to be a close connection between cultivating mātsarya and committing a "misdeed of speech" (*vāgduścarita*), like the above "act of harsh speech" (*kharaṃ vākkarma*) or the tendency to "berate" (*pari* + √*bhāṣ*),[31] for mātsarya gives rise to scatological physical acts, vicious verbal barbs, or both. Notice that while eight of the stories in this collection end with an injunction to rid oneself of mātsarya, one is enjoined to rid oneself of mātsarya and misdeeds of speech in "Blind from Birth" and to rid oneself only of misdeeds of speech in "Sons."[32] Here the text seems to conflate cause and effect, pathogen and disease, for mātsarya tends to be virulent, metastasizing into toxic acts that have severe karmic repercussions. The monk in "Jāmbāla" apparently recognizes this karmic danger, for first he begs the aggrieved arhat for forgiveness and then on his deathbed makes a fervent aspiration to try to negate the effects of his caustic words. But to no avail.[33] As a result of committing that act of harsh speech toward an arhat, "he experienced endless suffering in saṃsāra"—a severe punishment indeed.

Considering the monk's foul-mouthed suggestion to the arhat, one might say that seeing other monks encroach on what he believes to be his turf makes him "lose his shit." It is not a stretch to say that this being—first as a neurotically possessive monk and then, thanks to karmic justice, as a shit-eating boy—is anal. One might say that the monk is anal retentive in that he is sufficiently obsessed with his own version of propriety that he "shits on" others who don't follow it. And in his incarnation as a coprophagic boy, he is anal in that he "eats shit," literally if not figuratively.

Yet perhaps most helpful for making sense of the *Avadānaśataka* is the category of "mātsarya with regard to material gains." In the story called "Sugar Mill," a solitary buddha contracts a fatal disease, and a doctor prescribes that he drink sugarcane juice as a cure. So he goes to a sugar mill, and upon seeing him, the owner asks:

> "Does the noble one need anything?"
>
> "Yes, householder—sugarcane juice," the solitary buddha said.

> The householder instructed one of his workmen: "Provide the noble one with sugarcane juice."
>
> Then one day the householder went away on a business trip.
>
> During that time, there arose in the workman [who dispensed the sugarcane juice] a feeling of mātsarya with regard to another's property [in this case, his boss's]. "If I give the noble one sugarcane juice," he thought, "he'll just come back again." Hell-bent on descending into the three realms of existence that no one desires [the realms of hell beings, animals, and hungry ghosts], spurning the two realms of existence to which everyone aspires [the realms of gods and humans], and having strayed far, far away from any noble dharma, he produced a sinful thought and said to the solitary buddha: "Hey monk! Give me your bowl. I'll give you some sugarcane juice."
>
> . . . That wicked and cruel-hearted man took the bowl, went off to a place hidden from view, filled it up with urine, topped it off with sugarcane juice, and then returned and presented it to the solitary buddha.
>
> The solitary buddha reflected [on what the man had done] and thought, "This poor man has committed a great sin." Then he dumped out his bowl to one side and departed.

Here mātsarya arises in the workman with regard to physical "property" (*dravya*)—close to a synonym for "material gains" (*lābha*)[34]—even though this property isn't his; it belongs to his boss. The worker exhibits a kind of "organizational identification."[35] He so identifies with the business where he works that he treats the business's property as his own, and he clings to it accordingly. The peculiarity here is that he chooses to reject his boss's instructions. It's as though, following Buddhaghosa's commentary, he just "can't endure" giving some "material gain" that is his to another person, even if it means infuriating his boss and risking punishment, in this life or the next.[36]

But the text also suggests that mātsarya has made the workman "hell-bent on" (*namra*)—more literally, "bowing to," "attached to," "devoted to," or "worshiping"—a descent into the three lower realms of existence, where beings suffer terribly. In other words, the workman isn't simply confused; he is actually "hell bent," figuratively and apparently literally. He has strayed far away from any "noble dharma" or "Buddhist teaching" (*āryadharma*),[37] and in doing so seems to have constructed his own hellish dharma such that he can be "wicked," "badly behaved," or "depraved" (*durācāra*) and nevertheless justify and rationalize his own deviant behavior. And so, to give the solitary buddha food would be a kind of travesty of *his* justice. According to his justice, mendicants are freeloaders and should not be rewarded; they should be punished.

Medieval and Modern Masters

In the *Abhidhammatthavibhāvinī* (*Exposition of the Topics of Abhidhamma*), a twelfth-century Pali commentary, the author Sumaṅgala offers a creative (yet telling and helpful) etymology for *macchariya*: it is "the state of one who is mean, or meanness occurs as the thought 'May others not (*mā*) possess this wonderful thing (*acchariya*); let it be mine alone.'"[38] This is close to the understanding of mātsarya in the *Avadānaśataka*. It is a clinging to one's own material possessions while also wishing others not to gain any material advantage.

It is something like this sense of the term that we encounter in a modern explanation by Mahāsi Sayadaw, a renowned twentieth-century Burmese monk, as well as a prolific author and one of the most esteemed and influential meditation teachers of the last century. Most telling is his discussion of *macchariya* with regard to *lābha*.

> "Stinginess with regard to gain" (*lābhamacchariya*) is to be jealous of another person's gain. It is also stinginess regarding gain to be unwilling to share one's belongings with worthy people, such as respectable fellow monks and so on. It may not be stinginess, however, if one is too fond of something to give it away; it could also be attachment. Note that the characteristic of stinginess is to be unable to bear that others possess or use one's belongings, whereas the characteristic of greed is to be attached to one's belongings without being able to give them away.[39]

Notice that he begins by explaining "stinginess" with "jealousy," demonstrating not just a close link between *macchariya* and *issā* but a slippage between one and the other. He also distinguishes between *macchariya* proper and other forms of defilement like "greed" or "attachment" (*lobha*), for "not every apparent instance of stinginess [*macchariya*] is necessarily a sign of the fetter [*saṃyojana*] of stinginess."[40] What differentiates *macchariya* is a kind of unbearableness. Sounding like Buddhaghosa, he notes that someone suffering from *macchariya* proper is simply "unable to bear" others making use of his things. Or, as he notes elsewhere, even the thought that others would use his things or that he would offer them his consent.[41]

Ashin Janakābhivamsa, another renowned twentieth-century Burmese monk and prolific author who was the longtime abbot of the Mahagandayon Monastery in Amarapura, likewise offers helpful commentary:

> Stinginess is the nature of *macchariya*. Nowadays, those who are not charitable, and those who are reluctant to give anything to anybody, are called people with *macchariya*. But actually, *macchariya* is not the lack of a will to give or be charitable—it is a wishing that others do not get any-

> thing. Not wanting to give is only the clinging to one's possession—it is *lobha* [or "attachment"]. *Macchariya* is the wish that others do not get anything, by way of material gains or attributes, regardless of whether or not the materials or attributes belong to one.[42]

The venerable Janakābhivamsa was renowned for his skill at explaining Abhidhamma to lay audiences, as evidenced by his numerous popular books, so there is a temptation to dismiss this as a lay or perhaps modernist understanding of *macchariya*. And perhaps it is. But in this case, his understanding of the term offers considerable insight into mātsarya in the *Avadānaśataka*. It designates less a reluctance to give—as in being stingy or miserly, frugal or parsimonious—than a fervent and unjust wish[43] that others don't get anything, regardless of whether it is one's own property being given. Such a mean-spirited person is mean not in the sense of being stingy but in the sense—to use an appropriate euphemism for someone destined to be reborn as a hungry ghost—of being an asshole.[44]

Consider this example from the story "Drinking Water," in which we read of a monk, tormented by thirst, who finally comes upon a well, and standing beside it is a young woman who has just filled a pot with water.

> "Sister," the monk said to her, "I'm tormented by thirst. Please offer me some water."
>
> In that young woman there arose a feeling of mātsarya. Since she clung to her possessions, she said to the monk, "Monk, if you were dying, I still wouldn't give you any water. My water pot wouldn't be full."

This doesn't appear to be miserliness, avariciousness, or stinginess, nor close-fistedness or hoarding, attachment or greed, a contraction or a shrinking, a reluctance to give away something of one's own or a kind of unbearableness. It is, instead, a kind of self-righteous sadism.

The Madness of Mātsarya

In the *Avadānaśataka,* the idea seems to be that mātsarya, especially if it is "practiced, developed, and cultivated,"[45] gives rise to various "faults" (*doṣa*),[46] which manifest in wrong action and wrong thinking, along with the mistaken conviction that these are, in fact, just.

One consequence of cultivating mātsarya is something akin to faulty wiring. While Buddhist narratives are full of examples of householders seeing the Buddha or monastics or holy sites and then cultivating faith in their hearts, which lead them to acts of charity,[47] we find just the opposite in the story called "Food."

> At that time in Vārāṇasī there was a householder's wife who possessed mātsarya, was miserly, and clung to her possessions; she couldn't even bring herself to offer something to a crow, let alone beggars in need. When she saw an ascetic, a brahman, someone destitute, or a mendicant, she hardened her heart.

Another consequence, and this might be the most insidious, is that it leads to faulty logic and perverse conclusions such that one embraces an "ignoble dharma"—an unjust vision of justice—and yet thinks it true. And what is more, such individuals project onto those they disdain versions of those qualities that they themselves are exhibiting. They shift the blame away from themselves, perhaps to appease their guilt, like the adulterer who accuses his spouse of infidelity or the corrupt politician who accuses his opponent of breaking the law.

In the story called "Uttara," a son gives all the money he earns to his mother with instructions that she should use the money to feed ascetics, brahmans, and the poor.

> But his mother was greedy, possessed mātsarya, was miserly, and clung to her possessions. She would hide her son's money, and when ascetics and brahmans would arrive at their home in search of alms, she would berate them: "It's as though you were born as hungry ghosts, always begging for alms at people's homes!" And she would deceive her son: "Today I offered food to lots of monks!" Eventually she died and was reborn as a hungry ghost.

And in the story called "Maudgalyāyana," five hundred former merchants recount a similar pathology:

> We possessed mātsarya, were miserly, and clung to our possessions. On our own, we never gave gifts or made offerings, and when others were giving gifts or making offerings, we would obstruct them. And we would berate all those truly worthy of offerings by calling them "hungry ghosts": "It's as though you were born as hungry ghosts, always begging for alms at people's homes!" And so, after we died, we were reborn as hungry ghosts like this.

In both cases laypeople think of mendicants who receive gifts as hungry ghosts with insatiable yearnings. But this, according to the text, is a misunderstanding of the workings of karma. Begging for alms doesn't lead one to become a hungry ghost, but obstructing that process just might. The mātsarya-filled mother and the mātsarya-filled merchants aren't preventing an injustice; they're causing one. And they're incensed at what they perceive as a perversion of propriety.

One explanation for why these mātsarya-filled beings see religious mendicants and the poor as hungry ghosts is that their "faults" (*doṣa*) have so twisted their thinking, logic, and proverbial wiring that they are now psychologically deficient. They see the world in a distorted fashion, not so much half full or half empty but as a place teeming with hungry ghosts. Such deviance has enormous implications, for in many early Buddhist texts, as Rupert Gethin notes, "cosmology is essentially a reflection of psychology and vice versa."[48] We are what we think, quite literally.

Gethin offers this explanation:

> When a human being experiences unpleasant mental states, such as aversion, hatred, or depression, then there is a sense in which that being can be said to be experiencing something of what it is like to exist in a hell realm—in other words, he makes a brief visit to the hell realms . . . But if those states of aversion, hatred, and depression become the habitual states of mind for that being, the danger is that he will end up visiting the hell realms for rather longer than he might have envisaged—in other words, when the wholesome conditions that placed him in the human realm are exhausted and he dies, he might find himself not just visiting hell but being reborn there.[49]

Perhaps then it isn't so far off to say that the characters in these stories who are filled with mātsarya are, in fact, making a "brief visit" to the realm of hungry ghosts. And the irony is that they see those who beg for food as hungry ghosts when the truth is that it is they themselves who are hungry ghosts—only in mind for now but, with their next rebirth, in body as well. Mentally, in fact, they seem worse off as humans with a hungry-ghost mentality than as hungry ghosts proper. The latter, as I mentioned above, have come to know the error of their previous mātsarya-inspired ways and now suffer the consequences. The former are deluded or, better yet, delusional.[50]

Charity as Cure

So what's the point here? First and foremost, don't cultivate mātsarya. It leads to rebirth in the realm of hungry ghosts, which is filled with exquisite torments and tortures. One way not to cultivate mātsarya, and even to abandon it, is to be charitable. Consider this explanation that the Buddha gives to the monastic community in "Morsel," which appears in the fourth decade of stories in the text:

> If, monks, beings were to know the result of charity and the consequence of offering charity as I know the result of charity and the consequence of offering charity, then they would never eat the very last remaining morsel of food without giving it away or sharing it, if a worthy recipient of that food were to be found. And the mātsarya-filled thoughts that arise would not seize hold of their minds. But those beings who do not know the result of charity and the consequence of offering charity as I know the result of charity and the consequence of offering charity eat with a mind that is miserly, without giving their food away or sharing it. And the mātsarya-filled thoughts that arise do seize hold of their minds.[51]

Charity in other words functions as a kind of prophylactic against the cultivation of mātsarya. Give gifts and make offerings, and this should prevent mātsarya from seizing control of one's mind and, one hopes, fend off rebirth as a hungry ghost.[52]

But charity also serves a second purpose: it can help lessen the torments of those who are already hungry ghosts, and the ranks of whom might very well include one's deceased family members.[53] And remember: hungry ghosts are in an especially painful situation. Besides undergoing daily and excruciating torments, they are basically powerless to perform good deeds, earn merit for themselves, and alter their destiny.[54] And what makes this situation all the more painful is that hungry ghosts, unlike their previous human selves, know what deeds are karmically beneficial; they are just powerless to perform them.

Hungry ghosts—in an ironic twist of fate for those who once viewed beggars with such disdain—must now rely on the kindness and largesse of others.[55] These good deeds come in two forms. In the first instance, the Buddha appears before various hungry ghosts, offering a vision of himself or a dharma teaching, so that those hungry ghosts can cultivate faith in their hearts toward him. This cultivation of faith is the direct cause of a better rebirth, even leading to an auspicious rebirth among the gods of Trāyastriṃśa (Thirty-Three), home to Śakra, the leader of the gods.[56] Elsewhere, however, the cultivation of faith merely leads hungry ghosts to being reborn as "hungry ghosts with great power" (*pretamaharddhika*), who are then able to earn merit,[57] although they may find it difficult to do so.[58] Not cultivating faith could lead a hungry ghost to an even worse fate: rebirth in the realms of hells, where suffering is even greater.[59]

In the other instance, humans can make offerings to the monastic community, which can then assign the merit earned from those offerings to particular hungry ghosts.[60] While ordinary humans in these stories can't directly "feed" hungry ghosts,[61] they can offer food and the like to monks and nuns, who can then "convert" these offerings into merit, rendering them into a form (karmic currency rather than comestible) that hungry ghosts can accept.[62] Hungry ghosts may be perpetually hungry and thirsty, but merit is what they need most.

In addition to individual offerings to the monastic community, the text also counsels making collective offerings, which can be initiated by a layperson or monastic "going the rounds of the town and inviting subscriptions from all citizens."[63] In "Maudgalyāyana," for example, the five hundred hungry ghosts who had previously been mātsarya-filled merchants offer this counsel:

> Bhadanta Mahāmaudgalyāyana, our relatives live in Rājagṛha. Explain to them the deed that led us to this fate. Then initiate a general collection of alms, feed the monastic community led by the Buddha, and have the reward from the offering assigned in our names. Maybe then we can be liberated from this existence as hungry ghosts.[64]

A "general collection of alms" (*chandakabhikṣaṇa*) refers to a diverse set of practices,[65] yet a singular explanation of them is offered in "Cloth," which appears in the sixth decade of stories in the text. An extremely poor woman is puzzled as to why the householder Anāthapiṇḍada, who is fabulously wealthy, has initiated such a collective offering. She wonders why he can't just pay for everything himself.[66] A Buddhist layman offers this explanation:

> It is for the benefit of others who [are poor and thus] are unable to feed the Blessed One and his community of disciples. He performs this act of kindness for their sake. However much is collected will be presented to the Blessed One.[67]

Although one gains great merit from feeding the Blessed One and the monastic community, not everyone has the means to do so. Buddhist materials are filled with accounts of wealthy individuals—including Anāthapiṇḍada himself[68]—inviting the Buddha and/or a group of monastics to their homes for a meal. But the poor, or even the middle class, would likely have found it difficult to feed a large group of monastics, lacking either the money to buy the food or the physical space to house them. Initiating a "general collection of alms" is an "act of kindness" (*anugraha*), for it allows individuals to contribute, however little, to a monastic meal or ritual offerings and reap the karmic benefits. Charity, however small, is still the best mechanism for improving one's lot in life; it allows one to accrue the only currency that one can take with one into the next life: merit.

Words to the Wise

But how does the text convince its audience to give? First, it presents the stories it contains as both proof texts and models for behavior. Those who visit the realm of hungry ghosts and question the inhabitants about the deeds they performed as humans that led them to their current, wretched existence are invariably instructed to ask the Buddha instead. Although the hungry ghosts in these stories know the terrible deeds they committed and their karmic consequences, the Buddha still knows more. "When the sun has already risen, there's no need of a lamp"[69] is the common refrain, for the Buddha's wisdom outshines a hungry ghost's wisdom, as the sun outshines a lamp. And in the blazing sun, who needs a flickering flame?

Visitors to the realm of hungry ghosts are then offered instructions such as these:

> Ask the Blessed One about the matter. He will explain to you the deed that led me to this fate. And when other beings hear his account, they will refrain from this sinful deed.[70]

Visitors then go and question the Buddha, and he responds with a detailed account of the sinful, mātsarya-inspired deed that led the hungry ghost to his or her present condition. More specifically, the Buddha recounts the "karmic bonds" or, better yet, "connective threads" (*karmaploti*) that tie together one's karmic history, such that his account functions as a case study and proof text for the ill effects of mātsarya and the mechanics of karma. To cultivate mātsarya is to damn your future self to hellish torments as a hungry ghost. The listener, to be sure, is meant to trust the Buddha, and hence these stories, and to act accordingly.[71]

The text also tries to convince its audience of its message by employing scare tactics: cultivate mātsarya at your own peril! The hungry ghosts in these stores are meant to be negative role models, much like their compatriots in the *Petavatthu* (*Ghost Stories*),[72] a Pali anthology of fifty-one stories told in verse.[73] There, however, many hungry ghosts experience both miseries and joys, demonstrating not just that bad deeds lead to bad results—like being racked with sensations that are "searing, piercing, distressing, agonizing, and acute"[74]—but that good deeds lead to good results.[75] It is an oft-repeated karmic truism that "the result of absolutely evil actions is absolutely evil, the result of absolutely pure actions is absolutely pure, and the result of mixed actions is mixed,"[76] but the hungry ghosts in the *Avadānaśataka* experience only misery. And their misery offers a warning: mātsarya can be all consuming, devouring even the possibility of future joy.

The role of hungry ghosts, following Jeffrey Shirkey, is—

> somewhat analogous to modern felons who participate in "scared straight" programs. In such programs, felons who have broken society's laws and who are now suffering the consequences of poor choices during their youth, preach passionately to adolescents who may be on the verge of making similarly poor choices themselves. The goal, as the name for the program indicates, is to scare those youths straight, to get them to conform to ideals and laws they seem intent on transgressing.[77]

Hungry ghost are like felons in that they have direct experience that "crime doesn't pay," and while some would-be offenders might believe they can escape punishment from the state, no one, we are told, escapes karmic punishment: "Actions never come to naught, even after hundreds of eons."[78]

While the ghost stories in the *Avadānaśataka* can certainly be read as ethical injunctions on charity, with trust and fear the major motivators for right action, a major critique in these stories is certainly psychological, as I have already mentioned. And that critique exposes a kind of paradox, for the fruits of charity can be both blessing and curse. Good deeds generate good karma, which as the text tells us, leads to surplus wealth (as opposed to mere subsistence), and yet surplus wealth can lead to the cultivation of mātsarya.[79] And this mātsarya can generate a variety of faults, most notably a deviant form of thinking that leads one to fashion a false dharma and lash out at those who are in violation of it. Monks who ask for charity are like hungry ghosts or freeloaders, or like thieves, for they want something that is not theirs. Begging, in this view, is like stealing.

Helpful, at least for me, for making sense of this wrong view is the writings of a preacher who was once posted in my hometown of Northampton, Massachusetts—Jonathan Edwards, the famous eighteenth-century Protestant theologian and reformer. He recognized a similar paradox.

> Edwards stood in a long line of Calvinists who lived with a paradox: virtue led to wealth, yet wealth corrupted . . . Edwards associated the spread of market-induced acquisitiveness with selfishness which destroyed all sense of community, "the cement of any society and its happiness" . . . A prosperous society was a godly society; a godly society was a cohesive society; and in a cohesive society individuals sacrificed private interest for the public good . . . [Edwards] grounded his exhortations on the primacy of the body social over private property; individuals were merely stewards of the common wealth . . . Any refusal to give charity . . . implied a perverse insistence on the property rights of an individual over the rights of God. "You have no absolute right to [your goods]," he told his people, "only a subordinate right." The one who kept his wealth for himself "is therein guilty of robbing his master and embezzling his substance."[80]

Edward's critique was directed at the wealthy, and one might expect to find the same critique in the *Avadānaśataka*, for the wealthy have a lot to cling to.[81] But in the *Avadānaśataka*, those who are shown cultivating mātsarya are not economic or social elites; they are mostly subordinates, by wealth, gender, or both: a daughter-in law, a workman, a young woman at a well, a merchant's wife. They are, like the petty monk in "Jāmbāla," simply "ordinary people."[82] But they, like those that Edwards pillories, exert "a perverse insistence on [certain] property rights." They don't think of themselves as merely stewards, nor do they recognize that their reluctance to share is a kind of robbing or embezzling.

The text seems to follow a distinction, common in Buddhist discourse, between "ordinary people" (*pṛthagjana*) and "noble ones" (*ārya*), with the former referring to the masses, who are unlearned and unrestrained in terms of Buddhist ideas and practices, and the latter referring to spiritual nobility—those who have insight into Buddhist teachings and have progressed on the Buddhist path. The text is especially concerned with the former, as they are the ones who are shown cultivating mātsarya and sowing the seeds for their future rebirth as hungry ghosts. Like the previously mentioned workman in "Sugar Mill," they have strayed far away from Buddhism's "noble dharma," either because they've never heard it or because of an abiding "perverse insistence" on a different dharma. In "Jāmbāla," for example, even a monk who is a "permanent monastic resident"[83] and who has surely heard the dharma is classified as an "ordinary person," challenging any easy distinction between "monastic" and "lay" as proxy for "spiritually adept" and "spiritually inept."[84] To be bound by mātsarya, no matter how lofty one's status or position, is to be entrenched as an "ordinary person." And an "ordinary person," as Buddhaghosa reminds us in the *Visuddhimagga*, "is like a madman."[85]

The Audience

One might expect, therefore, that "ordinary people"—especially those with an intense (and likely Brahmanical) aversion to the impurity of excrement[86]—would be the primary audience for these stories. Learned monastics would recount these tales directly to these wayward individuals, be they workers, women, or monks, warning them of the dangers of meanness and the benefits of charity. As I mentioned previously, these stories were likely intended for both monks and laypeople,[87] and this scenario would account for both constituencies. But I think it is likely that among laypeople, the primary audience wasn't "ordinary people" per se; it was merchants.

Merchants were one of early Buddhism's primary constituencies,[88] and the various encomiums in these stories to the wealth of merchants suggest that wealthy businessmen were a target audience here as well, either in actuality or in aspiration. The text refers to them with the term *śreṣṭhin*—which I translate as "merchant," although the term could mean "a banker or merchant or the foreman of a guild."[89] The common characteristic of a *śreṣṭhin* in these stories is that he possesses a large surplus of wealth. In four of these stories a *śreṣṭhin* is described as "rich, wealthy, and prosperous, with vast and extensive holdings, and who had amassed a wealth like the god Vaiśravaṇa. Truly, he rivaled Vaiśravaṇa in wealth."[90] The same formula occurs in twenty-five of the one hundred stories in the *Avadānaśataka*—more times than in the entire *Mūlasarvāstivāda-vinaya*—suggesting a certain preoccupation, or even obsession, with the ultra rich.[91]

Although *śreṣṭhin*, or one of its Prakrit variants, is the most common mercantile designation in Indian Buddhist inscriptions, testifying to their importance as formal donors to Buddhist establishments,[92] the merchants in these stories make no donations to shrines or monasteries, either formal or informal. What offerings they do make are more mundane and domestic—the promise of wholesome food or some sugarcane juice, as in "A Pot of Shit" and "Sugar Mill," which I've already discussed—suggesting the quotidian practices of being a compassionate human being. These everyday acts of charity are not generally commemorated in monastic inscriptions, but they are frequently celebrated in Buddhist narratives. The latter are instructional tales, and like the stories in this collection, many of them are concerned with cultivating good intentions and inspiring acts of goodness,[93] and with fostering community and loyalty.[94]

But the hungry ghost stories in the *Avadānaśataka* also sound a cautionary note. The generally good intentions and trusting nature of merchants—with a few exceptions[95]—are contrasted with the bad intentions and spiteful deeds of those who are their subordinates. In "A Pot of Shit," a merchant offers wholesome food to a solitary buddha and instructs his daughter-in-law to do the same, but she, overcome with mātsarya and unbeknownst to him, offers shit instead. Likewise in "Sugar Mill," a merchant offers sugarcane juice to a solitary buddha and instructs his workman to do the same, but he too is overcome with mātsarya and surreptitiously offers urine. And in "Uttara," a merchant gives all his money to his mother and asks her to make offerings to religious mendicants and the needy, but in the grip of mātsarya she hides the money, berates those who ask for alms, and lies to her son, claiming she has fulfilled his request. These merchants, it seems, have misplaced their trust.

Men of the house, apparently, should be wary of their dependents. In addition to the above stories that feature a merchant betrayed, respectively, by his daughter-in-law, his workman, and his mother, other stories recount the malfeasance of a merchant's daughter (in "Blind from Birth"), a merchant's first wife (in "Sons"), and a householder's wife (in "Food"). And then there is the unaccompanied young woman who taunts a young monk dying of thirst (in "Drinking Water"). Many characters in the *Avadānaśataka* are "trustworthy" or "devout" (*śrāddha*)—a description that occurs in twenty-five of the stories in the *Avadānaśataka*, usually of a householder or a king—but not so a merchant's family and workers. And women appear to be especially suspect.[96] Beware, the text seems to say, of "ordinary people" who are, as they say, "hiding in plain sight" and "close to home." Their meanness can wreak havoc.[97]

Another audience for these stories was surely monastics, especially those in need of a reminder about the dangers of mātsarya-fueled acquisitiveness and spite. In "Jāmbāla," as already mentioned, a monk who is an "ordinary person" with "extreme mātsarya with regard to residence" thinks a visiting arhat is encroaching on *his* space, so he verbally abuses him and as a result experiences "endless suffering in saṃsāra." And in "Blind from Birth," a merchant's daughter goes forth as a nun and resides in a nunnery that her relatives have constructed on her behalf. But she is careless with respect to moral conduct, and the other nuns expel her. In mātsarya-fueled retribution, she suspends the general collection of alms that provided them with food and denounces her coreligionists. If she can't live in *her* monastery, she seems to indicate, then the nuns can go ahead and starve. And when she encounters virtuous monks, she shuts her eyes, making herself blind to those who are just and to justice itself. The "noble dharma" doesn't disappear, however, just because one wills oneself not to see it.

And finally, in "The Merchant," a *śreṣṭhin* who possesses the legendary luxuries of the god Vaiśravaṇa goes forth as a monk and gains renown as well as a hoard of monastic provisions. He comes to treat the latter as his personal property, suffering from the delusion that these goods are somehow inalienably his own. He too exhibits "a perverse insistence on [certain] property rights," to quote Edwards again, which is all the more egregious considering that as a monk he has formally abdicated such claims. Buddhist monks vow to be temporary custodians of monastic goods, and upon their death these goods are to be returned to the monastic community.[98] But the monk in this story is covetous, and after his death he is reborn as a hungry ghost, still in his old cell and still clutching his former bowl and robe. The Buddha brings the monastic community to witness this sad spectacle and instructs the hungry ghost: "Cultivate faith in your heart toward me! And cultivate dispassion in your heart for these monastic provisions!"

Monastics should have faith in the Buddha and forsake attachment to material goods, and they should beware of mātsarya-filled thoughts that delude them into thinking that they themselves own such goods or that they even could own them. Monastics should be "stewards," following Edwards, dispassionate caretakers whose hearts are not quickened by objects and tainted by possessiveness. Monks and nuns might think of themselves as "noble ones" (*ārya*), but they may be "ordinary people" (*pṛthagjana*) or what some Pali sources refer to as "foolish ordinary people" (*bāla-puttujjana*), who are "blind and lacking vision, unknowing and unseeing."[99] The oft-quoted *Dhammapada* offers an important reminder: "Blind is this world! Few here see clearly."[100] Monks and nuns should do their best to be among those few who see clearly.

Mātsarya, Meanness, and Bad Faith

The pathology of mātsarya in the *Avadānaśataka* has modern parallels in language, art, and life, and these, I think, are useful for thinking through the ways that the text might help us make sense of the modern world, and vice versa.[101] While mātsarya and the behaviors it induces in the text are very specific—even idiosyncratic, as I've already mentioned, when compared with other Buddhist texts—they nevertheless signal forms of deviancy that many might find recognizable, in others if not in themselves.

Modern English, for example, abounds with apposite metaphors and euphemisms for the various "anal" forms of behavior found in the text, suggesting that neither they nor the pathology that produced them is especially rarefied. Characters look like shit, eat shit, lose their shit, shit on others, and don't give a shit. Mātsarya induces shitty decision making and shitty outcomes, like serving excreta as food and then having them become one's only food. Whether one understands these forms of deviancy rhetorically, psychologically, or cosmologically, they are telling of a Buddhist imaginaire that is concerned with forms of depravity and their very real psychosomatic effects.[102]

Also apposite and telling for making sense of mātsarya is the English word that I've used for its translation: "mean." Following the *Oxford*

English Dictionary, "mean" is likewise associated with people "inferior in rank or quality . . . often opposed to *noble* . . . who are poor; poor in ability [and] learning; destitute of moral dignity; ignoble, small-minded; penurious, wanting in liberality, stingy; and vicious." Mean people, in other words, are the antithesis of "noble ones." They are neither wealthy nor learned, and they are immoral, miserly, and cruel. And according to *Merriam-Webster's Collegiate Dictionary*, the "meanness" they espouse is "the desire to cause pain for the satisfaction of doing harm," which is a kind of perverse parody of the early ideals of "nonviolence" (*ahiṃsā*).[103] So both *mātsarya* and *mean* connect thought and deed, stinginess and viciousness, and contain an implicit orientation toward economic and social class. The repeated use of either term in a text is no doubt telling of certain political dispositions, of the author and the intended audience, and of aspirations for change, perhaps even revolution.[104]

Meanness finds an iconic antihero in Flannery O'Connor's acclaimed short story "A Good Man Is Hard to Find," which features a sadistic murderer named The Misfit. Just after he kills a woman's son and grandson, and just before he kills her, he sermonizes:

> "Jesus was the only One that ever raised the dead," The Misfit continued, "and He shouldn't have done it. He thrown everything off balance. If He did what He said, then it's nothing for you to do but thow [sic] away everything and follow Him, and if He didn't, then it's nothing for you to do but enjoy the few minutes you got left the best way you can—by killing somebody or burning down his house or doing some other meanness to him. No pleasure but meanness," he said and his voice had become almost a snarl.[105]

Meanness here has reached a kind of perverse apogee, where one isn't sure if The Misfit experiences only meanness and not pleasure or meanness as his only pleasure. The latter reading harkens back to the definition from *Merriam-Webster's Collegiate Dictionary*, and to those mātsarya-filled characters in the *Avadānaśataka* who torment others and take self-righteous pleasure in doing so. Their schadenfreude is indicative of compassion gone awry. Misfits in a Buddhist world, they are unable (or unwilling) to cultivate "loving kindness" (*maitrī*), which according to many Buddhist texts provides one with well-being and protection, even as it helps others.[106] Granted, this conceit can be hard to embrace. You might be enjoined to "love your enemies" and be told that it offers fantastic rewards (Matthew 5:44–45), but do you actually do it? As the psychoanalyst Adam Phillips and the historian Barbara Taylor write in *On Kindness*, "most people, as they grow up now, secretly believe that kindness is a virtue of losers."[107] Would some of those among the intended audience for these stories have thought the same about loving kindness? Did they think that loving kindness would "open us up to the world (and worlds) of other people in ways that we both long for and dread?"[108] Was their world marked by "the pleasures of cruelty and the cruelty of pleasures"?[109] Were they Buddhist yeasayers, or were they misfits?

Meanness reaches a different kind of apogee with Gordon Gekko, the rapacious corporate raider played by Michael Douglas in the film *Wall Street* (1987). In a speech to the stockholders of a struggling company, Teldar Paper, who have just been urged by the management to reject his tender offer to buy their shares, Gekko explains why he deserves their trust and compliance:

> The point is, ladies and gentlemen, that greed, for lack of a better word, is good. Greed is right. Greed works. Greed clarifies, cuts through, and captures the essence of the evolutionary spirit. Greed, in all of its forms—greed for life, for money, for love, knowledge—has marked the upward surge of mankind. And greed, you mark my words, will not only save Teldar Paper, but that other malfunctioning corporation called the USA.

Gekko is certainly not trustworthy; he lies and cheats repeatedly, and wrecks companies simply because they are "wreckable," but his appeal to the efficacy of greed is apparently sincere. He considers the world "a zero sum game—somebody wins and somebody loses," and he always wants to win, at whatever the cost. Greed is apparently effective: Gecko himself is fabulously wealthy, and his appeal to greed, to save the corporation and the United States, does convince the stockholders to accept his tender. One honest broker explains that "the main thing about money . . . is that it makes you do things you don't want to do," but the film demonstrates something else: greed for money makes people overcome their objections to doing things that they once found highly objectionable. Greed seduces them into justifying the unjust, rationalizing their way from acquiescence to assent.

Gekko is surely "mean" in the sense of being immoral, miserly, and cruel, and although wealthy and learned, he is nevertheless stingy and vicious. He is a kind of avatar for the meanness of 1980s stock traders, engaging in insider trading to defraud others and enrich himself, like the notorious Ivan Boeski, who is one of the models for Gekko's character. Boeski was likewise feted as a trading savant, before being indicted, fined, and jailed, and he too indulged his greed, in deed and word. His commencement address at the University of California, Berkeley, School of Business in 1986 served as the template for Gekko's speech to the stockholders. "I think greed is healthy," Boeski told the graduates. "You can be greedy and still feel good about yourself."[110] In the movie's sequel, *Wall Street: Money Never Sleeps* (2010), Gekko's version of Boeski's speech is revised for a new generation so that art and life can comfortably coincide: "I once said, 'Greed is good.' Now it seems it's legal. Because everyone is drinking the same Kool-Aid." Everyone has apparently been drugged into the same delusion: greed has become a kind of law.[111]

Gekko and Boeski have both strayed far away from any "noble dharma" and have embraced greediness as a kind of virtue, such that maximizing wealth signals a form of moral excellence. But to what extent do they believe in the rightness, or righteousness, of their actions? Have they really strayed away from believing in a "noble dharma," or are they acting in *bad faith*, engaging in "a sustained form of deception which consists in entertaining or pretending to entertain one set of feelings, and acting as if influenced by another?"[112] In *Wall Street*, Gekko is certainly acting in bad faith when he negotiates with the trade union for Bluestar Airlines, exploiting the trust of the union leader's son, who is also his acolyte. His promises notwithstanding, Gekko doesn't intend to manage the company; he intends to liquidate it, selling off the assets and appropriating the overfunded pension for himself.[113] But is he acting in good faith when he praises the value of greed to a group of shareholders? Has he actually become convinced that greed is good, or is he somehow deceiving himself? And is he deceiving others? Is he being sincere or duplicitous? Is this another instance of a kind of bad faith?

Such ideas of "bad faith" and "good faith" are evident, if not explicit, in Buddhist narrative literature, and they are helpful for thinking about the complicated ways that intention comes to bear upon Buddhist ethics. For example, in "The Story of a Lonesome Fool" in the *Divyāvadāna*, a seemingly stupid monk named Panthaka eventually attains arhatship,[114] and the Buddha then orders him to instruct a group of nuns. The latter have watched him struggle for three months to memorize a single verse and think him a fool, not knowing that he has now become an arhat. When the venerable Panthaka approached the nuns,

> he saw that a lion throne had been specially prepared, and upon seeing it, he reflected, "Was this seat of honor prepared in good faith or with the intent of doing harm?" He saw that it had been prepared with the intent of doing harm. So the venerable Panthaka stretched out his arm like the trunk of an elephant and put the lion throne in its proper place.[115]

The nuns were acting in bad faith when they prepared a seat of honor for Panthaka. They didn't want to exalt him, as a "lion throne" (*siṃhāsana*),[116] elevated no less, would normally indicate; they wanted to ridicule him. They thought they were being disparaged by having a fool address them, and they wanted to return the proverbial favor, creating a situation where that same fool would be ashamed of his predicament and refrain from teaching—or worse, speak from a lofty seat to thousands of listeners, embarrass himself, and alienate his audience. The text sets up a dichotomy between acting "in good faith" (*prasāda-jātābhiḥ*)—perhaps glossed as "with faith" or "doing the duty of one who has faith" (*prasannādhikaraṇaṃ* + √*kṛ*)[117]—and acting "with the intent of doing harm" (*viheṭhanābhiprāyābhiḥ*). The faithful cultivate faith in themselves and others, but these nuns, being dishonest and duplicitous, engage in "a sustained form of deception," attempting to punish a monk and turn his listeners against him. They aren't simply acting without faith—they are, it is said, educated and eloquent nuns who know the Buddhist canon well—they are acting in bad faith, and cruelly so. Nevertheless, the venerable Panthaka sits down in the seat of honor and then performs a host of miracles, and while explaining the first half of the verse he finally memorized, he awakens twelve thousand beings. The nuns' bad intentions have been thwarted: "they were determined to ruin the venerable Panthaka, and yet they did him nothing but good."[118]

The twelve nuns in the story were certainly engaging in "a sustained form of deception," outwardly faithful and inwardly furious. Constructing an elevated lion throne is an act of mockery, as is announcing at the streets, roads, squares, and crossroads throughout the city of Śrāvastī that "a great instructor of ours is coming tomorrow!"[119] Thinking themselves—and by extension, all women—disrespected, they egg each other on: "Sisters, look at how women are insulted!"[120] Unlike "the followers of other religious traditions" (*anyatīrthikā*) who are rude, abusive, and disrespectful to Panthaka, the nuns don't seem to have embraced a different dharma. They are likewise "rude" (*avadhyāyanti*), but even as they act out vindictively, attempting to betray not only Panthaka and his audience of listeners but also the Buddha, who had ordered Panthaka to address them, they appear to be overcome only temporarily. To put it more crassly, they're bullshitting people in Śrāvastī, but they don't believe their own bullshit.

By comparison, the monastics in the *Avadānaśataka* who cultivate mātsarya are more compromised, with their good sense, to varying degrees, occluded. In "Jāmbāla," as mentioned above, a resident monk who is an "ordinary person" and has "extreme mātsarya with regard to residence" maligns a visiting arhat, spitefully accusing him of appropriating what was being given in good faith. The lay donor who constructed the monastery where the monk resides—and who is thus the provisional owner of the property to which the monk is attached[121]—had recognized a visiting monk as an arhat and invited him and the monastic community for a steambath and a meal. The resident monk, not knowing that a visitor had been invited to join them, enters the steambath and finds the owner of the monastery massaging the visiting monk with various perfumed substances. And then:

> In the resident monk there arose a feeling of mātsarya, and with a mind polluted with bad thoughts, he uttered harsh words at the visiting monk: "Monk, it would better for you to smear your own body with shit instead of commandeering the services of a donor like this one!"

The resident monk has lost his temper, presumably outraged that the owner of the monastery would share goods and services with an outsider and convinced that the visiting monk had somehow extorted them. The arhat accepts this rebuke silently, inwardly lamenting the horrific karmic consequences of this verbal outburst, and so the resident monk doesn't realize his folly until the next general meeting of the monastic community. There he hears someone say,

> "You polluted your mind with bad thoughts toward an arhat!"
>
> Hearing this, he felt regret. Then he fell prostrate at the arhat monk's feet and said, "Forgive me, noble one, for I have uttered cruel words against you."

The resident monk immediately recognizes the truth of the charge, feels "regret" and "remorse" (*vipratisāra*), and then asks for forgiveness, acknowledging that he had, in fact, uttered words that were "harsh," "unkind," and "cruel" (*paruṣa*)—not in good faith or to promote the faith, but with the intention to do harm. The arhat then rises into the air and performs various miracles, and the resident monk feels "even greater regret." He then "confesses, declares, and proclaims that what he has done is a sin," owning up to his misdeed but nonetheless destined to suffer the karmic consequences. The resident monk could be reminded of the truth and could be moved by both the arhat's word and deeds, demonstrating that he hadn't strayed so far from the dharma that he couldn't be brought back into the fold. He was just an "ordinary person," petty and proprietary, with little self-control.

The merchant's daughter who becomes a nun in "Blind from Birth," however, has strayed further from the dharma and has apparently "lost faith." At first she longs for the dharma and, from listening to it, comes to see "the faults of conditioned existence and the virtues of nirvāṇa." With this knowledge of the dharma, she goes forth as a nun, but because of her "heedlessness" and "carelessness" (*pramāda*), she becomes so lax with respect to moral conduct that the other nuns consider her "immoral" (*duḥśīlā*) and expel her from the order. Her "morality" (*śīla*) has gone "bad" (*duḥ*), and so too, it seems, has her faith. Cultivating mātsarya, she intervenes to prevent the nuns from getting alms and "denounces" (*avarṇo bhāṣitaḥ*) them all, novices and masters alike. Ironically enough, she offers a "denunciation" as though the nuns were somehow "outcastes" (*avarṇa*), when it was she who cast aside the religion. And she closes her eyes when she encounters monks who are "virtuous"—those who, unlike her, "possess morality" (*śīlavata*). She has fully rejected the faith, and she never comes to feel regret or ask for forgiveness.

Other characters in the stories can't "lose faith" because they never had it in the first place. All the stories in the decade seem to take place during the dispensation of a buddha,[122] and yet the lay characters who cultivate mātsarya seem unaware of the Buddhist dharma or just oblivious. The nun in "Blind from Birth" can abandon Buddhism, as well as concerns for the next life, regret, forgiveness, and so on, but others can't abandon what they have never embraced. Although the term isn't mentioned in this decade, these characters are *aśrāddha*—"without faith or belief in the noble dharma," seemingly on the cusp between immoral and amoral.[123] They aren't Buddhists or lapsed Buddhists, or followers of another teacher or doctrine. They are, knowingly or otherwise, followers of mātsarya. They are, to coin a term, Mātsaryans, or perhaps Meanists.[124]

Yet it is unclear how these Mātsaryans understand their own actions, inclinations, and emotions. To the extent that they have embraced an "ignoble dharma," are they—as with Gordon Gekko—being sincere or duplicitous? Is their faith simply absent or is it somehow bad? Buddhist texts offer numerous descriptions of characters gaining "faith" (*prasāda*)—seeing the Buddha or listening to him speak are particularly effective[125]—but what is the experience of Mātsaryans who don't gain faith and who don't come to believe in the Buddhist dharma? Are they self-aware or self-deceiving?

While Buddhist philosophical and psychological texts offer answers to such questions, I find it instructive, for making sense of both the world of the text and the world outside the text, to consider Jean-Paul Sartre's understanding of "bad faith" (*mauvaise foi*), especially his insights into the ways we can and do deceive ourselves.[126] In "Lying to Oneself: A Sartrean Perspective," Joseph Catalano offers this assessment of how Sartre's work on bad faith is related to an attempt to hide from a kind of personal responsibility:

> Bad faith . . . does not really change in the face of new evidence, because it is not really about evidence. Bad faith aims at a stability of beliefs that evidence cannot provide. It is thus more a belief in belief itself rather than a belief arising from evidence. What makes it "bad" and self-deceptive is that it sees itself as of the same type as a belief that arises from evidence . . . Ontologically, good and bad faith are two radically different kinds of things; the same name of 'belief' is used, since they both have something to do with evidence. A good-faith belief is actually based on specific evidence, while a bad-faith belief does not need this or any other specific evidence . . . In bad faith, and specifically in self-deception, I have no real interest in altering my understanding about myself, since my belief is aimed at sustaining a certain attitude whatever the cost . . . Since no belief can be *perfectly* justified, bad faith appears to be justified belief. Thus a person in bad faith can hide from conceptualizing its bad faith as "bad" and as self-deceptive.[127]

Mātsaryans are convinced that mendicants who receive gifts, especially those who beg for them, are freeloaders, veritable hungry ghosts, insatiable in their needs, and this justifies and empowers them to lie, deceive, and act with the intention to harm and humiliate. But how is all this justified? For Sartre, "bad faith does not hold the norms and criteria of truth as they are accepted by the critical thought of good faith,"[128] and here too the justifications don't seem particularly convincing. Mātsaryans in the *Avadānaśataka* likely see mendicants as hungry ghosts because, as discussed previously, they themselves think like hungry ghosts, not like normal humans. Their logic, like bad faith, "appears to be justified belief," but it is not based on what normal humans would think of as "the norms and criteria of truth." Hungry ghost logic is a breed apart.

But why cultivate bad faith in the first place? According to Sartre, "the goal of bad faith"—the purpose of such posturing and provocation—"is to put oneself out of reach; it is an escape."[129] Mātsaryans certainly seem to be trying to escape, from giving charity and from helping those in need but also perhaps from certain forms of self-understanding. For Sartre, bad faith is an attempt "to constitute myself as being what I am not. It apprehends me positively as courageous when I am not so."[130] Mātsaryans would likely think of themselves as courageous, speaking truth to power as they rally against what they perceive as injustices. The *Avadānaśataka* is clear that they are "sinners" (*pāpakāriṇī*),[131] but they would no doubt like to be what they are not, and only a kind of bad faith lets that happen.

So . . . the hungry ghost stories in the *Avadānaśataka* show ordinary folks who, when confronted with those they think of as freeloaders, are overwhelmed by stinginess, which leads them to cultivate a "righteous" indignation (which they may or may not realize isn't righteous) and prompts them to lash out in a spiteful and scatological fashion, in deeds or words, to teach the perceived freeloaders a lesson. Those who cultivate mātsarya are triggered by the prospect of others receiving goods or services that they haven't earned. For them, charity isn't righteous. It's a form of misappropriation, and worse still, it enables and empowers those who ask for charity to ask again, perpetuating and normalizing an unjust practice. As the workman in "Sugar Mill" observes, "If I give the noble one sugarcane juice, he'll just come back again." Charity is the engine of an unjust system.

This kind of thinking likely sounds familiar. Although the hungry ghost stories in the *Avadānaśataka* were written long ago in a milieu very different from our own, they address deluded ways of thinking and being that were thought to be common, not constrained by age, gender, geography, or time period. "Ordinary people" of diverse kinds were considered susceptible to mātsarya, and although the stories offer examples from the time of the Buddha and the distant past, one could presumably find examples of mātsarya-induced behavior closer to home—or perhaps even in one's own home. According to the venerable Janakābhivamsa, the modern Burmese scholar mentioned earlier, *macchariya* is now "rampant" among monks and nuns, and "quite common" among the laity.[132] According to the Latin saying, "envy keeps no holidays" (*invidia festos dies non agit*),[133] and it seems one could say the same about mātsarya.

Perhaps it is the sheer ordinariness of mātsarya that accounts for the mātsarya-like mean-spiritedness that is now "quite common," maybe even "rampant." Many people, outraged at the prospect of what they perceive to be unjust redistribution, espouse the idea that "welfare is theft" and taxation as well. A quick bit of internet sleuthing leads to such popular (and populist) memes as: "Everything you get from the government was stolen from someone else," and "Redistribution is not fairness, it's theft." And, yes, internet searches for "throwing shit on the homeless" or "pissing on welfare recipients" yield numerous results. The website angry.net, for example, features diatribes with titles like "Welfare scum," "Welfare whores," and "Useless pieces of shit on welfare."[134]

Considering the numerous ways that morals and markets are mutually imbricated and constituted, it comes as little surprise that with the advent of neoliberalism and the seeming "commoditization of everything," a new "market truth" would arise, along with its proponents.[135] Elements in society that were considered impossible to marketize, such as water, pollution, and social welfare, have now been commoditized, transformed from public goods to tradable entities. The young woman in "Water Pot" who wouldn't help a desperately thirsty monk could now put a price tag on the water and service she withholds. Even human urine and excrement, like those offered in "Sugar Mill" and "A Pot of Shit," are now commodities, nutrient or pollutant to be purchased or disposed of at a price. In a world of "everything for sale,"[136] why give away something for nothing?

It isn't necessarily the case that hypercommoditization leads to an increase in the arising of mātsarya, but there are certainly many modern cases of apparent meanness to productively ponder—to construe "either as authoritative or as involving opposition to, or better questioning of, Buddhist ideology (or both)."[137] Consider, for example, a very brief text: Donald Trump Jr.'s tweet about his three-year-old daughter on Halloween in 2017. "I'm going to take half of Chloe's candy tonight & give it to some kid who sat at home. It's never to [sic] early to teach her about socialism."[138] Trump Jr.'s tweet generated an enormous number of likes and retweets, as well some pointed commentary: "Imagine thinking that teaching your child to share is bad"; "My man, 'socialism' was her getting that free candy in the first place. You taking half for reasons she can't understand is capitalism"; and "It's telling that junior thinks that 'walking around getting gifts from people' is a good metaphor for 'earning money.'"[139] Was Donald Trump Jr.'s tweet in good faith or with the intention to harm? Was he being sincere or duplicitous? Has he cultivated "mātsarya with regard to material gains," and as such, does he find (certain) others acquiring them, without having earned them, unbearable? Has he strayed from the noble dharma and embraced an ignoble dharma, or is he lying to others and maybe to himself? Is his logic sound, his beliefs justified, his faith good?[140]

So what can we do to resolve our own confusion? In the *Avadānaśataka*, when monks are "in doubt" about an individual's moral psychology and karmic trajectory, past and future, they question the Buddha, for he is "the remover of all doubts."[141] And, likewise, when hungry ghosts are questioned about what led them to their fate, they invariably tell the questioner to ask the Buddha. We have no such recourse. But the stories themselves make excellent teachers. They can be read as karma stories, demonstrating action and its consequences; as phenomenological treatises, connecting thought, action, and judgment; as psychological accounts, explicating profound truths about human cupidity; as poetic tales, conjuring vivid images and intense feelings; as legal tracts, schooling us in a code of communal conduct; as moral texts, offering insight into the complexities of human action; as apocalyptic texts, chronicling the torments that untold humans will inevitably endure; as ideological texts, forming us as faithful and giving subjects; as ethical texts, letting us refashion ourselves through contemplation of the human condition; as human texts, chronicling the pettiness and struggles of everyday life; as divine texts, guiding us to a more compassionate, charitable, and joyful existence; and on and on.

In this collection, the Buddha frequently instructs those who seek his counsel to "listen" and then "concentrate well and closely."[142] This is excellent advice. Characters in these stories who listen closely to the Buddha's words often have life-changing experiences. Maybe it will be the same for you.

Hungry Ghosts through Images

IT IS HELPFUL to consider hungry ghosts not only as they are represented in texts but also as they appear in images. This approach is telling, for in some places such images are simply missing, and in other cases they abound, and it isn't always clear why. As Monika Zin notes, "Hells are frequently represented in Tibetan painted scrolls and mural paintings . . . [but] not a single picture has survived from ancient India."[143] And images of hungry ghosts share a similar fate.[144] Yet later images of hungry ghosts proliferate not only in Tibet but also across much of Asia. And there are vast differences in the ways that hungry ghosts are represented, stylistically and aesthetically, from illustration to icon, and equally vast differences in their reception, from instilling fear and revulsion to offering hope and redemption. Could the absence of early Indian images of hungry ghosts be indicative of a kind of prohibition? And what does it tell us about contemporary Japan that two Japanese scrolls from the twelfth century, known as the *Scroll of Hungry Ghosts* (*Gaki zōshi*), which feature graphic images of hungry ghosts consuming human excrement, urine, blood, sweat, pus, and earwax, are now housed at the Tokyo National Museum and Kyoto National Museum and recognized as national treasures?[145] Such images provide insight into various Buddhist imaginaries and ritual protocols, as well as the changes they have undergone across geography, time period, and sectarian affiliation.

Crucial to making sense of these images of hungry ghosts is

recognizing what they are not: these images are not simply representations of descriptions in Buddhist texts, as though the artists who created them were merely transcribing the texts in visual form. These images have their own logic, which is usually constituted by the artist having engaged with texts, written or oral, with varying degrees of fidelity and creativity, depending on the artist's skill and intent, and then indulging in some measure of artistic exigency and license, depending on the medium and moment. Wu Hung offers a similar assessment about the relationship between Buddhist art and literature from Dunhuang, where "the process of image-making has its own logic that differs from those found in writing and oral recitation" and where there are cases of seemingly "irregular" sequences of scenes that "may have resulted from a deliberate effort to increase the dramatic effect of the story by rearranging the events."[146] Thinking about Buddhist art more generally, texts and images have often existed in a reciprocal relationship, with artists adapting narratives and authors adapting art, and both working together to create various doctrines and rituals.[147]

With all this in mind, it is important to resist what Carlo Ginzburg calls an easy "physiognomic" reading of hungry ghost images, whereby "the historian reads into them *what he has already learned* by other means, or what he believes he knows, and wants to 'demonstrate.'"[148] Christopher Pinney uses this quotation as the epigraph for his book *"Photos of the Gods": The Printed Image and the Political Struggle in India* and explains how eighteenth- and nineteenth-century chromolithographs "could easily be used to produce a narrative that conforms with what we already know about India, serving as evidence of what (as Carlo Ginzburg suggests) we have proved 'by other means.' What, however, if pictures have a different story to tell, what if—in their luxuriant proliferation—they were able to narrate to us a different story, one told, in part, on their own terms?"[149] Likewise, images of hungry ghosts could easily be used to produce a narrative that conforms to what we already know about Buddhism, where disjunctions between text and image would be explained away as unfortunate aberrations.

While Pinney tries "to rearrange Indian history so that a central place can be found for the visual,"[150] my plan here is more constrained, offering less of an image-based history than a series of image-based history lessons. In what follows, I have compiled some images of hungry ghosts from different regions, eras, and traditions, and I've tried to make sense of them, reading them in conjunction with various texts while also noting the divergences. The goal is to demonstrate some of the "luxuriant proliferation" of hungry ghost imagery, the complicated ways these images relate to the representations of hungry ghosts in texts, and what all this might begin to tell us about various Buddhist imaginaries.

A Nature to Suffer

One helpful way of thinking about all these images of hungry ghosts, regardless of their provenance, is to consider the ways that the bodies of hungry ghosts are designed and destined for suffering. Their bodies are like torture chambers, and one cannot escape the torments they mete out. Reflecting on hungry ghosts in medieval Japan, William LaFleur notes,

> Hunger is in its name because it is constituted by hunger, not merely conditioned by it. For other kinds of beings—mankind, animals and the like—hunger will come and go but for the *gaki* [hungry ghost] there is only an ongoing, unalleviated gnawing of the stomach and parching of the throat. When the Buddhist canon again and again depicts this creature as one "with a stomach as huge as a mountain but a throat as narrow as a needle," there may be hyperbole in the dimensions, but the antinomy of the structure is of central importance to the definition of this type. That body is this being's horrible dilemma: voracious appetites and absolutely minimal equipment [that] cannot even begin to satisfy it.[151]

These hungry ghosts are racked with excruciating and inescapable hunger and thirst; such is the logic and justice of karma. And this condition is exacerbated by the fact that the karma of hungry ghosts ensures that they only have access to repulsive and polluting substances for possible nourishment. Such is the case for the hungry ghosts in the *Scroll of Hungry Ghosts*, described above, or those in "Jāmbāla," the last of the stories translated in this volume, whose only food is pus-filled blood and shit, which they eat, then vomit and defecate, then eat again.

As an additional torment, hungry ghosts are often pictured in flames. This burning is likewise excruciating and inescapable, functioning as an external source of pain to complement the inner burning of hunger and thirst. According to LaFleur, a hungry ghost in medieval Japan was thought to be "a consumer of fires . . . In its blind, deluded passion to fulfill the hunger and thirst within, the *gaki* mistakes fire for food, thus incrementally aggravating its condition. This is why it both emits fire from its mouth and takes more of it into its body."[152] But how does one make sense of the image in what follows from a Thai manuscript (plate 6) in which hungry ghosts have flames emerging not from their mouths but from their hands, knees, foreheads, and shoulders? What karmic misdeeds generate such a fate? Perhaps the artist had in mind the famed "Fire Sermon," regarded as the third formal discourse of the Buddha's ministry, in which the Buddha proclaims that "all is burning" and then explains in exacting detail how our senses and sensations are burning with the fires of passion, hatred, delusion, and more.[153] A body in flames would be a fitting retribution for such an enflamed sensorium. One can't know for sure—the manuscript mentions no such affliction—but one can productively ponder, relating the image to other texts and teachings, and maybe in doing so one can illuminate not just the life of a few images but also the life outside such images, both in the past and present.

In the spirit of productive pondering, one might consider LaFleur's idea that certain Japanese images of hungry ghosts partake in an "exquisite realism," offering viewers a kind of "ontological x-ray" of the world they inhabit but to which they generally remain blind. As such, these images offer the viewer two (in)sights:

> first, that *gaki,* in fact, commingle invisibly with humans in their own world and, second, that men, women and children ordinarily live their lives oblivious to the gruesome beings hunched over next to them.[154]

All this accords with the stories in this volume. While some traditions imagine hungry ghosts primarily living in the bowels of the earth, here hungry ghosts are much like animals—they live in our midst but generally go unnoticed, either because we haven't been trained to see them or because they choose to keep their distance.[155] And much like solitary buddhas, they live in secluded woodlands on the outskirts of cities, unobserved by the city's inhabitants. In the stories in this volume, they often appear just outside of cities in and around various groves and parks, on the banks of the Ganges River, and near Vulture's Peak, a retreat outside of the city of Rājagṛha. But they sometimes dwell in far more urban and less bucolic places, like the hungry ghosts in "Jāmbāla" who live in a moat that surrounds Vaiśālī, immersed "in a muck of bile and urine."

So, why are humans oblivious to the hungry ghosts who live in such close proximity to them, on the margins of their cities or in the nearby countryside? It isn't because hungry ghosts are simply invisible. According to the stories, monks are the ones who most often see hungry ghosts, and some of these monks are arhats with special powers of sight. But ordinary humans can see them as well. In "Uttara," when the venerable Uttara invites a hungry ghost who previously had been his mother to a meal for the Buddha and monastic community, with the merit from the offering going to her, "hundreds of thousands of beings" gathered around and saw the hungry ghost's deformed body. And in "Jāmbāla," the young boy Jāmbāla would roam around Vaiśālī doing good deeds, and when he saw the five hundred hungry ghosts living in the moat around the city, he descended into the muck and joined them.

It isn't difficult to read this as a form of social commentary, especially in its early Indian context. A group of starving individuals live on the margins of society, either wandering outside city limits, homeless and hungry, or toiling in the city's cesspools, immersed in the inhabitants' excreta. They suffer enormously in truly shitty conditions, and yet they remain unseen by nearly everyone. Most people have developed an ingrained blindness to this underclass and its painful predicament; they are a kind of invisible poor, both out of sight and out of mind. If asked to appear in public, they are likely to be trepidatious about being seen, like the hungry ghost in "Uttara," who has been invited to a meal in her honor and yet is "ashamed and embarrassed" at appearing in public with no clothes. In her previous life as a human, she had abused whoever came to her home looking for alms, calling them "hungry ghosts." Would an actual hungry ghost showing up at someone's home for a meal be subject to such verbal abuse, or worse?

The situation of these hungry ghosts bears a striking resemblance to India's "manual scavengers," members of the lowest caste, who have served as an underclass in the Indian subcontinent for thousands of years. Like hungry ghosts, they have often been regarded as a "stigmatized people whose stigma is derived through birth-ascribed group membership and is shared throughout the group."[156] These individuals generally live in ghettos on the margins of society, nearly homeless in ramshackle shelters; they are chronically underfed and suffer from a host of illnesses; and they are stigmatized and persecuted, owing to their caste-mandated job of removing human excreta from toilets. Much like the hungry ghosts in medieval Japanese images, they are "invariably . . . present in latrines and cesspools,"[157] either because they are cleaning them or because they are forced to dump the removed excreta into cesspools that are in the ghettos where they live. This waste matter is frequently referred to as "night soil," for these individuals usually clean the latrines at night so that no one sees them. If they are seen, they are often subject to violence, as their very presence is thought to be polluting. While the plight of manual scavengers in India has improved in the past century, especially after their employment was made illegal in 1993, the law did not end manual scavenging or its ravages, as a recent report makes clear in its title: *Burden of Inheritance: Can We Stop Manual Scavenging? Yes, But First We Need to Accept It Exists.*[158]

Yet the images of hungry ghosts offer an especially potent form of verisimilitude. They aren't simply suggestive of starving and disregarded individuals living on society's margins; they seem to depict them in gruesome detail. LaFleur suggests that the painters of the *Scroll of Hungry Ghosts* based their images of hungry ghosts on famine victims who were suffering advanced forms of starvation.[159] Hungry ghosts are defined by the fact that they are starving, so one can understand why artists might have based their images of hungry ghosts not just on descriptions found in texts but also on their observations of actual starving people—individuals who, like their counterparts in the texts, beg for food and water and bemoan their fate. The maladies suffered by hungry ghosts and human victims of extreme starvation are eerily similar. Severe malnutrition in humans leads to the disorder known as kwashiorkor, with symptoms like stomach bloating from fluid retention, hair loss, tooth loss, hair depigmentation, and dry and cracked skin.[160] Sufferers from this ailment have skeletal bodies, spindly limbs, and incongruously large stomachs, making them a "physiological oxymoron."[161] They are seemingly fabricated but all too real, like survivors of famines and concentration camps whose bodies bear unimaginable ravages that many might wish not to see—and not to take responsibility for helping.

One might simply dismiss the suffering of such individuals, reasoning that it has been earned by a kind of karmic calculus, whereby one reaps exactly what one sows and gets exactly what one deserves, whether that be rebirth as a hungry ghost or a manual scavenger.[162] In fact, the hungry ghosts in the stories acknowledge that they are living proof of karma's unerring inevitability, whereby mātsarya-inspired deeds result in rebirth as a hungry ghost with a body that is a corporeal chamber of horrors.[163]

But what if directly acknowledging the suffering of such individuals could be liberative? In "Uttara," after hundreds of thousands of beings gather around and look at the hungry ghost's deformed body, they "are deeply moved and cultivate faith in their hearts for the Blessed One." The text is presenting a recognized spiritual progression: one experiences *saṃvega*—being "deeply moved," "stirred," and "shocked"—and then one cultivates *prasāda* (Pali, *pasāda*)—"faith"—and these two events transform the individual, catapulting them forward on the Buddhist path. This spiritual progression is the explicit goal of certain classical texts and contemporary songs,[164] yet here individuals are transformed not by reading or listening but simply by gathering around a hungry ghost and looking at her—seeing her for who and what she is. And that's enough.

And maybe it's enough just to look at the sick and afflicted in our midst. In the *Buddhacarita* (*Life of the Buddha*), Aśvaghoṣa's poetic biography of the Buddha from the first or second century CE, the Buddha's father is worried that his son, destined to be either a great king or a great seer, will choose the latter path, so he keeps him confined in the palace, shielded from experiencing or witnessing suffering. When Gautama, the Buddha to be, hears about the enchanting beauty of the city's groves and parks, he wants to see them, so his father orders an excursion. And to keep his son happy and shielded,

> He prevented ordinary people with afflictions
> from gathering on the royal highway, thinking,
> "The tender-minded young prince
> must not experience *saṃvega*!"
>
> Then, with supreme gentleness, they sent away from all corners
> those with missing limbs or defective senses,
> the old, the sick, the poor, and the like,
> and made the royal highway supremely beautiful.[165]

The king is afraid that if his son sees "ordinary people" (*pṛthagjana*) who are less than paragons of good health, his mind will become flooded with *saṃvega*. So the king turns the natural world into something artificial, removing those who, like the hungry ghost in "Uttara," are somehow deformed. The king fears that such sights will catapult his son forward on the spiritual path. And his fears are well founded. Thanks to the contrivances of the gods, the Buddha does see the old, the sick, and the dead, and that does push him out of the palace onto the spiritual path.

Like the old, the sick, and the dead, hungry ghosts can make great teachers. Their self-recriminations about mātsarya-inspired deeds are offered as lessons to be passed on to their relatives so they will know better and do better. But the account in "Uttara" suggests that hungry ghosts could also be teachers in the lineage of solitary buddhas, who "teach the dharma not with words but with their bodies."[166] Yet instead of flying into the air and performing miracles to convert onlookers, as solitary buddhas are wont to do, the hungry ghost in the story simply stands still, like a figure in a painting, making suffering visible. As the group of five hundred hungry ghosts in "Jāmbāla" explain, "We are horrifying, and our nature is to suffer." To see beings who so fully embody suffering, who are "suffering" (*duḥkha*) by "nature" (*prakṛti*)—suffering incarnate—is an opportunity to witness the truth of suffering: it permeates existence, it has a cause, it can end, and there is a path leading to its cessation. The Buddha elucidates these four noble truths in his discourses on the dharma, and these hungry ghosts do so with their bodies, which function as corporeal dharma teachings. And these teachings are made all the more visceral by the close connection between hungry ghosts and ancestors,[167] which makes the suffering of hungry ghosts especially personal, poignant, and difficult to disregard.

And yet to disregard suffering—to not see it, either by choice or habit, consciously or otherwise, or like the Buddha's father, to not want others to see it—is all too common. C. W. Huntington Jr., in his evocative memoir about his struggles with terminal cancer and the ways we deny suffering only to increase it, cites an especially telling passage from Thomas Merton's autobiography:

> Indeed, the truth that many people never understand, until it is too late, is that the more you try to avoid suffering, the more you suffer, because smaller and more insignificant things begin to torture you, in proportion to your fear of being hurt. The one who does most to avoid suffering is, in the end, the one who suffers most: and his suffering comes to him from things so little and so trivial that one can say that it is no longer objective at all. It is his own existence, his own being, that is at once the subject and the source of his pain, and his very existence and consciousness is his greatest torture.[168]

Part of this strategy for avoiding suffering is a propensity to desubjectify, to think of subjects as objects, living beings as somehow not quite living, worthy of neither our compassion nor our grief. Consider, for example, the ways that the enslaved in America were "degraded from the human rank, and classed with those irrational animals which fall under the legal denomination of property."[169] One becomes inured to the suffering of others, unable to see it or feel it, such that others are no longer grievable.[170] Yet, as Merton reminds us, this form of denial only exacerbates one's own suffering. Perhaps what we need is an experience akin to *saṃvega* that will shake and shock us out of complacency and facilitate a kind of awakening and new awareness.

For Huntington that shaking-and-shocking experience is a terminal diagnosis, and it overwhelms his valiant efforts at denial:

> I well knew, from my hospice work, my study of Buddhism, and all my other reading that I was in denial, but it was the sort of denial that all of us habitually indulge. For all I know

> we may need to live this way; to confront the truth squarely on its own terms may not be possible for anyone other than saints and buddhas. But for me things have changed. In facing my own imminent death, all the attitudes and techniques that I had honed over the years in my search for the approval of others have become useless, or worse . . . In order to live what is left of my life and die in peace, the wrathful deity of death is teaching me to give myself over to the human community and to a felt kinship with the nonhuman world, a world to which I have always belonged while never fully appreciating the significance of that belonging, a world where this failing body of mine is, like all bodies, a tiny, fleeting shadow in the immensity of creation.[171]

But maybe it isn't only saints and buddhas and those with terminal diagnoses who can overcome denial and directly observe suffering, their own and others, and act with care and compassion. In "Jāmbāla," the boy Jāmbāla simply sees five hundred hungry ghosts in the moat around the city, descends into it, "and there he joined with them, gathered with them, exchanged pleasantries, and developed friendships." No mention is made of Jāmbāla previously having any friends; he passed his time alone on garbage heaps and in latrines. And considering that he was physically deformed, compulsively pulling out his hair, smeared in excrement, stinking, and eating excrement as well, one can imagine that he was socially ostracized and shunned. The text describes him as "absolutely disgusting,"[172] the same term used to describe a hungry ghost in "The Merchant," suggesting he was truly a hungry ghost among humans.

Jāmbāla was no Buddhist when he met those hungry ghosts. Other than the love and care he had received from his parents, he seems to have been neither socialized nor educated in his present life.[173] And yet, somehow, without any prompting, he could see hungry ghosts, and when he did, he joined them in conversation and offered them friendship. This wasn't a learned behavior; rather, it was an act of a kind of innate and innocent wisdom. Jāmbāla here is reminiscent of Panthaka, who was likewise seemingly ignorant yet actually wise and destined to become an arhat. Panthaka thought himself "a fool, an absolute fool, an idiot, a complete idiot," and so the Buddha explained to him,

> One ignorant because of his innocence
> is actually wise in this case.
> But one ignorant and thinking himself wise
> is rightly recognized as a fool.[174]

Jāmbāla exemplifies this innocent wisdom, and it allows him to see what others somehow can't see or won't see, like the young child in Hans Christian Andersen's "The Emperor's New Clothes," who alone allows himself to see that the emperor wears nothing at all.[175] Exemplars like Jāmbāla and Panthaka suggest the value of cultivating the proverbial beginner's mind and the unlearning that it entails so that we might attain an atavistic, childlike understanding of the world. Perhaps seeing hungry ghosts, like seeing the most dehumanized among us, requires stripping away various forms of socialization, unlearning the casteism, classism, conformity, and bigotry that blind us, or never having been socialized into them in the first place.

So how does one look at images of hungry ghosts? One can read the images in conjunction with texts, as I do in much of what follows, assuming that the artists were familiar with Buddhist discourses about hungry ghosts and that they responded to them with varying degrees of fidelity and creativity. Or one might choose to look at the images without the texts, without reading my descriptions, and try to be like Jāmbāla or the mass of humanity in "Uttara," and see them for what they are: images of beings who suffer terribly. One might then be deeply moved and gain some insight into the ways that suffering permeates existence and the ways that we are blind to it. And one might even be inspired to discover those suffering beings in our midst we have not noticed and, like Jāmbāla, offer them friendship.

Plate 1

In this painting, the caravan leader Śroṇa Koṭikarna encounters an iron city filled with hungry ghosts. The gate to the city stands before him, and the hungry ghosts, emaciated and skeletal, beseech him with arms outstretched. In the version of the story recounted in the *Divyāvadāna*,[176] Śroṇa Koṭikarna encounters two iron cities filled with hungry ghosts; he enters each of them in search of water, only to be surrounded by thousands of hungry ghosts who themselves are absolutely desperate for water. According to the text, the hungry ghosts look like burned-out tree stumps, raised-up skeletons covered with hair from head to toe, with stomachs like mountains and mouths like pinholes.

Plate 2

Pictured are four hungry ghosts, emaciated with visible ribs, gangly with long arms and necks, their wire-like hair sticking straight up.[177] The topmost three figures have their mouths wide open, so perhaps the flames that surround them signify their burning hunger. This detail comes from an elaborate cave mural with scenes of various hells.[178] The murals in this cave are a composite of various artistic traditions, which makes it difficult to identify the sources and inspirations for these hungry ghost images.[179]

Plate 3

This painting, *Path of the Hungry Ghosts*, comes from a set of eight extant painted scrolls—originally there were sixteen or more—each of which depicts ten distinct figures from different classes of beings.[180] There are ten figures from each of the six realms of existence (i.e., gods, antigods, humans, animals, hungry ghosts, hell beings), as well as ten Daoist deities and ten local deities. These paintings were most likely created in or near the port city of Ningbo, on the eastern coast of China, and were intended for use in the *shuilu fahui* (rite for deliverance of creatures of water and land), one of the most popular and elaborate rituals in the Chinese Buddhist repertoire. The *shuilu* rite was designed for the liberation of all beings, especially those who had met an untimely end or were improperly buried. To that end, beings of all different types are invited to the ritual, either to facilitate the proceedings or to be propitiated or indoctrinated. The figures in these paintings represent the panoply of beings invited to the ritual. According to Daniel Stevenson, the paintings were neither icons nor the focus of ritual action; instead, they constituted "the simulacrum in which that action and its intentions [would] unfold."[181]

This particular painting features ten figures from the hungry ghost realm, each of whom has unique features. Based on various literary sources, one can make some best guesses about the various figures portrayed. For example, according to a short tract about hungry ghosts by Tiantai master Ciyun Zunshi (964–1032) entitled "On the Visualizations [That Accompany a] Charitable Bestowal of Food [on Hungry Ghosts], in Reply to Questions of the Official Cui Yucai," there are three basic types of hungry ghosts: (1) those deprived of provisions, (2) those with meager provisions, and (3) those with bountiful provisions.[182] Among the first type—those deprived of provisions—there are three subsets of hungry ghost:

> (1.1) the fire or flaming-mouth ghosts, insofar as flames blaze constantly from their mouths; (1.2) the needle-throat ghosts, whose bellies are huge as mountains but throats as thin as needles. The sūtra at hand mentions principally these two types, with all the others generically clustered around [in attendance]; and, finally, (1.3) the stinking or

> stench-mouth hungry ghosts, whose mouths are filled with stinking filth and rot, causing them agony from their own loathsomeness.[183]

These three kinds of hungry ghosts appear to be represented in the upper right of this painting. There are three hungry ghosts who are skeletal with large bellies, signaling their dire hunger, and who have protruding foreheads, noses, and jaws, giving them a simian quality. These are likely a flaming-mouth hungry ghost, with fiery breath; a needle-throat hungry ghost, with a small throat that inhibits eating; and a stinking-mouth hungry ghost, who is holding his nose, attempting perhaps to block the smell of his own terrible breath.

Zunshi then enumerates three kinds of hungry ghosts of the second type—those with meager provisions:

> (2.1) the needle-fur ghosts, whose fur is sharp like needles and stabs them whenever they move about; (2.2) the stench-fur ghosts, whose [noxious hairs] are sharp, causing pain and distress when they stab [the ghost] or when [the ghost] tries to pull them out; and (2.3) the goiter ghosts, whose throats swell or droop large goiters that exude noxious pus when they chew.

These three kinds of hungry ghosts appear to be represented in the middle of the painting, standing side by side in a row. These are likely a needle-fur hungry ghost, with needle-like white hair all over his body; a stench-fur hungry ghost, with a dark complexion, who is holding his nose, likely trying to block his own rank smell; and a goiter hungry ghost, with a wildly enlarged thyroid gland, which would make it very difficult for him to consume his meager provisions, and which he supports with both hands.

And finally, Zunshi enumerates three kinds of hungry ghosts of the third type—those with bountiful provisions:

> (3.1) ghosts who obtain cast-off or discarded [provisions], so named because they are regularly able to obtain foods discarded from ritual libations and offerings;[184] (3.2) ghosts who obtain lost [goods], insofar as they lurk about and get hold of foods that have been dropped or discarded in alleyways and streets; and (3.3) ghosts endowed with actual power[s], which comprises beings such as yakṣas, rākṣasas, piśācas, and so on. Their pleasures are categorically akin to those of human beings and gods, but they belong to the [lower] evil paths.

These latter three kinds of hungry ghosts may be represented in the lower left of the painting, but the identities of the figures there are more difficult to discern. Not including the figure in the lower-left corner, there are three figures with straightened windswept hair, with hands respectfully folded, and with what seem to be "bountiful provisions." The top two figures are physically similar, with bulging eyes and eyebrows, a central cranial protuberance, and large mops of hair—one blue and one red. They are both similarly dressed, with matching earrings, bracelets, and armlets, and with long green cloaks draped over shoulders and forearms. The figure with red hair has a third eye and what seems to be a flame-shaped jewel in his hair. Perhaps the blue-haired figure is a kind of minor deity (*yakṣa*), and the red-haired figure is a kind of demon (*rākṣasa*), as a third eye is fairly common in depictions of the latter. The third figure wears a robe and crown and carries a scepter, all of which are signifiers of kingly status in Chinese painting, and his face is more human and less animalistic than the two figures above him. This figure is a kind of royalty among ghosts and likely represents Yama, the king of hungry ghosts.

The final figure, in the lower-left corner, wears matching earrings, bracelets, armlets, and anklets, along with a jeweled tiara and matching sandals, and has a long red cloak draped over shoulders and forearms. He has wispy, near waist-length hair that is styled with two topknots, and his eyes are downcast. This figure looks like a brahman seer (*brahmarṣi*)—high caste, high class, and vaguely foreign.[185]

Plate 4

This painting, *Flaming-Mouth Ghost King*, has its basis in a story.[186] According to various Buddhist texts,[187] the venerable Ānanda encountered a terrifying hungry ghost aptly named "Flaming Mouth," who told Ānanda that after three days the latter would die and be reborn as a hungry ghost unless before then he could somehow feed a nearly infinite number of hungry ghosts. Terrified, the venerable Ānanda approached the Buddha, who then taught him a special incantatory text that had the power to feed all those hungry ghosts and more. Ānanda followed the Buddha's guidance, and in doing so he saved himself and innumerable hungry ghosts. This story serves as the basis for an elaborate ritual known as the *Yuqie yankou* (Yoga Rite of Flaming Mouth), which began as a simple rite in the Tang dynasty (618–907) and developed into a complex liturgy that remains popular today in China and elsewhere.[188]

In the bottom left corner is the venerable Ānanda, with a *vajra* in one hand and a bell in the other, wearing a red "five-buddha crown." Such crowns are now worn by the main officiant of the ghost-feeding ritual that Ānanda is said to have initiated. In fact, real-world monks with five-buddha crowns likely performed the ghost-feeding ritual with this painting on the altar for hungry ghosts, creating a kind of kinship between those officiants and Ānanda. In the painting, Ānanda stands before the officiant's altar with various requisites for the ritual, including candles, vases, an incense burner, and an open text, perhaps even the manual for the ritual being performed. Ānanda is flanked by two monastic assistants, the bottom one standing before the open text with palms reverently pressed together. A hungry ghost with what looks like a manuscript page in hand approaches the officiant's altar, and below him another hungry ghost, with what looks like a pile of manuscript pages on his back, has turned his head to watch the proceedings. These hungry ghosts appear to be offering their assistance to the liturgist.

In the bottom center is the altar for hungry ghosts, featuring three mountains of food offerings—vegetables on the left,[189] steamed buns in the middle, and rice on the right. These mountains of offerings are decorated with flags (that in contemporary ritual practice often bear dedicatory inscriptions) and topped with finials, such that they look like stūpas. The central offering of steamed buns appears to be a favorite for the hungry ghosts. On the altar and below it, hungry ghosts can be seen eating and hoarding the steamed buns. On the right side of the image, hordes of hungry ghosts stream down to the offerings, and on the left side of the image, they stream back, with steamed buns in hand, in mouth, or filling their bowls.

In the center of the image sits Flaming Mouth, with his mouth agape and breathing fire, with hair sticking straight up around a central bald spot, and with dilated pupils and visible viscera. He is adorned with a cloak and with earrings, bracelets, anklets, and an elaborate necklace. He sits enthroned on a rocky pedestal in full-lotus posture, with his hands in his lap in a classic meditative position, and with a steamed bun, no doubt obtained from the offerings below, resting in them. While the steamed bun marks Flaming Mouth as a recipient of the offering, his halo and frontal orientation mark him as an icon for the outside viewer of this image.

Flaming Mouth is often understood to be a manifestation of the ever-compassionate bodhisattva Guanyin, who expediently assumed the form of Flaming Mouth and precipitated Ānanda's crisis in order to facilitate the Buddha's creation of the *Yuqie yankou* ritual. Pictured above Flaming Mouth is a roundel borne aloft by clouds that contains Guanyin, with her white robes, vase of healing elixir in one hand and willow sprig in the other. The snaking wisp of clouds that connects her to Flaming Mouth signals her power over him. In fact, the principal officiant of the *Yuqie yankou* ritual visualizes himself as Guanyin, and he feeds hungry ghosts at least in part by controlling Flaming Mouth, regarded as the leader of all the other hungry ghosts.

In the bottom left corner is a tablet with a lotus-blossom base and an inverted lotus-leaf top, which is inscribed with a colophon: "On the first day of the tenth month of Chongzhen 16 [1643], the disciple Weiyin resolved to gather people to fund the creation [of this work]."

Plate 5

This is a detail from a Tibetan painted scroll of the wheel of existence,[190] whose date and provenance is uncertain.[191] The lower portion of the hungry ghost realm features hungry ghosts with tiny necks, extended bellies, and spiky hair, and with limbs akimbo and flailing. They breathe fire, indicating that they are unable to eat or drink and are perennially hungry and thirsty. Among these flailing hungry ghosts are two larger and more static figures. There is a maternal figure, likely the goddess Hārītī,[192] who offers a hand of support to each of the two small children that cling to her neck. Her breasts are large yet desiccated; like other hungry ghosts, she is malnourished, with no access to food or drink, and so she can't breastfeed her children. There is also a figure sitting in a pavilion, likely Yama, the proverbial Lord of Death,[193] bearing a skeleton staff. Its shaft is made of a spinal column topped with a skull that is crowned with a jewel.[194]

In the upper left are three figures in cloud-thrones: on top is the bodhisattva Mañjuśrī, with a flaming sword in one hand and a wisdom text in the other; below him to the left is the protector deity Vajrapāṇi, the Buddha's de facto bodyguard in a halo of flames; and below him to the right is the buddha for the hungry ghost realm, golden begging bowl in both hands, ready to feed the hungry ghosts, with food if not with merit.[195] In the upper right is the deity Tārā, surrounded by floral vines with lotus buds and blossoms, and beneath her are three hungry ghosts, raised above the rest, looking up to her and, likely owing to her blessing, no longer breathing fire.

At the bottom left of this image one can see into the lowest "realm of existence" (*gati*)—hell—with excruciating cold and heat, and its even more horrific torments, like having one's head sawed in half and being speared in one's genitals.

Plate 6

This image[196] comes from the first page of an illustrated manuscript of the *Phra Malai Klon Suat*,[197] a popular recitation version of the story of the legendary miracle-working monk Phra Malai that includes detailed descriptions of his travels to the realms of heaven, hell, and hungry ghosts.[198] Phra Malai is pictured emerging from an opening in the clouds, with a fan in his left hand and his right hand outstretched in a gesture of benevolence. Below him are five hungry ghosts, each on fire and suffering unique torments, and each with hands joined in veneration toward him.

The outer two characters are male, bug-eyed with wispy beards and mouths agape, and with slightly bloated stomachs, signifying hunger. The character on the far right has flames emerging from his knees and forehead. The character on the far left has flames for hands and suffers from an enormous scrotum, perhaps a gigantic hydrocele, which is draped over his shoulder. According to the text of the *Phra Malai Klon Suat*, "this consequence awaits corrupt government officials who take advantage of their position at the expense of the peasants."[199]

The three characters in the middle are likely female, with visible ribs and protruding spines. The character in the center has a pagoda-shaped protuberance on the top of her head, shaped much like her raised hands, and flames coming from her left elbow. Her head has hair and ears, but her eyes, nose, and mouth are located at her waist, with one beady eye looking up at the character to her right. The *Phra Malai Klon Suat* describes a similar type of hungry ghost—headless, with a mouth at the urethra, eyes at the chest, head on the belly, and a protruding nose—who suffers this fate because in his previous life as a human he had been a thief.[200] The character who looks down to meet her gaze has the face, ears, and horns of what looks like a water buffalo, with flames emerging from knee and shoulder. The *Phra Malai Klon Suat* describes a type of hungry ghost with an animal's head, including some who have a human body and the head of a water buffalo. This fate awaits one who believes in witches and is guided by wickedness.[201] The leftmost character in the middle likewise has a protuberance on the top of her head and has hair and ears but no face; flames emerge from her thighs. Not all the hungry ghosts depicted in this image are described in the text, and the text describes various types of hungry ghosts that are not represented in the image, like those whose flesh is devoured by packs of wild beasts because in a previous existence they killed animals for food and had no remorse.[202]

According to the *Phra Malai Klon Suat,* the various hungry ghosts plead with Phra Malai—with palms pressed together in veneration, just as depicted in the image—asking him to inform their relatives in the human world of their miserable condition as hungry ghosts so that their relatives can make merit on their behalf. Phra Malai readily agrees.[203]

Plate 7

This image is representative of the genre of Indian prints known as *karnī bharnī* ("reap as you sow").[204] Such images, which were imported from Jain soteriology into mainstream Hinduism in the late nineteenth century, depict the karmic consequences of moral transgression. Paired together are human misdeeds and the unique torments they generate in the next life, offering a visual representation of karmic causality that is reminiscent of the textual accounts found in the hungry ghost stories in this volume. This print shows the hellish results that await one who pierces an animal's septum, slaughters fish, forges documents, drinks alcohol, abuses one's parents, hunts animals, has illicit sex, preaches falsehoods, commits adultery, torments a rival's child, and overloads beasts of burden.

Plate 8

Four hungry ghosts are pictured, with tiny necks and extended stomachs, visible spines and spindly limbs, long nails and scraggly hair, and vacant eyes.[205] Behind them is a forbidding wooden fence and gate, both run down and overgrown. The hungry ghosts are on a desolate street, with scraps of paper, twigs, weeds, rocks, pools of urine, and piles of shit. The central figure sits on the ground, slouching with desiccated breasts, mouth agape, looking disconsolate. The three other figures, who are presumably male, are in various states of eating excrement. The character in the back is licking up a pile of shit, and the character in the front appears to be preparing to do the same. The character on the far right, with hands and mouth full of shit, stares back at the viewer.

Matthew Meyer, who created this image for an illustrated database of Japanese folklore, offers these insights:

> I studied Buddhist art and culture in college, and ever since I have been interested in the imagery of hungry ghosts (*gaki*). The general look is always the same—distended bellies, desperate looks on their faces. It's all very Hieronymus Bosch.
>
> In my line of work, I come into contact with lots of ghost paintings and monster scrolls. One genre I particularly enjoy is hell scrolls. These are big paintings, which many Japanese temples possess, that depict the layers of hell and often the realm of hungry ghosts. I've seen scrolls where hungry ghosts are just sitting outside of peoples' homes, seemingly living in our world but in a darker, more grotesque version of it. There are houses, gates, and everything you'd see in a painting of a normal town, only more grim and less colorful.
>
> When designing the present image, I took inspiration from the imagery that had been in my head for a long time. I placed my *gaki* in front of a gate to a wealthy home, where

the only thing they could even attempt to eat is the refuse sitting in the street. Being ghosts, they probably don't see the beauty in the world; it's all a dull grayish tone. My image is more brown because the scrolls that I enjoy so much have all browned with age, and so that is the color tone that I associate with ghosts and *gaki*.[206]

Plate 1. Śroṇa Koṭikarna encounters an iron city filled with hungry ghosts. A painting from cave 212 (the so-called Seafarer's Cave) of the Kizil cave complex in Xinjiang, China, from the fifth century CE. The reproduction comes from Grünwedel 1920, plates 15–16. The painting is now housed in the Museum für Asiatische Kunst in Berlin, no. III 8401. See p. 55.

Plate 2. Four hungry ghosts. Detail of a wall painting from Bezeklik Cave 18 of the Bezeklik cave grottoes near Turpan in Xinjiang, China, from the eleventh–twelfth century CE. Inv. no. III 8453, © Museum für Asiatische Kunst, Staatliche Museen zu Berlin; photo: Ines Buschmann. See p. 55.

Plate 3. *Path of the Hungry Ghosts*, one of the *Six Paths*. China, Southern Song period, thirteenth century. Ink and colors on silk, 41 ¼ x 18 ½ inches. Shin Chion-in, Shiga Prefecture, Japan. Photograph courtesy of Otsu City Museum of History. See pp. 55–59.

Plate 4. *Flaming-Mouth Ghost King*. China, Ming dynasty, 1643. Ink and colors on silk, 57 ⅞ x 31 ⅞ inches. Rokudōchinnō-ji, Kyoto, Japan. Photograph courtesy of Osaka City Museum of Fine Arts. See pp. 59–61.

Plate 5. Detail of the hungry ghost realm from a Tibetan painted scroll (*thangka*) representing the "wheel of existence" (*saṃsāra-cakra, bhāva-cakra*). © State Museum of Ethnology Munich, no. 69-5-1; photo: Marianne Franke. See pp. 61–62.

Plate 6. Detail from an illustrated manuscript from circa 1862 of the *Phra Malai Klon Suat* from Wat Manee Sathit Kapittharam (alias Wat Thung Kaeo), Uthai Thani province, central Thailand. Photo courtesy of Fragile Palm Leaves Foundation / Henry Ginsburg Fund, Bangkok. See pp. 62–63.

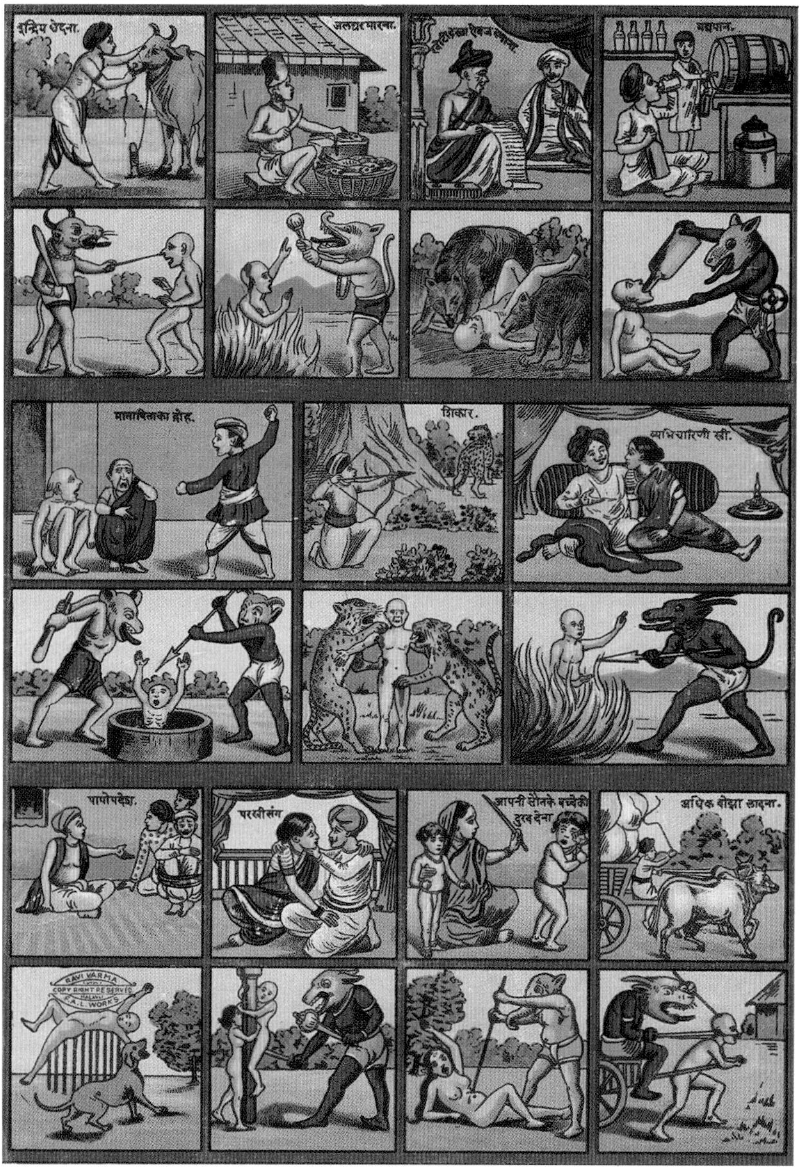

Plate 7. *Reap as You Sow.* "Narakvās Number 2." Chromolithograph, Ravi Varma Press, Malavi (near Lonavala), circa 1915. See pp. 63.

Plate 8. Matthew Meyer, *Hungry Ghosts*, 2015. Digital illustration from pencil drawing, 6 x 8 inches. See pp. 64–65.

Technical Notes

Sources

THE FOLLOWING TRANSLATION is based on the Sanskrit edition of the *Avadānaśataka* compiled by J. S. Speyer in 1906 (= Avś). Speyer made use of five manuscripts to create his edition (mss. B, D, P, C, and F),[207] but as he explains, he primarily relied on only one, "the Cambridge Add. 1611, which I denote as [ms.] B. The other three mss. I have collated, CDP have been copied from it. There cannot be the least doubt thereabout."[208] Speyer also examined other avadāna texts for parallels and consulted the Tibetan version of the *Avadānaśataka* for problematic words and passages, although only indirectly. Not skilled in the language himself, he reached out to Léon Feer, who had made extensive use of the Tibetan when he translated the *Avadānaśataka* in 1891. Feer, as Speyer notes, "with the greatest helpfulness and sympathy supplied me with the Tibetan correspondences of which I stood in need up to the 6th decade."[209]

I also reviewed P. L. Vaidya's Sanskrit edition of the *Avadānaśataka* from 1958 (= Avś-V). It is a near verbatim rendering of Speyer's edition but without the latter's copious notes and appendices; nevertheless, it does contain some new readings, both inspired and spurious. As such, in my translation I include page numbers in square brackets that refer to Speyer's edition, and in my notes, when especially helpful or noteworthy, I reference Vaidya's edition. Also useful is the edition of the text that is currently available on GRETIL (Göttingen Register of Electronic Texts in Indian Languages).[210] It is based on the work of both Speyer and Vaidya, although it contains no new readings.

Particularly helpful for my translation was the canonical Tibetan translation of the text, which is now preserved in the Kangyur. This Tibetan text does not differ dramatically in content from the Sanskrit text of Speyer's edition, but it is often helpful for clarifying the Sanskrit and, occasionally, for correcting it. In cases of the latter, I refer to the Tibetan recension of the *Avadānaśataka* that is preserved in the Derge (= D) edition of the Buddhist canon.

In addition to Sanskrit and Tibetan editions of the text, I also consulted other texts for helpful parallels and discrepancies, especially the *Divyāvadāna*, another avadāna compilation, and the *Mūlasarvāstivāda-vinaya,* which is closely affiliated with the *Avadānaśataka*.[211] For the latter, I made use of the *Gilgit Manuscripts* (Dutt 1984), the facsimile edition of the *Gilgit Buddhist Manuscripts* (Vira and Chandra 1995), critically edited portions of the text (e.g., Vogel and Wille 1996), and Tibetan recensions.

I also benefited enormously from the research of other scholars, both past and present. Eugène Burnouf translated portions of the text way back in 1844, and Léon Feer translated the complete text in 1891. Their work is astonishingly good. Reading it is both an education and a schooling, simultaneously a learning and a humbling experience. Unlike these pioneers, I have been able to rely on the work of many scholars, making use of new editions (e.g., Demoto 2006, 23–26, and Silk 2008, 265–66), new translations (e.g., Schopen 1995, 500–502, Appleton 2013, Appleton 2014a, and Appleton 2020), recent studies (e.g., Demoto 2006 and Muldoon-Hules 2017), and a wide variety of reference works. The field of Buddhist studies has expanded dramatically since the nineteenth century, and Buddhist scholars now have many interlocutors, in prose and in person.

Conventions

In the first note to each of the ten stories in this volume, I provide a reference to the corresponding Tibetan and, if relevant, additional editions, translations, studies, and/or parallels. Each story is then annotated with technical notes, primarily intended for specialists, that record important textual and grammatical issues as well as some alternate readings and likely reconstructions. I do not note every one of the text's peculiarities, nor every time the Tibetan recension preserves an alternate reading, nor (alas) what is preserved in the Chinese, but my notes do help make sense of the more problematic and opaque passages.

In terms of style, I follow many of the same conventions that I followed in my translation of the *Divyāvadāna*:

> I try to translate prose as prose and verse as verse, and I offset certain stereotypical passages for ease of reading. I do not translate proper names and place names, although the first time they occur in each story I include a translation in parentheses (if a translation is helpful or possible). Some of these names are found in the glossary, but not place names . . . Technical terms have been translated when possible, and when not, they have been left in the original Sanskrit and italicized. There are, however, some exceptions. Terms that have been adopted in vernacular English, such as *dharma*, *brahman*, and *saṃsāra*, have been left untranslated and unitalicized, as have terms that appear frequently and are part of the naturalized lexicon of the text, such as *arhat* . . . and *tathāgata*. Conversely, some rather technical terms have been translated, such as *antigod* (for *asura*) . . . and *great snake* (for *mahoraga*). Although all of these terms could be usefully glossed, I think the vernacular understanding of the former and the translations of the latter are sufficient for the reader to understand these stories in their complexity. These

technical terms, whether translated or not, can be found in the glossary.[212]

Also in terms of style, I have tried to follow the text's diction, being colloquial, technical, crass, or eloquent as signaled by the text. For example, when a character "berates" another or commits an "act of harsh speech," it should sound appropriately brash. These stories are alternatively, if not simultaneously, treatises for the learned and tales for the layman, and I have tried to preserve this heterogeneous character.

Abbreviations

Avś	*Avadānaśataka*. See Speyer 1902–9.
Avś-V	*Avadānaśataka*. See Vaidya 1958.
BHSD	*Buddhist Hybrid Sanskrit Dictionary*. See Edgerton 1993, vol. 2.
D	Derge edition of the Tibetan Tripiṭaka
Skt.	Sanskrit
Tib.	Tibetan

Sanskrit Pronunciation

The vowels and consonants in Sanskrit listed below are pronounced much like the italicized letters in the English words that follow them. Note that an *h* after a consonant is not a separate letter. It signifies instead that the consonant it follows is to be aspirated. The Sanskrit letters are listed in Sanskrit alphabetical order.

Vowels

a	b*u*t
ā	f*a*ther
i	p*i*t

ī *see*

u f*oo*t

ū dr*oo*l

ṛ *ri*g

ṝ no obvious English equivalent; lengthened *ṛ*

e r*a*y

ai h*i*gh

o h*o*pe

au r*ou*nd

Gutturals (pronounced by slightly raising the back of the tongue and closing off the throat)

k *k*ick

kh blo*ckh*ead

g *g*o

gh do*gh*ouse

ṅ ri*n*g

Palatals (pronounced with the tongue lying on the bottom of the mouth)

c *ch*ip

ch mat*chh*ead

j *j*ob

jh he*dge*hog

ñ i*n*jury

Retroflex (pronounced by curling the tip of the tongue to touch the roof of the mouth)

ṭ *t*ry

ṭh *t*art

ḍ *d*rum
ḍh no obvious English equivalent; strongly aspirated *ḍ*
ṇ ti*n*t

Dentals (pronounced by placing the tip of the tongue against the back of the upper teeth)

t s*t*ick
th an*th*ill
d *d*inner
dh roun*dh*ouse
n *n*ice

Labials (pronounced with the lips together)

p s*p*in
ph u*ph*eaval
b *b*in
bh clu*bh*ouse
m *m*other

Semivowels, sibilants, and additional sounds

y *y*es
r d*r*ama
l *l*ife
v a sound between English *v* and *w* (e.g., between *v*ine and *w*ine)
ś *sh*ip
ṣ retroflex *ś*
s *s*ip
h *h*ope
ṃ *anusvāra:* nasalizes the preceding vowel
ḥ *visarga:* an aspiration with an echoing of the preceding vowel (e.g., *devaḥ* as *devaha*)

Translation

Avadānaśataka STORIES 41–50

[241] A summary of the decade:

(1) Sugar Mill, (2) Food, (3) Drinking Water, (4) A Pot of Shit,
(5) Maudgalyāyana, (6) Uttara, (7) Blind from Birth,
(8) The Merchant, (9) Sons, and (10) Jāmbāla.[213]

1. Sugar Mill

41. Guḍaśālā[214]

The Lord Buddha was respected, honored, revered, and venerated by kings, royal ministers, the wealthy, city dwellers, merchants, caravan leaders, gods, nāgas, yakṣas, antigods, heavenly birds, kinnaras, and great snakes. Worshiped as such by gods, nāgas, yakṣas, antigods, heavenly birds, kinnaras, and great snakes, the Lord Buddha—who was renowned and possessed great merit[215]—received provisions of robes, begging bowls, bedding and seats, and medicines to cure the sick. Once he was staying in the city of Rājagṛha with the community made up of his disciples at the bamboo grove in Kalandakanivāpa (Squirrel Feeding Place).

When the Blessed One awakened to unsurpassed perfect awakening, the venerable Śāriputra and Maudgalyāyana made this promise: "We will not eat any almsfood as long as there remains even a single being that we have not released from the realms of hell, the animal realm, and the realm of hungry ghosts." Thereafter, from time to time, those two venerable ones would journey through the realms of hell and journey through the realms of animals and hungry ghosts. In the realm of hungry ghosts, they [would hear][216] the incoherent wailing of beings as they suffered various torments. When they returned [from these journeys],[217] they would inform the fourfold assembly, who upon listening to them would be deeply moved. [242] Especially for them, those two venerable ones would give explanations of the dharma[218] such that many beings would attain spiritual distinction and became vessels for stories about listening to the dharma.[219]

One time the venerable Mahāmaudgalyāyana was journeying through the realm of hungry ghosts, and he saw a hungry ghost [with a face] like a mountaintop,[220] a stomach like an ocean, a mouth like the eye of a needle, and who was totally covered with hair. He was ablaze, completely aflame, a single fiery mass, a perpetual cremation.[221] Racked with sensations that were searing, piercing, distressing, agonizing, and acute, he was crying out in pain. Wherever he wandered, the ground turned into excrement and urine, and so he made his way with difficulty.

"Friend," the elder asked the hungry ghost, "what deed have you done such that you are racked with sensations that are searing, piercing, distressing, agonizing, and acute?"

"When the sun has already risen, there's no need of a lamp," the hungry ghost said. "Ask the Blessed One about the matter. He'll explain to you the deed that led me to this fate."

Then the venerable Mahāmaudgalyāyana approached the Blessed One. At that time the Blessed One had just emerged from meditative seclusion and was giving the fourfold assembly an explanation of the sweet dharma—sweet like pure honey. [243] The assembly of many hundreds [of people] listened to the sweet dharma of the Blessed One with faculties unwavering.

Now lord buddhas speak first [out of propriety], speak kindly, offer words of welcome—"Come near!"—and smile first and foremost. And so the Blessed One said this to the venerable Mahāmaudgalyāyana: "Come near, Maudgalyāyana! Welcome. Where are you coming from?"

"Bhadanta," Maudgalyāyana said, "I am coming from a journey through the realm of hungry ghosts. There I saw a hungry ghost whose mouth was like the eye of a needle, whose stomach was like a mountain, who was totally covered with hair, and who was foul smelling—really foul smelling." Then he said,

Throat and lips parched, suffering terribly,
body unstable like a lofty mountain,[222]
hairy face, naked as the sky,
mouth like the eye of a fine needle, skinny,

naked and hirsute,
[emaciated] like an upright skeleton,
skull in hand, horrific,[223]
running around screaming,

exhausted by hunger and thirst,
tormented by misfortune,
racked with searing sensations,
and crying out in pain.

What terrible sin did he commit
in the world of mortals? [244]

"Maudgalyāyana," the Blessed One said, "that hungry ghost is a sinner. Do you want to hear the deed that led him to this fate?

"Yes, Bhadanta."

"Then listen to this, Maudgalyāyana. Concentrate well and closely. I will speak."

Long ago, Maudgalyāyana, in the city of Rājagṛha, there was a certain merchant who was rich, wealthy, and prosperous, with vast and extensive holdings, and who had amassed a wealth like the god Vaiśravaṇa. Truly, he rivaled Vaiśravaṇa in wealth. He owned five hundred sugarcane mills where sugar was pressed.

When no buddhas are born, solitary buddhas can arise in the world. They have compassion for the poor and neglected, they live in remote areas, and they alone are worthy of people's offerings.

At that time there was a certain solitary buddha who had compassion for the poor and neglected and who stayed in remote areas. One morning, he got dressed, took his bowl and robe, and entered Rājagṛha for alms.

That Bhadanta had contracted a fatal disease, and a doctor had prescribed sugarcane juice for him as a cure. So he approached the merchant's factory.

The merchant saw the solitary buddha, who inspired faith through his body and through his mind, and upon seeing him, he said, "Does the noble one need anything?"

"Yes, householder—sugarcane juice," the solitary buddha said.

The householder instructed one of his workmen: "Provide the noble one with sugarcane juice."

Then one day the householder went away on a business trip. During that time, there arose in the workman [who dispensed the sugarcane juice] a meanness with regard to another's property [in this case, his boss's]. "If I give the noble one sugarcane juice," he thought, "he'll just come back again." Hell-bent on descending into the three realms of existence that no one desires [the realms of hell beings, animals, and hungry ghosts], spurning the two realms of existence to which everyone aspires [the realms of gods and humans], and having strayed far, far away from any noble dharma, he produced a sinful thought and said to the solitary buddha: "Hey monk![224] Give me your bowl. I'll give you some sugarcane juice."

Now the knowledge and insight of arhats, disciples, and solitary buddhas does not operate unless they focus their attention.[225] [245] So the solitary buddha, having compassion for the poor and neglected, thought, "This man is just a worker for hire. Something good should be done for him." And he offered him his bowl.

That wicked and cruel-hearted man took the bowl, went off to a place hidden from view, filled it up with urine, topped it off with sugarcane juice, and then returned and presented it to the solitary buddha.

The solitary buddha reflected [on what the man had done] and thought, "This poor man has committed a great sin." Then he dumped out his bowl to one side and departed.

"What do you think, Maudgalyāyana?" the Blessed One said. "The workman at that time and at that juncture is now this hungry ghost. As a result of his deed, he has experienced unending suffering in saṃsāra. Even now, as a hungry ghost, he experiences excruciating suffering. Therefore, Maudgalyāyana, work hard to rid yourself of meanness![226] That way you won't develop faults like that hungry ghost.[227]

"And so, Maudgalyāyana, the result of absolutely evil actions is absolutely evil, the result of absolutely pure actions is absolutely pure, and the result of mixed actions is mixed. Therefore, Maudgalyāyana, you should reject absolutely evil actions and mixed ones as well and strive to perform only absolutely pure actions. It is this, Maudgalyāyana, that you should learn to do."

This was said by the Blessed One. With their minds uplifted, the venerable Maudgalyāyana and various gods, antigods, heavenly birds, and so on rejoiced at the words of the Blessed One.

2. *Food*

42. Bhaktam[228]

[246] The Lord Buddha was respected, honored, revered, and venerated by kings, royal ministers, the wealthy, city dwellers, merchants, caravan leaders, gods, nāgas, yakṣas, antigods, heavenly birds, kinnaras, and great snakes. Worshiped as such by gods, nāgas, yakṣas, antigods, heavenly birds, kinnaras, and great snakes, the Lord Buddha—who was renowned and possessed great merit—received provisions of robes, begging bowls, bedding and seats, and medicines to cure the sick. Once he was staying in the city of Śrāvastī with the community made up of his disciples at the Jeta Grove in the park of Anāthapiṇḍada (Almsgiver to the Poor).

At that time the venerable Mahāmaudgalyāyana was sitting at the base of a tree for a midday rest when he heard the sound of a hungry ghost crying out in pain. She was racked with sensations that were searing, piercing, distressing, agonizing, and acute—all the while, she was looking for food: "Friends, I'm hungry!" she said. "Friends, I'm thirsty!"

The elder Mahāmaudgalyāyana saw the hungry ghost and questioned her: "What sin did you commit such that you experience[229] such forms of suffering?"

"When the sun has already risen, there's no need of a lamp," the hungry ghost said. "Ask the Blessed One about the matter. He'll explain to you the deed that led me to this fate."

Then the venerable Mahāmaudgalyāyana approached the Blessed One. At that time the Blessed One had just emerged from meditative seclusion and was giving the fourfold assembly an explanation of the sweet dharma—sweet like pure honey. The assembly of many hundreds [of people] listened to the sweet dharma of the Blessed One with faculties unwavering.

Now lord buddhas speak first [out of propriety], speak kindly, offer words of welcome—"Come near!"—and smile first and foremost. [247] And so the Blessed One said this to the venerable Mahāmaudgalyāyana: "Come near, Maudgalyāyana! Welcome. Where are you coming from?"

"Bhadanta," Maudgalyāyana said, "I'm coming from a journey through the realm of hungry ghosts. There I saw a hungry ghost whose mouth was like the eye of a needle, whose stomach was like a mountain, and who was naked and totally covered with hair. Racked with sensations that were searing, piercing, distressing, agonizing, and acute, she was crying out in pain." Then he said,

Throat and lips parched, suffering terribly,
body unstable like a lofty mountain,
hairy face, naked as the sky,
mouth like the eye of a fine needle, skinny,

naked and hirsute,
[emaciated] like an upright skeleton,
skull in hand, horrific,
running around screaming,

exhausted by hunger and thirst,
tormented by misfortune,
racked with searing sensations,
and crying out in pain.

What terrible sin did she commit
in the world of mortals
so that she now experiences
such horrific suffering?

"Maudgalyāyana," the Blessed One said, "that hungry ghost is a sinner. Do you want to hear the deed that led her to this fate?

"Yes, Bhadanta."

"Then listen to this, Maudgalyāyana. Concentrate well and closely. I will speak."

Long ago, Maudgalyāyana, in a time gone by, when people lived for twenty thousand years, there arose in the world a perfectly awakened buddha named Kāśyapa who was

perfect in knowledge and conduct,
a sugata,
a knower of the world,
an unsurpassed guide for those in need of training, [248]
a teacher of gods and mortals,
a buddha,
and a blessed one.

Once he was staying near the city of Vārāṇasī at the deer park in Ṛṣipatana (Where Seers Fly).

At that time in Vārāṇasī there was a householder's wife who was mean, miserly, and clung to her possessions; she couldn't even bring herself to offer something to a crow, let alone beggars in need. When she saw an ascetic, a brahman, someone destitute, or a mendicant, she hardened her heart.[230]

One day a beggar who survived on alms entered her house, and when she saw him, there arose in her a meanness. She hardened her heart and had this thought: "If I offer him hospitality, he'll just come back again." Then that sinner, not considering the unwanted dangers of the next world, invited the monk in only to shut the door on him, cutting him off from any food. She berated him and said, "Monk, this hospitality is for you . . . so that you won't enter this house again!"[231]

Since that woman practiced, developed, and cultivated her meanness, she was reborn as a hungry ghost and so experiences such forms of suffering. Therefore, Maudgalyāyana, work hard to rid yourself of meanness! That way you won't develop the same faults as that hungry ghost.

This was said by the Blessed One. With their minds uplifted, the venerable Maudgalyāyana and various gods, antigods, heavenly birds, kinnaras, and great snakes rejoiced at the words of the Blessed One.

3. *Drinking Water*

43. Pānīyam[232]

[249] The Lord Buddha was respected, honored, revered, and venerated by kings, royal ministers, the wealthy, city dwellers, merchants, caravan leaders, gods, nāgas, yakṣas, antigods, heavenly birds, kinnaras, and great snakes. Worshiped as such by gods, nāgas, yakṣas, antigods, heavenly birds, kinnaras, and great snakes, the Lord Buddha—who was renowned and possessed great merit—received provisions of robes, begging bowls, bedding and seats, and medicines to cure the sick. Once he was staying near the city of Rājagṛha with the community made up of his disciples at the bamboo grove in Kalandakanivāpa (Squirrel Feeding Place).

Meanwhile the venerable Mahāmaudgalyāyana was wandering through the realm of hungry ghosts. There he saw a hungry ghost who looked like a burned-out tree stump,[233] totally covered with hair, with a mouth like the eye of a needle and a stomach like a mountain. She was ablaze, alight, aflame, a single fiery mass, a perpetual cremation. Tormented by thirst, she was racked with sensations that were searing, piercing, distressing, agonizing, and acute. Just by her sight, rivers and wells would dry up. And when the heavens sent rain, on her would fall a shower of sparks and embers.

Seeing her, the venerable Mahāmaudgalyāyana asked, "What sin did you commit such that you experience suffering like this?"

"I am a sinner, Bhadanta Mahāmaudgalyāyana," the hungry ghost said. "Ask the Blessed One about the matter. He will explain to you the deed that led me to this fate. And when other beings hear his account, they will refrain from this sinful deed."

Then the venerable Mahāmaudgalyāyana approached the Blessed One. At that time the Blessed One had just emerged from meditative seclusion and was giving the fourfold assembly an explanation of the sweet dharma—sweet like pure honey. The assembly of many hundreds [of people] listened to the sweet dharma of the Blessed One with faculties unwavering. [250]

Now lord buddhas speak first [out of propriety], speak kindly, offer words of welcome—"Come near!"—and smile first and foremost. And so the Blessed One said this to the venerable Mahāmaudgalyāyana: "Come near, Maudgalyāyana! Welcome. Where are you coming from?"

"Bhadanta," Maudgalyāyana said, "I'm coming from a journey through the realm of hungry ghosts. There I saw a hungry ghost who looked like a burned-out tree stump, totally covered with hair, with a mouth like the eye of a needle and a stomach like a mountain. She was ablaze, alight, aflame, a single fiery mass, a perpetual cremation. Tormented by thirst, she was racked with sensations that were searing, piercing, distressing, agonizing, and acute, and she was crying out in pain. Just by her sight, rivers and wells would dry up. And when the heavens sent rain, on her would fall a shower of sparks and embers."

"Mahāmaudgalyāyana," the Blessed One said, "that hungry ghost is a sinner. Do you want to hear the deed that led her to this fate?"

"Yes, Bhadanta."

"Then listen to this, Maudgalyāyana. Concentrate well and closely. I will speak."

Long ago, Maudgalyāyana, at a time in the past during this present auspicious age, when people lived for twenty thousand years, there arose in the world a perfectly awakened buddha named Kāśyapa who was

perfect in knowledge and conduct,
a sugata,
a knower of the world,
an unsurpassed guide for those in need of training,
a teacher of gods and mortals,
a buddha,
and a blessed one.

Once he was staying near the city of Vārāṇasī at the deer park in Ṛṣipatana (Where Seers Fly). And it was there that a monk walked by who was tormented by thirst. Then he came upon a well. A young woman who had just filled a pot with water was standing beside it.

"Sister," the monk said to her, "I'm tormented by thirst. Please offer me some water."

In that young woman there arose a meanness. Since she clung to her possessions, she said to the monk, "Monk, if you were dying, I still wouldn't give you any water. My water pot wouldn't be full." [251]

The monk, tormented by thirst and despairing, continued on his way.

That young woman, who had practiced, developed, and cultivated her meanness, then died and was reborn as a hungry ghost. And so she is racked with sensations that are searing, piercing, distressing, agonizing, and acute.

Therefore, Maudgalyāyana, this is the lesson to be learned: Work hard to rid yourself of meanness! It is this, Maudgalyāyana, that you should learn to do.

This was said by the Blessed One. With their minds uplifted, the venerable Maudgalyāyana and various gods, antigods, heavenly birds, kinnaras, great snakes, and so on rejoiced at the words of the Blessed One.

4. A Pot of Shit

44. Varcaghaṭaḥ[234]

[252] The Lord Buddha was respected, honored, revered, and venerated by kings, royal ministers, the wealthy, city dwellers, merchants, caravan leaders, gods, nāgas, yakṣas, antigods, heavenly birds, kinnaras, and great snakes. Worshiped as such by gods, nāgas, yakṣas, antigods, heavenly birds, kinnaras, and great snakes, the Lord Buddha—who was renowned and possessed great merit—received provisions of robes, begging bowls, bedding and seats, and medicines to cure the sick. Once he was staying near the city of Rājagṛha with the community made up of his disciples at the bamboo grove in Kalandakanivāpa (Squirrel Feeding Place).

One morning the venerable Maudgalyāyana got dressed, took his bowl and robe, and entered Rājagṛha for alms. After wandering through Rājagṛha for alms, he ate his meal, and after eating, he returned from his almsround. Then he put away his bowl and robe, washed his feet, and approached Vulture's Peak. Having approached, he made his way up Vulture's Peak and then sat down at the base of a tree for a midday rest.

Then the venerable Maudgalyāyana saw a hungry ghost who looked like a burned-out tree stump, naked and totally covered with hair, with a mouth like the eye of a needle and a stomach like a mountain. She was ablaze, alight, aflame, a single fiery mass, a perpetual cremation. Tormented by thirst, she was racked with sensations that were searing, piercing, distressing, agonizing, and acute, and she was crying out in pain. [253] She was foul smelling—really foul smelling. She looked like shit, and she was feeding on feces. And even those, she only procured with difficulty.[235]

Upon seeing her, the venerable Maudgalyāyana was deeply moved, and he questioned the hungry ghost:

> What sin did you commit such that
> you experience a result like this?

"I am a sinner, Bhadanta Mahāmaudgalyāyana," the hungry ghost said. "Ask the Blessed One about the matter. He will explain to you the deed that led me to this fate. And when other beings hear his account, they will refrain from this sinful deed."

Then the venerable Mahāmaudgalyāyana approached the Blessed One. At that time the Blessed One had just emerged from meditative seclusion and was giving the fourfold assembly an explanation of the sweet dharma—sweet like pure honey. The assembly of many hundreds [of people] listened to the sweet dharma of the Blessed One with faculties unwavering.

Now lord buddhas speak first [out of propriety], speak kindly, offer words of welcome—"Come near!"—and smile first and foremost. And so the Blessed One said this to the venerable Mahāmaudgalyāyana: "Come near, Maudgalyāyana! Welcome. Where are you coming from?"

"Bhadanta," Maudgalyāyana said, "I'm coming from a journey through the realm of hungry ghosts. There I saw a hungry ghost who looked like a burned-out tree stump, naked and totally covered with hair, with a mouth like the eye of a needle and a stomach like a mountain. She was ablaze, alight, aflame, a single fiery mass. Racked with sensations that were searing, piercing, distressing, agonizing, and acute, she was crying out in pain. Just by her sight, rivers and wells would dry up. [254] And when the heavens sent rain, on her would fall a shower of sparks and embers. She was foul smelling—really foul smelling. She looked like shit, and she was feeding on feces. And even those, she only procured with difficulty." Then he said,

> [Naked and hirsute,
> emaciated like an upright skeleton,][236]
> racked with searing sensations,
> and crying out in pain.
>
> She runs around suffering,
> piles of shit everywhere,[237]
> [wailing] "I drink and eat only shit!"[238]
> And even that she gets with difficulty.
>
> What terrible sin did she commit
> in the world of mortals
> so that she now experiences
> such horrific suffering?

"Maudgalyāyana," the Blessed One said, "that hungry ghost is a sinner. Do you want to hear the deed that led her to this fate?

"Yes, Bhadanta."

"Then listen to this, Maudgalyāyana. Concentrate well and closely. I will speak."

Long ago, Maudgalyāyana, in the city of Vārāṇasī, there was a solitary buddha who had compassion for the poor and neglected and who stayed in remote areas. Afflicted with an illness, he entered Vārāṇasī for alms, after a doctor had prescribed for him [a diet] of wholesome food. [255] He approached the home of a merchant.

The merchant saw him and asked, "Noble one, do you need anything?"

"Homemade nutritious food," he said.

Then the merchant instructed his daughter-in law: "Give wholesome food to the noble one."

In his daughter-in law there arose a meanness. "If I give him food today, he'll just come back again tomorrow." She retreated indoors, filled a bowl with shit, then covered it with food and proceeded to give it to the solitary buddha.

Now the knowledge and insight of disciples and solitary buddhas does not operate unless they focus their attention. So the solitary buddha accepted the bowl, and only after accepting it did he realize how much it smelled. "She must have filled it with excrement," he thought. Then that great being dumped out his bowl to one side and departed.

"What do you think, Maudgalyāyana?" the Blessed One said. "The merchant's daughter-in-law at that time and at that juncture is now this hungry ghost. Since she performed such a sinful deed, as a result, ever since, she is always reborn as a hell being, animal, or hungry ghost, and she always feeds on feces. Therefore, Maudgalyāyana, work hard to rid yourself of meanness! That way you won't develop the same faults as that hungry ghost. It is this, Maudgalyāyana, that you should learn to do."

This was said by the Blessed One. With their minds uplifted, the venerable Maudgalyāyana and various gods, antigods, heavenly birds, kinnaras, great snakes, and so on rejoiced at the words of the Blessed One.

5. *Maudgalyāyana*

45. Maudgalyāyanaḥ[239]

[256] The Lord Buddha was respected, honored, revered, and venerated by kings, royal ministers, the wealthy, city dwellers, merchants, caravan leaders, gods, nāgas, yakṣas, antigods, heavenly birds, kinnaras, and great snakes. Worshiped as such by gods, nāgas, yakṣas, antigods, heavenly birds, kinnaras, and great snakes, the Lord Buddha—who was renowned and possessed great merit—received provisions of robes, begging bowls, bedding and seats, and medicines to cure the sick. Once he was staying near the city of Rājagṛha with the community made up of his disciples at the bamboo grove in Kalandakanivāpa (Squirrel Feeding Place).

At that time, between Rājagṛha and the bamboo grove, there were five hundred hungry ghosts who looked like burned-out tree stumps, naked and totally covered with hair, with stomachs like mountains and mouths like the eye of a needle. They were ablaze, alight, completely aflame, a single fiery mass. Racked with sensations that were searing, piercing, distressing, agonizing, and acute, they were crying out in pain. And they were spinning in the air like whirlwinds, never finding rest on stable ground.

One morning the venerable Maudgalyāyana got dressed, took his bowl and robe, [257] and set off to enter[240] Rājagṛha for alms. He saw those hungry ghosts, and those hungry ghosts saw him.

As a single group those hungry ghosts approached the venerable

Mahāmaudgalyāyana and, having approached, spoke in a single voice, their words heavy with sorrow and sadness: "Bhadanta Mahāmaudgalyāyana, we were once five hundred merchants [living] in Rājagṛha. We were mean, miserly, and clung to our possessions. On our own, we never gave gifts or made offerings, and when others were giving gifts or making offerings, we would obstruct them. And we would berate all those truly worthy of offerings by calling them 'hungry ghosts': 'It's as though you were born as hungry ghosts, always begging for alms at people's homes!' And so, after we died, we were reborn as hungry ghosts like this.

"Bhadanta Mahāmaudgalyāyana, our relatives live in Rājagṛha. Explain to them the deed that led us to this fate. Then initiate a general collection of alms, feed the monastic community led by the Buddha, and have the reward from the offering assigned in our names. Maybe then we can be liberated from this existence as hungry ghosts."

The venerable Mahāmaudgalyāyana accepted the hungry ghosts' request with his silence. Then the venerable Mahāmaudgalyāyana initiated a general collection of alms from the homes of the relatives of those hungry ghosts and invited the monastic community led by the Buddha for a meal the following day. He then informed the hungry ghosts: "The Blessed One along with the monastic community has been invited for a meal tomorrow. You should come."

Then he announced to the relatives [of those hungry ghosts]: "[Tomorrow] you should come to the meal you have sponsored, offered on behalf of your relatives. There we will see them [in their current state as] hungry ghosts."

After this, the venerable Mahāmaudgalyāyana, all by himself, began to prepare the food. [258] As night turned into dawn, the food was made ready, but when the time arrived to sound the gong [for the meal], the venerable Mahāmaudgalyāyana didn't see those hungry ghosts. Making use of his divine sight, he began to focus his attention on them. He didn't see them anywhere in all of Magadha. Then, systematically, he began to search through the four continents. He didn't see them there either. Then he activated his knowledge and insight and continued searching. Even then he didn't see them.

The venerable Mahāmaudgalyāyana was troubled, and he informed the Blessed One: "Blessed One, the beneficiaries of the gift are nowhere to be seen!"

"Maudgalyāyana," the Blessed One said, "Don't despair. There are world systems beyond the reach of every disciple and solitary buddha, and beyond measure as well. They are set in motion by the winds of karma.[241] Now, Maudgalyāyana, observe the power of a tathāgata. I will make visible the knowledge and insight of one who is omniscient. I will demonstrate the miraculous power of a tathāgata. Strike the gong!"

When the gong was struck, the entire monastic community assembled. The relatives of the hungry ghosts, along with others who came out of curiosity, also assembled, eager to see the hungry ghosts. The Blessed One, making use of his magical powers, created a vision such that the hungry ghosts could see the Lord Buddha and the community made up of his disciples as they ate, and then retain it in their awareness.

"Our relatives feed the monastic community led by the Blessed One for our benefit!" they reflected.

Then the Blessed One, in a voice endowed with the five good qualities, assigned the reward from the offering: [259]

> May the merit from this gift
> follow these hungry ghosts!
> May they quickly rise from
> the brutal world of hungry ghosts!

Especially for them, the Blessed One gave an explanation of the dharma such that when [those assembled] heard it, many hundreds and thousands of beings rid themselves of the filth of meanness and attained a vision of truth. Those [five hundred] hungry ghosts cultivated faith in their hearts for the Blessed One, then died and were reborn in the select company of the gods of Trāyastriṃśa (Thirty-Three).

It is a rule of nature that just after beings are reborn as sons and daughters of the gods, they have three thoughts:

> From where did I die and pass away?
> Where have I been reborn?
> As a result of what deed?

The [newly born gods] saw that they had died and passed away from the realm of hungry ghosts. They had been reborn in the select company of the gods of Trāyastriṃśa. And this was the result of having cultivated faith in their hearts toward the Blessed One.

Then it occurred to those divine children who had previously been hungry ghosts: "It wouldn't be right for us to wait until our time here [in heaven][242] is finished before we went to see the Blessed One. We really should go to see the Blessed One even before our time here is done."

That very night those divine children who had previously been hungry ghosts—wearing earrings flawless and dangling and crowns resplendent with precious jewels, their bodies adorned with strings and necklaces of pearls and smeared with saffron, *tamāla* leaves, fenugreek, and so on—filled their laps with divine flowers: blue and red waterlilies, white lotuses, coral-tree flowers, and more. Then, illuminating the entire bamboo grove in Kalandakanivāpa with a great blaze of light, [260] they showered the Blessed One with those flowers and sat down in front of him to listen to the dharma.

Then the Blessed One, knowing the inclinations, propensities, makeup, and nature of those divine children who had previously been hungry ghosts, gave them an explanation of the dharma such that when they heard it, they attained great distinction. [Pleased] like traders who have just made a profit, they circumambulated the Blessed One three times and then vanished on the spot.

The Blessed One then addressed the venerable Mahāmaudgalyāyana: "Well done! Well done, Mahāmaudgalyāyana! Your service to the dharma has been successful. You have established those[243] hungry ghosts among the gods! On this night they came before me, and I instructed them in the dharma. They benefited and profited, and then they departed."

Then the venerable Mahāmaudgalyāyana explained [all this] to the relatives [of those former hungry ghosts who were now children of the gods]. Listening to him, they were astonished. Then they cultivated faith in their hearts toward the Blessed One and honored him all the more.

"Therefore, Maudgalyāyana, work hard to rid yourself of meanness![244] That way you won't develop the same faults as those hungry ghosts."

This was said by the Blessed One. With their minds uplifted, the venerable Maudgalyāyana and various gods, antigods, heavenly birds, kinnaras, great snakes, and so on rejoiced at the words of the Blessed One.

6. Uttara

46. Uttaraḥ[245]

[261] The Lord Buddha was respected, honored, revered, and venerated by kings, royal ministers, the wealthy, city dwellers, merchants, caravan leaders, gods, nāgas, yakṣas, antigods, heavenly birds, kinnaras, and great snakes. Worshiped as such by gods, nāgas, yakṣas, antigods, heavenly birds, kinnaras, and great snakes, the Lord Buddha—who was renowned and possessed great merit—received provisions of robes, begging bowls, bedding and seats, and medicines to cure the sick. Once he was staying near the city of Rājagṛha with the community made up of his disciples at the bamboo grove in Kalandakanivāpa (Squirrel Feeding Place).

In Rājagṛha there was a certain merchant who was rich, wealthy, and prosperous, with vast and extensive holdings, and who had amassed a wealth like the god Vaiśravaṇa. Truly, he rivaled Vaiśravaṇa in wealth. He brought home a girl from an appropriate family as his wife, and with her he fooled around, enjoyed himself, and made love. After some time, from fooling around, enjoying himself, and making love, his wife became pregnant. Eight or nine months later, she gave birth to a boy. After celebrating the occasion of the boy's birth, his relatives selected a named for him.

"What should this boy's name be?"

"He was born under the lunar mansion Uttara," the relatives said. "So let his name be Uttara."

The boy Uttara was raised and nourished, and in time he grew up. Then his father died, and Uttara became the master of the house. He set up a shop where he bought things and sold them and thus made his living in trade.[246]

Each day Uttara would go before the Blessed One, and from seeing him and listening to the true dharma, he developed faith in the Blessed One's order. The thought came to him that he should go forth as a monk, so he asked his mother, "Mother, give me permission to go forth as a monk in the Blessed One's order."

"Son," his mother, "you're my only child. [262] For as long as I live, don't go forth as a monk. When I'm dead, do as you must."

Uttara would give all that he earned to his mother and say, "Mother, use this to make offerings to ascetics and brahmans, to the poor and destitute."

But his mother was greedy, mean, miserly, and clung to her possessions. She would hide her son's money, and when ascetics and brahmans would arrive at their home in search of alms, she would berate them: "It's as though you were born as hungry ghosts, always begging for alms at people's homes!" And she would deceive her son: "Today I offered food to lots of monks!" Eventually she died and was reborn as a hungry ghost.

After the loss of his mother, Uttara gave gifts, performed meritorious deeds, and then went forth as a monk in the Blessed One's order. After striving, struggling, and straining, he came to understand that ever-turning five-spoked wheel of saṃsāra; he destroyed rebirth with all its conditioning factors, since it is subject to decay and decline, scattering and destruction; and by ridding himself of all defilements, he directly experienced arhatship. Becoming an arhat,

he was free from attachment in the three realms;
he regarded clods of earth and gold as equal in value;
he possessed equanimity toward the sky
and the palm of his hand;

he didn't distinguish between being cut by a blade
  and being anointed with sandalwood paste;
he crushed the eggshell [of his ignorance] with knowledge;
he obtained the special knowledges, superhuman faculties,
  and analytic insights;
and he was averse to worldly attainments, temptations,
  and honors.
He became worthy of respect, honor, and obeisance
  from the gods, including Indra and Upendra.

On the banks of the Ganges River, he made a hut out of leaves, and in it he meditated.

His mother, reborn as a hungry ghost, looked like a burned-out tree stump, naked and totally covered with hair, with a mouth like the eye of a needle and a stomach like a mountain. She was ablaze, completely aflame, a single fiery mass. Crying out in pain, she approached the venerable Uttara. The venerable Uttara saw the hungry ghost and asked, "Who are you? Why are you like this?"

The hungry ghost said:

I am your loving mother,
from whom you were born, dear son.
I have entered the realm of hungry ghosts,
which has no food or drink. [263]

Twenty-five years have passed
since I met my death.
I no longer recognize water,
let alone the look of food.

When I approach trees filled with fruit,
because of me they become barren.

When I approach lakes filled with water,
because of me they go dry.[247]

It is peaceful at the base of the Bhadanta's tree.
Cool water fills your water pot.
Have compassion for one who suffers.
Give me water! I am tormented by thirst![248]

Then Uttara said to his mother: "Mother, surely in the past, when you were human, you made offerings and performed meritorious deeds."

"Dear son," the hungry ghost said, "back then meanness consumed me, [264] so I didn't make offerings or perform meritorious deeds. With bad thoughts in mind, I buried all our valuables under the ritual fire pit. So now, dear son, go to our relatives' homes, initiate a general collection of alms, feed the monastic community led by the Buddha, have the reward from the offering assigned in my name, and have the Buddha teach.[249] Maybe then I can be liberated from this existence as a hungry ghost."

"Mother," Uttara said, "so it shall be. But you'll need to stand near the Buddha."

"Son," the hungry ghost said, "being naked, I'd be ashamed and embarrassed."

"Mother," Uttara said, "you weren't ashamed when you sinned. So why feel shame now, when your deeds have come to fruition?"

"Okay then," the hungry ghost said, "I'll come."

Then Uttara initiated a general collection of alms from the homes of his relatives and invited the monastic community led by the Buddha for a meal the following day. At the time of the gong [for the meal], the monastic community led by the Buddha assembled. The hungry ghost stood near the Buddha. Many hundreds and thousand of beings gathered around wishing to see her. When they saw the hungry ghost's deformed body, they were deeply moved and cultivated faith in their hearts for the Blessed One.

Then the venerable Uttara served fine foods to the monastic community led by the Buddha and had the reward from the offering assigned in the name of that hungry ghost. The Blessed One himself, in a voice endowed with the five good qualities, assigned the reward from the offering:

> May the merit from this gift
> follow this hungry ghost!
> May she quickly rise from
> the brutal world of hungry ghosts!

Especially for them, the Blessed One gave an explanation of the dharma to that hungry ghost and that large crowd of people such that when they heard it, many hundreds and thousands of beings attained a vision of truth. With faith in her heart, the hungry ghost died and was reborn as a hungry ghost with great power. [265] The venerable Uttara focused his attention and saw that she had been reborn as a hungry ghost with great power.

"Mother," the venerable Uttara said, "now you can do it. Give offerings and gifts."

"But son, I can't do it," the hungry ghost with great power said. "I have no desire to give."

Then the venerable Uttara said to that hungry ghost with great power:

> Even now your body is bloated yet
> emaciated, only skin, bones, and hide.
> Eyes veiled with the darkness of greed,
> you have returned to the realm of hungry ghosts.

Sometime after issuing this forceful rebuke, the venerable Uttara acquired twin pieces of cloth,[250] which he gave to the monastic community. A monk then purchased[251] the set from the monastic community and put it on a peg for hanging clothes.[252] That night the hungry ghost [that had been Uttara's mother] came and stole it. The monk informed the venerable Uttara, [266] so Uttara went and berated the hungry ghost, then recovered the cloth and returned it. This happened three times—the cloth was stolen from the monk, and then the venerable Uttara recovered it and returned it. Then the monk ripped the twin pieces of cloth into pieces and sewed them together into a floor covering on behalf of the monastic community from the four directions. The hungry ghost never stole it again.

"Now that you have seen how meanness makes beings ridiculous, you should, for this reason, focus your thinking on getting rid of meanness. That way you won't develop faults like that hungry ghost."

This was said by the Blessed One. With their minds uplifted, the venerable Maudgalyāyana and various gods, antigods, heavenly birds, kinnaras, great snakes, and so on rejoiced at the words of the Blessed One.

7. Blind from Birth

47. Jātyandhā[253]

[267] The Lord Buddha was respected, honored, revered, and venerated by kings, royal ministers, the wealthy, city dwellers, merchants, caravan leaders, gods, nāgas, yakṣas, antigods, heavenly birds, kinnaras, and great snakes. Worshiped as such by gods, nāgas, yakṣas, antigods, heavenly birds, kinnaras, and great snakes, the Lord Buddha—who was renowned and possessed great merit—received provisions of robes, begging bowls, bedding and seats, and medicines to cure the sick. Once he was staying in the city of Śrāvastī with the community made up of his disciples at the Jeta Grove in the park of Anāthapiṇḍada (Almsgiver to the Poor).

One morning the venerable Nandaka got dressed, took his bowl and robe, and [entered Śrāvastī for alms].[254] After wandering through Śrāvastī for alms, he ate his meal, and after eating, he returned from his almsround. Then he put away his bowl and robe and set off on a journey into the realm of hungry ghosts.

There the venerable Nandaka saw a hungry ghost who looked like a burned-out tree stump, congenitally blind, totally covered with hair, with a mouth like the eye of a needle and a stomach like a mountain. She was foul smelling and looked like a [corpse at a] cremation ground.[255] Crows, vultures, dogs, and jackals swarmed around her, and they were ripping her apart and devouring her flesh. Battered by sensations deep within, and racked with those sensations, which were searing, piercing, distressing, agonizing, and acute, she was crying out in pain.

The venerable Nandaka was deeply moved, and he questioned her: "Sister, what sinful deed did you commit such that you now experience suffering like this?"

"When the sun itself has already risen, there's no need of a lamp," the hungry ghost said. "Ask the Blessed One about the matter. He will explain to you the deed that led me to this fate. And when other beings hear his account, they will refrain from this sinful deed."

Then the venerable Nandaka approached the Blessed One. [268] At that time the Blessed One had just emerged from meditative seclusion and was giving the fourfold assembly an explanation of the sweet dharma—sweet like pure honey. The assembly of many hundreds [of people] listened to the sweet dharma of the Blessed One with faculties unwavering.[256]

Now lord buddhas speak first [out of propriety],[257] offer words of welcome—"Come near!"—and smile first and foremost. And so the Blessed One said this to the venerable Nandaka: "Come near, Nandaka! Welcome. Where are you coming from?"

"Bhadanta," Nandaka said, "I'm coming from a journey through the realm of hungry ghosts. There I saw a hungry ghost who looked like a burned-out tree stump,[258] totally covered with hair, with a mouth like the eye of a needle and a stomach like a mountain. She was foul smelling and looked like a [corpse at a] cremation ground. Crows, vultures, dogs, and jackals swarmed around her; they were ripping her apart and devouring her flesh. Battered by sensations deep within, and racked with those sensations, which were searing, piercing, distressing, agonizing, and acute, she was crying out in pain." Then he said,

> Throat and lips parched, suffering terribly,
> body unstable like a lofty mountain,
> hairy face, naked as the sky,
> mouth like the eye of a fine needle, skinny,

naked and hirsute,
[emaciated] like an upright skeleton,
skull in hand, horrific,
running around screaming,

exhausted by hunger and thirst,
tormented by misfortune,
racked with searing sensations,
and crying out in pain.

What terrible sin did she commit
in the world of mortals
so that she now experiences
such horrific suffering?

"Nandaka," the Blessed One said, "that hungry ghost is a sinner. Do you want to hear the deed that led her to this fate?

"Yes, Bhadanta."

"Then listen to this, Nandaka. Concentrate well and closely. I will speak." [269]

Long ago, Nandaka, in this present auspicious age when people lived for twenty thousand years,[259] there arose in the world a perfectly awakened buddha named Kāśyapa, who was[260]

perfect in knowledge and conduct,
a sugata,
a knower of the world,
an unsurpassed guide for those in need of training,
a teacher of gods and mortals,
a buddha,
and a blessed one.

Once he was staying near the city of Vārāṇasī at the deer park in Ṛṣipatana (Where Seers Fly). In Vārāṇasī there was a certain merchant's daughter who longed for the dharma. Eventually, from listening to the dharma, she came to see the faults of conditioned existence and the virtues of nirvāṇa. She then obtained her parents' permission and went forth as a nun in the Blessed One's order. On her behalf, her relatives constructed a nunnery,[261] and it was there that she lived, together with other nuns, both novices and masters.

Over time, because of her heedlessness, she became lax with respect to moral conduct. The other nuns, considering her immoral, expelled her. In response, the merchant's daughter [suspended][262] the general collection of alms that was gathered from the homes of the monastery's donors[263] [and was destined for the nuns]. She also denounced the nuns, both novices and masters. And when she saw virtuous monks, she'd shut her eyes.

"What do you think, Nandaka? The merchant's daughter is now this hungry ghost. Since she indulged her meanness while she was in the nunnery, she was reborn as a hungry ghost. Since she suspended the regular provisions of food [that her relatives offered to the nuns], she is now mauled by crows, vultures, dogs, and [jackals].[264] Since she denounced the nuns, both novices and masters, a foul smell clings to her. And since when she saw virtuous monks she would shut her eyes, she was born blind.

"And so, Nandaka, the result of absolutely evil actions is absolutely evil, the result of absolutely pure actions is absolutely pure, and the result of mixed actions is mixed. Therefore, Nandaka, you should reject absolutely evil actions and mixed ones as well, and strive to perform only absolutely pure actions. It is this, Nandaka, that you should learn to do." [270]

While this explanation of the dharma was being delivered, tens of hundreds and thousands of beings had a vision of truth. Then the Blessed

One addressed the monks: "[Monks,][265] these beings and others [like them] know that there is great danger in meanness and misdeeds of speech. [Therefore] work hard to rid yourselves of meanness and misdeeds of speech! It is this, monks, that you should learn to do."

This was said by the Blessed One. With their minds uplifted, the monks and various gods, antigods, heavenly birds, kinnaras, great snakes, and so on rejoiced at the words of the Blessed One.

8. The Merchant

48. Śreṣṭhī[266]

[271] The Lord Buddha was respected, honored, revered, and venerated by kings, royal ministers, the wealthy, city dwellers, merchants, caravan leaders, gods, nāgas, yakṣas, antigods, heavenly birds, kinnaras, and great snakes. Worshiped as such by gods, nāgas, yakṣas, antigods, heavenly birds, kinnaras, and great snakes, the Lord Buddha—who was renowned and possessed great merit—received provisions of robes, begging bowls, bedding and seats, and medicines to cure the sick. Once he was staying in the city of Śrāvastī with the community made up of his disciples at the Jeta Grove in the park of Anāthapiṇḍada (Almsgiver to the Poor).

In Śrāvastī there was a certain merchant who was rich, wealthy, and prosperous, with vast and extensive holdings, and who had amassed a wealth like the god Vaiśravaṇa. Truly, he rivaled Vaiśravaṇa in wealth. One day he went out to the Jeta Grove and saw the Lord Buddha,

who was adorned with the thirty-two marks of a great man,
whose body was radiant with the eighty minor marks,
who was adorned with a halo extending an arm's length,
whose brilliance was greater than a thousand suns,
and who, like a mountain of jewels that moved,
  was beautiful from every side.

Upon seeing him, the merchant venerated the Blessed One's feet and sat down in front of him to listen to the dharma.[267]

The Blessed One gave him an explanation of the dharma designed to cause disgust with conditioned existence. Hearing it, the merchant saw the faults of conditioned existence and the virtues of nirvāṇa and went forth as a monk in the Blessed One's order.

Sometime after going forth as a monk, he came to be renowned and possess great merit, and so he received provisions of robes, begging bowls, bedding and seats, and medicines to cure the sick. He accepted those provisions,[268] hoarding whatever he obtained and not sharing with his fellow monks. Since he practiced, developed, and cultivated this meanness, he came to covet his possessions. And so when he died, he was reborn in his same monastic cell as a hungry ghost. [272]

His fellow monks struck the funeral gong[269] and then carried off his body. They performed a funeral ceremony for his corpse and afterward returned to the monastery. Once there they opened the door to [the deceased monk's] cell and began to look for his bowl and robe [to return them to the monastic community]. Just then they saw that hungry ghost, whose hands, feet, and eyes were deformed and whose body was absolutely disgusting. He was clutching [the deceased monk's] bowl and robe.[270] At such a hideous sight, the monks were deeply moved and informed the Blessed One.

Then the Blessed One—in order to do a good deed for that deceased son of a good family, to inspire trepidation in an assembly of students,[271] and to make perfectly clear the calamitous results of meanness—went to that place [in the monastery], leading the monastic community that surrounded him.

That hungry ghost saw the Lord Buddha,

> who was adorned with the thirty-two marks of a great man,
> whose body was radiant with the eighty minor marks,
> who was adorned with a halo extending an arm's length,

whose brilliance was greater than a thousand suns,
and who, like a mountain of jewels that moved,
was beautiful from every side.

As soon as the hungry ghost saw him, he developed faith in the Blessed One and became ashamed [of his past behavior].

Then the Blessed One, in a voice that was thundering, deep, and booming,[272] berated the hungry ghost: "Friend, hoarding your bowl and robe like this is self-destructive![273] That's why you were reborn in one of the terrible realms of existence. So cultivate faith in your heart toward me! And cultivate dispassion in your heart for these monastic provisions! If not, when you die [and pass away] from here, you will be reborn in the realms of hell."

Then the hungry ghost returned the bowl and robe to the monastic community, fell prostrate at the Blessed One's feet, and confessed his sin. The Blessed One then assigned the reward from the offering in the hungry ghost's name.

May the merit from this gift
follow this hungry ghost!
May he quickly rise from
the brutal world of hungry ghosts! [273]

The hungry ghost cultivated faith in the Blessed One, then died and was reborn as a hungry ghost with great power.

That very night that hungry ghost with great power—wearing earrings flawless and dangling and a crown resplendent with precious jewels, his body adorned with strings and necklaces of pearls and smeared with saffron, *tamāla* leaves, fenugreek, and so on—filled his lap with divine flowers: blue, red, and white waterlilies, white lotuses, and coral-tree flowers. Then, illuminating all of the Jeta Grove with a great blaze of light, he showered the Blessed One with those flowers and sat down in front of him to listen to the dharma. The Blessed One gave him an explanation of the dharma such that when he heard it, he became filled with faith. Then he departed.

The monks [in the monastery] had remained awake meditating in the first and last watches of the night[274] and had seen a great blaze of light near the Blessed One. In doubt about what they had seen, they [went and] asked the Blessed One: "Blessed One, last night did Brahmā, the lord of the world, Śakra, the leader of the gods, or the four world protectors come to see the Blessed One?"

"No, monks," the Blessed One said. "It wasn't Brahmā, the lord of the world, nor Śakra, the leader of the gods, nor the four world protectors who came to see me. Instead, it was that hungry ghost who died and has now been reborn as a hungry ghost with great power. Last night he came before me, and I instructed him in the dharma. When he departed, he was filled with faith.

"Therefore, monks, work hard to rid yourselves of meanness! That way you won't develop the same faults as that merchant who became a hungry ghost. It is this, monks, that you should learn to do."

This was said by the Blessed One. With their minds uplifted, the monks and various gods, antigods, heavenly birds, kinnaras, great snakes, and so on rejoiced at the words of the Blessed One.

9. *Sons*

49. Putrāḥ[275]

[274] The Lord Buddha was respected, honored, revered, and venerated by kings, royal ministers, the wealthy, city dwellers, merchants, caravan leaders, gods, nāgas, yakṣas, antigods, heavenly birds, kinnaras, and great snakes. Worshiped as such by gods, nāgas, yakṣas, antigods, heavenly birds, kinnaras, and great snakes, the Lord Buddha—who was renowned and possessed great merit—received provisions of robes, begging bowls, bedding and seats, and medicines to cure the sick. Once he was staying near the city of Rājagṛha with the community made up of his disciples at the bamboo grove in Kalandakanivāpa (Squirrel Feeding Place).

One morning the venerable Nālada got dressed, took his bowl and robe, and entered Rājagṛha for alms. After wandering through Rājagṛha for alms, he ate his meal, and after eating, he returned from his almsround. Then he put away his bowl and robe and set off on a journey into the realm of hungry ghosts.

Near Vulture's Peak he saw a hungry ghost who looked like one of the demons of Yama [the god of death]; she was covered in blood and surrounded by skeletons, as though she were in the middle of a cremation ground. Each night and each day she gave birth to five sons and experienced such intense suffering that, despite her maternal love, the ravages of hunger compelled her to eat her children.

"What sin did you commit," the elder Nālada asked, "so that you experience suffering like this?"

"When the sun has already risen, there's no need of a lamp," the hungry ghost said. "Ask the Blessed One about the matter. He will explain to you the deed that led me to this fate. And when other beings hear his account, they will refrain from this sinful deed."

Then the venerable Nālada approached the Blessed One. [275] At that time the Blessed One had just emerged from meditative seclusion and was giving the fourfold assembly an explanation of the sweet dharma—sweet like pure honey. The assembly of many hundreds [of people] listened to the sweet dharma of the Blessed One with faculties unwavering.

Now lord buddhas speak first [out of propriety], speak kindly, offer words of welcome—"Come near!"—and smile first and foremost. And so the Blessed One addressed the venerable Nālada: "Come near, Nālada! Welcome. Nālada, where are you coming from?"

"Bhadanta," Nālada said, "I am coming from a journey through the realm of hungry ghosts. There I saw a hungry ghost who looked like one of the demons of Yama; she was covered in blood and surrounded by skeletons, as though she were in the middle of a cremation ground. And she said,

> By day I eat five children,
> by night I eat five more.
> After giving birth to them,
> I never feel sated.

[And the venerable Nālada asked,]

> What terrible sin did she commit
> in the world of mortals
> so that she now experiences
> such horrific suffering?

"Nālada," the Blessed One said, "that hungry ghost is a sinner. Do you want to hear the deed that led her to this fate?

"Yes, Bhadanta."

"Then listen to this, Nālada. Concentrate well and closely. I will speak."

Long ago, Nālada, in a time gone by, in the city of Vārāṇasī, there was a certain merchant who was rich, wealthy, and prosperous, with vast and extensive holdings, and who had amassed a wealth like the god Vaiśravaṇa. Truly, he rivaled Vaiśravaṇa in wealth. He brought home a girl from an appropriate family as his wife, and with her he fooled around, enjoyed himself, and made love. From fooling around, enjoying himself, and making love, he had neither son nor daughter. With cheek in hand, he sat lost in thought. [276] "My home is filled with many treasures, and yet I have no son or daughter. Since my estate has no heir, after I die, it will automatically go to the king."[276]

Having no son but eager for one, he prayed to the likes of Śiva, Varuṇa, Kubera, Śakra, and Brahmā, as well as other more specialized deities: park deities, forest deities, courtyard deities,[277] crossroads deities, and deities who receive oblations. He also prayed to his hereditary deities, who shared his nature and constantly followed him.

It is popularly said that as a result of such prayers, sons are born and daughters as well. But this isn't the case. If it were, every man would have a thousand sons, just like a wheel-turning king. Instead, it's because of the presence of three things that sons are born and daughters as well. Which three? The mother and father must come together in love, the mother must be healthy and fertile, and a being seeking rebirth must be standing by. It's because of the presence of these three things that sons are born and daughters as well. And so, although he propitiated these deities, he had neither son nor daughter.

Then this thought occurred to him, "I'll take a second wife. Eventually she'll become pregnant." So he brought home a second girl from an appropriate family as a wife, and with her he fooled around, enjoyed himself, and made love. After some time, from fooling around, enjoying himself, and making love, his second wife became pregnant. She was pleased, satisfied, and delighted and informed her husband, "Congratulations, dear husband! I'm pregnant! And since the fetus has settled on the right side of my womb, it will definitely be a boy."

In high spirits, he puffed up his chest, extended his right arm, and uttered this inspired utterance:

> So it is that I may finally get to see my son's face,
> a sight I've long desired to see!
> May my son not be ignoble.
> May he perform those duties I expect of him.
> May he, having been supported by me, support me in return.
> May he be the one to claim my inheritance. [277]
> May my family lineage long endure.
>
> And may he, when we are dead and gone, make offerings, whether few or many,[278] and perform meritorious deeds and then direct the reward in our names with these words—"This merit shall follow these two wherever they are born and wherever they go."

Knowing that his wife was pregnant, the merchant kept her in the upper story of their palatial home, free from any restraints, with all the necessities for the cold in the cold season and all the necessities for the heat in the hot season. She was given the foods that doctors prescribed, those not too bitter, not too sour, not too salty, not too sweet, not too pungent, and not too astringent, and those foods free from bitterness, sourness, saltiness, sweetness, pungency, and astringency. Her body was adorned with strings and necklaces of pearls, and like a nymph wandering in the divine Nandana Grove, she moved from bed to bed and from seat to seat, never descending to the ground below. And she heard no unkind words until the fetus matured.

When the first wife, who had previously been the merchant's only spouse, saw the second wife being honored and cherished, she was filled with jealousy. "If this second wife gives birth to a son," she thought, "he'll surely torment me. Some skillful solution must be arranged, at any cost." As they say, one who indulges in sensual pleasures doesn't shy away from doing something sinful.

The first wife was foolishly [perched] at the precipice of the [three] realms of existence that no one desires—[the realms of hell beings, animals, and hungry ghosts]. She gained the second wife's trust and then gave her a drug that would induce an abortion. As a result of consuming the drug, that poor woman had a miscarriage.

The second wife then gathered together all her relatives and questioned the first wife: "You gained my trust and then gave me a drug to induce an abortion! That's why I had a miscarriage!"

Then the first wife, in the midst of those relatives, took an oath: "If I gave you a drug to induce an abortion, then may I become a hungry ghost and devour my children as they are born!" [278]

"What do you think, Nālada?" the Blessed One said. "The merchant's wife is now this hungry ghost. Since she was jealous by nature, she administered a drug that induced an abortion and so was reborn as a hungry ghost. Since she lied while taking an oath, as a result of that deed, each night and each day she gives birth to five sons, and she eats them.

"Therefore, Nālada, you work hard to rid yourself of misdeeds of speech! That way you won't develop faults like that hungry ghost. It is this, Nālada, that you should learn to do."

This was said by the Blessed One. With their minds uplifted, the monks and various gods, antigods, heavenly birds, kinnaras, great snakes, and so on rejoiced at the words of the Blessed One.

10. Jāmbāla

50. Jāmbālaḥ[279]

[279] The Lord Buddha was respected, honored, revered, and venerated by kings, royal ministers, the wealthy, city dwellers, merchants, caravan leaders, gods, nāgas, yakṣas, antigods, heavenly birds, kinnaras, and great snakes. Worshiped as such by gods, nāgas, yakṣas, antigods, heavenly birds, kinnaras, and great snakes, the Lord Buddha—who was renowned and possessed great merit—received provisions of robes, begging bowls, bedding and seats, and medicines to cure the sick. Once he was staying near the city of Vaiśālī with the community made up of his disciples in the Kūṭāgāra Hall on the banks of the Markaṭahrada (Monkey Pond).

At that time in Vaiśālī, in the moat around the city,[280] there lived five hundred hungry ghosts who vomited and excreted what they ate, dwelled in a muck of bile and urine, and whose only food was pus-filled blood and shit. They were horrifying, and their nature was to suffer. And they said,[281]

> We vomit and expel what we eat,
> dwell in a muck of bile and urine,
> and our only food is pus-filled blood and shit.
> We are horrifying, and our nature is to suffer.

Now in Vaiśālī there was a certain brahman. He brought home a girl from an appropriate family as his wife, and with her he fooled around, enjoyed himself, and made love. From fooling around, enjoying himself, and making love, his wife became pregnant. [280] A terrible smell then began to emanate from her body. The brahman summoned soothsayers and questioned them [about his wife's condition].

"It is the influence of the child in her womb," they said.

After eight or nine months, the brahman's wife gave birth to a boy who was ugly, unsightly, and misshapen, whose body was smeared in excrement, and who smelled terrible. His mother and father, bound to him by the bonds of love, raised him with care nonetheless, even though he was absolutely disgusting. He loved latrines, he would sit on garbage heaps or in the mud and pluck out his hair, and he would put excrement into his mouth. And so the boy came to be known as Jāmbāla (Muddy). [281]

One time, while Jāmbāla was wandering around and about, Pūraṇa Kāśyapa saw him and thought, "Since he loves such places, he must be a holy man! I really should initiate him." So Pūraṇa Kāśyapa initiated him.[282]

Naked, Jāmbāla would roam about and do good deeds. While roaming about, he saw those five hundred hungry ghosts in the moat around Vaiśālī. Connected to them as a result of his former deeds, he descended into that moat around the city, and there he joined with them, gathered with them, exchanged pleasantries, and developed friendships.

One day the boy Jāmbāla dashed off on some undertaking[283] and entered Vaiśālī just as the Blessed One arrived at that moat around the city. Those hungry ghosts saw the Lord Buddha,

who was adorned with the thirty-two marks of a great man,
whose body was radiant with the eighty minor marks,
who was adorned with a halo extending an arm's length,
whose brilliance was greater than a thousand suns,

and who, like a mountain of jewels that moved,
was beautiful from every side.

As soon as they saw the Blessed One, they fell prostrate at his feet.

"What torments you?" the Blessed One asked them.

"Blessed One," they said, "we are tormented by thirst."

Then the Blessed One sent forth five streams of water endowed with the eight good qualities, one from each of his five fingers, and satisfied the thirst of those five hundred hungry ghosts. They, in turn, cultivated faith in their hearts for the Blessed One, then died and were reborn in the select company of the gods of Trāyastriṃśa (Thirty-Three).

Now it is a rule of nature that just after beings are reborn as sons and daughters of the gods, they have three thoughts: [282]

From where did I die and pass away?
Where have I been reborn?
As a result of what deed?

They saw that they had died and passed away from the realm of hungry ghosts. They had been reborn in the select company of the gods of Trāyastriṃśa. And this was the result of having cultivated faith in their hearts toward the Blessed One.

Then it occurred to those divine children who had previously been hungry ghosts: "It wouldn't be right for us to wait until our time here [in heaven] is finished before we went to see the Blessed One. We really should go to see the Blessed One even before our time here is done."

That very night those divine children who had previously been hungry ghosts—wearing earrings flawless and dangling and crowns resplendent with precious jewels, their bodies adorned with strings and necklaces of pearls and smeared with saffron, *tamāla* leaves, fenugreek, and so on—filled their laps with divine flowers: blue, red, and white waterlilies, white lotuses, and coral-tree flowers.[284] Then, illuminating the entire Kūṭāgāra Hall with a great blaze of light, they showered the Blessed One with those flowers and sat down in front of him to listen to the dharma.

Then the Blessed One, knowing the inclinations, propensities, makeup, and nature of those divine children who had previously been hungry ghosts, gave them an explanation of the dharma that elucidated the four noble truths. When those five hundred divine children heard it, with their thunderbolts of knowledge they broke though that mountain, which is the false view of individuality that arises with its twenty peaks of incorrect views, and obtained the reward of the stream enterer.

After having this vision of truth—like traders who have just made a profit, like farmers with a bounty of grain, like warriors victorious in battle, and like patients cured of every illness—they came into the presence of the Blessed One with dignity, and with that same dignity they circumambulated the Blessed One three times and then returned to their [heavenly] home.

Meanwhile Jāmbāla returned to that moat around the city. He didn't see the hungry ghosts, so he began to look for them. He searched all around for them to the point of exhaustion, but he still never found them. [283]

Now there is nothing that lord buddhas do not know, see, realize, and understand. It is a law of nature that lord buddhas have great compassion,[285]

> they are intent on doing good deeds for mankind,
> they have a single guardian [which is mindfulness],
> they abide in the meditative states of tranquility and insight,
> they are expert in the three objects for self-control,
> they have crossed the four floods [of corruptions],
> they have planted the soles of their feet
> on the four bases of success,
> they have long since developed an expertise in the four means
> of attracting beings to the religious life,

they have destroyed the five [bad] qualities,
they have crossed over the five realms of existence,
they have acquired the six [good] qualities,
they have fulfilled the six perfections,
they are replete with the flowers of the seven factors
of awakening,
they are teachers of the eightfold path,
they are expert in attaining the nine successive states
of quiescence meditation,
they are powerful with the ten powers,
they have fame that fills up the ten directions,
and they are superior to the thousand gods who have control
over others.

As lord buddhas survey the world with their buddha vision, three times in the night and three times in the day, knowledge and insight arise as to the following:

Who will get worse?
Who will get better?
Who will encounter trouble?
Who will encounter difficulty?
Who will encounter danger?
Who will encounter trouble, difficulty, and danger?
Who is inclined toward a terrible realm of existence?
Who is drawn toward a terrible realm of existence?
Who is disposed toward a terrible realm of existence?
Whom shall I lift up from a terrible realm of existence
and establish in heaven and liberation?
To whom, mired in the mud of sense pleasures,
shall I offer a helping hand?
Who, without noble wealth, shall I establish in the lordship
and dominion of noble wealth?[286]

For whom with roots of virtue unplanted shall I plant them?
For whom with roots of virtue already planted
shall I cause them to mature?
And who with roots of virtue already matured
shall I cause to be released?

And it is said,

Although the sea, home to monsters,
may allow the time of the tides to pass,
the Buddha never allows the time to pass
for training his beloved children.

The next morning, in order to do a good deed for that noble son Jāmbāla, the Blessed One got dressed, took his bowl and robe, and leading the monastic community that surrounded him entered Vaiśālī for alms. As he progressed on his almsround, [284] he entered a marketplace.[287] Jāmbāla, who had been wandering around and about, found himself standing in front of the Blessed One. Then he saw the Lord Buddha,

who was adorned with the thirty-two marks of a great man,
whose body was radiant with the eighty minor marks,
who was adorned with a halo extending an arm's length,
whose brilliance was greater than a thousand suns,
and who, like a mountain of jewels that moved,
was beautiful from every side.

As soon as Jāmbāla saw him, he developed faith in his heart for the Blessed One. Filled with faith, he fell prostrate at the Blessed One's feet, respectfully cupped his hands together, and said, "Blessed One, I would like to be initiated[288] as a monk according to the dharma and monastic discipline that have been so well expressed—that is, if beings like me are allowed to be initiated."

Then the Blessed One, whose heart was filled with great compassion, who knew the inclinations and propensities of others, and who knew Jāmbāla's destiny,[289] stretched out his golden-colored arm like the trunk of an elephant and said, "Come, O monk! Follow the religious life!"

As soon as the Blessed One finished speaking, there Jāmbāla stood[290]—bowl and water pot in hand, with a week's growth of hair,[291] and the disciplined deportment of a monk who had been ordained for one hundred years.

> "Come," the Tathāgata said to him.
> With head shaved and body wrapped in robes,
> he instantly attained tranquility of the senses,
> and so he remained by the will of the Buddha.[292]

Then the Blessed One gave him the power of mental concentration.

After striving, struggling, and straining, Jāmbāla came to understand that ever-turning five-spoked wheel of saṃsāra; he destroyed rebirth with all its conditioning factors, since it is subject to decay and decline, scattering and destruction; [285] and by ridding himself of all defilements, he directly experienced arhatship. Becoming an arhat,

> he was free from attachment in the three realms;
> he regarded clods of earth and gold as equal in value;
> he possessed equanimity toward the sky
> and the palm of his hand;
> he didn't distinguish between being cut by a blade
> and being anointed with sandalwood paste;
> he crushed the eggshell [of his ignorance] with knowledge;
> he obtained the special knowledges, superhuman faculties,
> and analytic insights;
> and he was averse to worldly attainments, temptations,
> and honors.

He became worthy of respect, honor, and obeisance
from the gods, including Indra and Upendra.

Even after he obtained arhatship, he still loved hardship.[293] Regarding this, the Blessed One addressed the monks: "Monks, among those monks who are my disciples, the foremost in devotion to hardship is the monk Jāmbāla."

Some monks in doubt asked the Lord Buddha, the remover of all doubts, "What deed, Bhadanta, did the elder Jāmbāla do such that he experiences suffering like this?"

"Monks," the Blessed One said, "the deeds that Jāmbāla himself has performed and accumulated in previous lives have now come together, and their conditions have matured. They remain before him like an oncoming flood and will certainly come to pass. Those deeds were performed and accumulated by Jāmbāla. Who else will experience their results? For those deeds that are performed and accumulated, monks, do not mature outside of oneself—neither in the element of earth nor in the element of water, in the element of fire, or in the element of wind. Instead, those deeds that are performed, both good and bad, mature in the aggregates, the elements, and the sense bases that are appropriated when one is reborn.

Actions never come to naught,
even after hundreds of eons.[294]
When the right conditions gather and the time is right,
then they will have their effect on embodied beings."

[The Buddha then recounted the deed that led Jāmbāla to his present condition.] Long ago, monks, at a time in the past during this present auspicious age, when people lived for forty thousand years, there arose in the world a perfectly awakened buddha named Krakucchanda,

perfect in knowledge and conduct,
a sugata, [286]
a knower of the world,
an unsurpassed guide for those in need of training,
a teacher of gods and mortals,
a buddha,
and a blessed one.

Once he was staying near the capital Śobhāvatī.[295] Now in the capital a certain householder had built a monastery where monks from different regions could come and go as they pleased. In that monastery, one of the permanent monastic residents was just an ordinary person, and he was exceptionally mean with regard to that residence.[296] When he saw monks visiting the monastery, he would lose his temper and become irritated, hostile, exasperated, and outraged. But when he saw those monks leaving the monastery, he would be full of joy and pleasure. And he would go out and insult them.

One day a monk who was an arhat arrived from the countryside. Now the owner of the monastery, [the lay donor who had the monastery built,][297] was a nonreturner, and he recognized that the monk was an arhat just by the way he carried himself. Filled with faith, he invited the monk along with the monastic community [to come] the following day for a meal and a steam bath.[298] At that time, however, the resident monk wasn't there.

Now on the following day, when the steam bath was prepared and the food was made ready, the resident monk arrived. He entered the steam bath, and there he saw the owner of the monastery, wearing only a loincloth, attending to the visiting monk and slathering his body with various perfumed substances.[299] In the resident monk there arose a meanness, and with a mind polluted with bad thoughts, he uttered harsh words at the visiting monk: "Monk, it would better for you to smear your own body with shit instead of commandeering the services of a donor like this one!"

The arhat accepted this rebuke with his silence. "This poor man," he thought. "May he not suffer the consequences of this grave deed."

Soon the time came for a general meeting of the monastic community. [287] The resident monk heard these words: "You polluted your mind with bad thoughts toward an arhat!"

Hearing this, he felt regret. Then he fell prostrate at the arhat monk's feet and said, "Forgive me, noble one, for I have uttered cruel words against you."

Then the arhat, to increase the resident monk's faith, rose up into the air and began to display various miracles. The resident monk felt even greater regret. In front of that arhat, the resident monk confessed, declared, and proclaimed that what he had done was a sin. Nevertheless, he was unable to generate the highest knowledge.

Time passed, and when the resident monk was on the brink of death, he made this fervent aspiration: "Although I polluted my mind with bad thoughts toward an arhat and uttered harsh words, may I not suffer the result of that action. Instead, since I read, studied, made offerings, and served the monastic community, as a result of those actions, may I please and not displease perfectly awakened buddhas in the future!"

"What do you think, monks? The resident monk at that time and at that juncture was none other than Jāmbāla. As a result of committing an act of harsh speech toward an arhat, he experienced endless suffering in saṃsāra. And because of the residual karma from that act, even now, in his last existence, he smells terrible, absolutely terrible, and he has a strong inclination to inhabit latrines and toilets. But since he read, studied, and became well versed in the aggregates, well versed in the elements, well versed in the sense bases, well versed in interdependent arising, and well versed in what is possible and impossible,[300] [288] he went forth as a monk into my order, where by ridding himself of all defilements, he directly experienced arhatship.

"Therefore, monks, this is the lesson to be learned: Work hard to rid yourselves of meanness! Why? That way you won't develop the same faults as Jāmbāla, who had previously been just an ordinary person. Instead, amass a great collection of virtues such that one obtains arhatship! It is this, monks, that you should learn to do."

This was said by the Blessed One. With their minds uplifted, the monks and those other gods, antigods, heavenly birds, kinnaras, great snakes, and so on rejoiced at the words of the Blessed One.

So ends the fifth decade of inspired utterances in the *Avadānaśataka*.

Glossary

aggregates (*skandha*). See *five aggregates.*

analytic insights (*pratisaṃvid*). There are four: with regard to dharma, meaning (*artha*), languages and linguistic usage (*nirukti*), and eloquence (*pratibhāna*).

Anāthapiṇḍada. The Buddha's chief patron. After purchasing a park from Prince Jeta, son of King Prasenajit, he had a monastery constructed there for the Buddha to pass the rainy season.

antigod (*asura*). One of a class of demigods whose home is beneath the waters at the base of Mount Meru. Positioned just below the lowest heavenly sphere, these "not [quite]" (*a*) "gods" (*sura*) often vie with the gods above them.

arhat. A "worthy one," who has destroyed all of his defilements and thereby attained awakening. Often an epithet of a buddha. According to Paul Griffiths (1994, 62), it is used as a title for a buddha "to indicate both Buddha's worthiness to receive the homage (*pūjārhattva*) and offerings of non-Buddhists and, using a different etymology, Buddha's success in killing (*han-*) the enemies (*ari*) to awakening."

auspicious age (*bhadrakalpa*). An eon, such as the present one, in which five buddhas appear. In our present eon, the buddhas Krakucchanda, Kanakamuni, Kāśyapa, and Śākyamuni have already appeared, and Maitreya will be the fifth and last.

bhadanta. A respectful term used to address Buddhist monks.

blessed one (*bhagavān*). An epithet of a buddha. I translate *bhagavān* as "Blessed One" when it refers to Gautama Buddha, and as "lord" when it modifies a buddha (e.g., the lord Vipaśyin).

Brahmā. The highest deity in the "Brahmā world" (*brahmāloka*), which consists of the first three heavens in the form realm (*rūpadhātu*): Mahābrahmā (Great Brahmā), Brahmapurohita (Brahmā's Priests), and Brahmakāyika (Brahmā's Assembly).

brahman (*brāhmaṇa*). One of the four hereditary classes (*varṇa*) according to Brahmanical Hinduism (i.e., *brahman*, *kṣatriya*, *vaiśya*, *śūdra*). The primary duties of this class involve ritual activity.

buddha. One who has attained the highest possible awakening—who is, literally, an "awakened one." In the text, "the Buddha" is often used as a title to refer to Śākyamuni.

buddha vision (*buddhacakṣu*). Buddhas are said to possess five faculties of vision (*pañcacakṣu*): the physical eye (*māṃsacakṣu*), the divine eye (*divyacakṣu*), the wisdom eye (*prajñācakṣu*), the dharma eye (*dharmacakṣu*), and the buddha eye (*buddhacakṣu*). This last quality I translate as "buddha vision."

community (*saṅgha*). The Buddhist order of monks (*bhikṣu*) and nuns (*bhikṣuṇī*). The text often speaks, however, of a community of monks (*bhikṣusaṅgha*).

coral tree (*māndāraka*). *Erythrina indica.* One of the five celestial trees. Flowers from this tree are sometimes said to rain down from heaven as a divine greeting of respect.

corruptions (*āsrava*). These negative karmic forces, which must be interrupted to escape from saṃsāra, are sometimes translated as "cankers" or "outflows." They are often equated with the *four floods*.

disciple (*śrāvaka*). A follower of the Buddha is known as a "hearer" (*śrāvaka*), signaling the importance in early Buddhism of listening to the Buddha's dharma. In many avadānas, however, devotees are enjoined to look, as much as to hear, for visual practices are represented as the primary means of cultivating faith. Cf. Rotman 2009.

divine sight (*divyacakṣu*). The quality of clairvoyance, one of the aspects of *buddha vision*. It is also one of the *superhuman faculties*.

eightfold path (*āṣṭāṅgamārga*). The multifaceted path of conduct that leads to nirvāṇa: right view (*samyagdṛṣṭi*), right intention (*samyaksaṅkalpa*), right speech (*samyagvāc*), right action (*samyakkarmānta*), right livelihood (*samyagājīva*), right effort (*samyagvyāyāma*), right mindfulness (*samyaksmṛti*), and right concentration (*samyaksamādhi*).

eight good qualities (*aṣṭāṅga*) *of water*. It is (1) cool, (2) refreshing, (3) sweet, (4) soft, (5) clear, (6) free from bad smells, (7) soothing, and (8) wholesome. See Rigzin 1997, 78.

eighty minor marks (*aśītyānuvyañjana*). The secondary characteristics of a great man. Following Robert Thurman's enumeration (1983, 156–57), these are:

> [1] fingernails the color of brass, [2] shiny [3] and long; [4] round fingers; [5] tapered fingers; [6] fingers wide-spreading; [7] veins not protruding, [8] and without tangles; [9] slender ankles; [10] feet not uneven; [11] lion's gait; [12] elephant's gait; [13] swan's gait; [14] bull's gait; [15] gait tending to the right; [16] graceful gait; [17] steady gait; [18] his body is well covered, [19] clean, [20] well proportioned, [21] pure, [22] soft, and [23] perfect; [24] his sex organs are fully developed; [25] his thighs are broad and knees round; [26] his steps are even; [27] his complexion is youthful; [28] his posture is not stooped; [29] his bearing is expansive, [30] yet extremely poised; [31] his limbs and fingers and toes are well defined; [32] his vision is clear and unblurred; [33] his joints are not protruding; [34] his belly is relaxed, [35] symmetrical, [36] and not fat; [37] his navel is deep [38] and wound to the right; [39] he is completely handsome; [40] he is clean in all acts; [41] he is free of spots or discolorations of the skin; [42] his hands are soft as cotton; [43] the lines of his palms are clear, [44] deep, [45] and long; [46] his face is not overlong [47] and is bright as a mirror; [48] his tongue is soft, [49] long, [50] and red; [51] his voice is like an elephant's trumpet or like thunder, [52] yet sweet and gentle; [53] his teeth are rounded, [54] sharp, [55] white, [56] even, [57] and regularly arranged; [58] his nose is long [59] and straight; [60] his eyes are clear [61] and wide; [62] his eyelashes are thick; [63] the pupils and whites of his eyes are clearly defined, and the irises are like lotus petals; [64] his eyebrows are long, [65] soft, [66] evenly haired, [67] and gently curved; [68] his ears [69] are long-lobed and symmetrical; [70] his hearing is acute; [71] his forehead is high [72] and broad; [73] his head is very large;

[74] his hair is as black as a bee, [75] thick, [76] soft, [77] untangled, [78] not unruly, [79] and fragrant; [80] and his feet and hands are marked with lucky signs [of the *śrīvatsa*, svastika, and *nandyāvarta*].

Thurman follows *Mahāvyutpatti* §§ 269–348. Edgerton (BHSD, s.v. *anuvyañjana*) constructs a slightly different list.

elements (*dhātu*). "The psycho-physical constituent elements of the personality in relation to the outside world," to quote Franklin Edgerton (BHSD). There are eighteen: the six sense organs (i.e., eye, ear, nose, tongue, body, mind), the six objects of the sense organs (i.e., the visible, sound, odor, taste, tactile objects, mental objects), and the resultant six consciousnesses (i.e., eye consciousness, ear consciousness, nose consciousness, tongue consciousness, body consciousness, mind consciousness).

five aggregates (*pañcaskandha*). These constitute the physical and mental constituents of a person. They are matter (*rūpa*), feeling (*vedanā*), recognition (*saññā*), conditioning factors (*saṃskāra*), and consciousness (*vijñāna*).

five [bad] qualities (*pañcāṅga*). Equivalent to the five hindrances (*pañcanīvaraṇa*). These are sensual desire (*kāmacchanda*), ill will (*vyāpāda*), tiredness and sleepiness (*styānamiddha*), excitement and lethargy (*auddhatyakaukṛtya*), and doubt (*vicikitsā*).

five good qualities (*pañcāṇga*) *of the Buddha's voice*. It is (1) deep like thunder, (2) soothing and comforting to the ear, (3) pleasant and delightful, (4) lucid and articulate, (5) suitable and consistent. See Rigzin 1997, 293–94.

five realms of existence (*pañcagati*). The various categories of living beings. These are gods (*deva*), humans (*manuṣya*), animals (*tiryagyoni*), hungry ghosts (*preta*), and hell beings (*naraka*). Often the category of antigods (*asura*) is added between humans and hungry ghosts.

four bases of success (*caturṛddhipāda*). The bases that lead one to acquire magical power and spiritual success. These are the desire to act (*chanda*), strength (*vīrya*), mind (*citta*), and investigation (*mīmāṃsā*). For more, see Gethin 1992, 81–103.

four continents (*caturdvīpa*). The four continents that humans inhabit. These are Jambudvīpa (Black Plum Island, or India) to the south, Kuru to the north, Godanīya to the west, and Videha to the east.

four floods [*of corruptions*] (*caturogha*). These are desire (*kāma*), existence (*bhava*), ignorance (*avidyā*), and views (*dṛṣṭi*). One who has crossed over these four negative flows of karma is an arhat.

four means of attracting beings [*to the religious life*] (*catvāri saṅgrahavastūni*). These are generosity (*dāna*), kind speech (*priyavacana*), beneficial conduct (*arthacaryā*), and exemplary behavior (*samānārthatā*).

four noble truths (*caturāryasatya*). The classic formulation of the Buddha's teaching. It is true that there is suffering (*duḥkha*), that it has a cause (*samudaya*), that it can end (*nirodha*), and that there is a path (*mārga*) that leads to its cessation.

four world protectors (*catvāro lokapālāḥ*). The guardians of the four directions: Dhṛtarāṣṭra in the east, Virūḍhaka in the south, Virūpākṣa in the west, and Kubera (= Vaiśravaṇa, Dhanada) in the north. Elsewhere known as the *four great kings* (*catvāro mahārājānaḥ*).

fourfold assembly (*catasraḥ parṣadaḥ*). The monks, nuns, and male and female lay devotees who are adherents of the Buddha.

great man (*mahāpuruṣa*). One who has the thirty-two marks and as such is destined to become either a wheel-turning king ruling the four quarters of the earth or a buddha.

great snake (*mahoraga*). One of a class of celestial beings that is said to have a human body with a serpent head.

heavenly bird (*garuḍa*). One of a class of birdlike supernatural beings. They are said to be an enemy of the snakelike nāgas.

interdependent arising (*pratītyasamutpāda*). The Buddhist doctrine of causal interdependence, which describes the cycle of existence (*saṃsāra*). By extension, the doctrine that all things are interdependent.

insight (*vipaśyanā*). A type of analytic meditation that promotes a direct understanding of the true nature of reality.

karma. Often translated as "deed" or "action," although left untranslated when it refers to the force exerted by the results of such deeds—for example, in determining the quality of one's rebirth, present experience, or inclinations.

Kāśyapa. The twenty-fourth buddha, and the third of the present *auspicious age*. He is not to be confused with *Pūraṇa Kāśyapa*, an influential non-Buddhist teacher.

kinnara. A class of beings often said to be half human and half animal, as indicated by their name—literally, "What (*kiṃ*) sort of man (*nara*)?"

Kolika (or *Kolita*). The venerable Maudgalyāyana's given name. He was named after the village in which he was born. See *Maudgalyāyana*.

Krakucchanda. The twenty-second buddha, and the first of the present *auspicious age*.

lord (*bhagavān*). See *blessed one*.

magical power (*ṛddhi*). A set of special powers acquired through spiritual practice; also one of the *superhuman faculties*. There are often said to be eight: (1) being one he becomes many, being many he becomes one; (2) becoming invisible; (3) passing through solid objects; (4) traveling through the earth; (5) walking on water; (6) flying through the air; (7) touching and stroking the sun and moon with one's hand; (8) ascending to the world of the god Brahmā.

Mahāmaudgalyāyana. An honorific meaning "The Great Maudgalyāyana." See *Maudgalyāyana*.

Maudgalyāyana. One of the Buddha's chief disciples, regarded as foremost in the attainment of psychic powers.

Mount Meru. A sacred mountain, 80,000 leagues high, located in Jambudvīpa and considered to be the center of the world. On its terraces reside the four world protectors and on its summit the gods of Trāyastriṃśa heaven.

nāga. A serpent, capable of taking on human form, who lives in the water and possesses miraculous powers. Although often dangerous to humans, these beings can be instructed in the dharma. Virūpākṣa, one of the four world protectors, is their lord.

Nandana Grove (*nandanavana*). Quite literally "a grove of delight" in Trāyastriṃśa heaven.

nine successive states of quiescence meditation (*navānupūrvavihāra*). The four meditations or contemplations (*dhyāna*) of the form realm; the four formless spheres—i.e., the sphere of infinite space (*ākāśānantyāyatana*), the sphere of infinite consciousness (*vijñānānantyāyatana*), the sphere of nothingness (*akiñcanyāyatana*), and the sphere of neither consciousness nor unconsciousness (*naivasaṃjñānāsaṃjñāyatana*); and lastly, the cessation of conceptualization and sensation (*saṃjñāvedayitanirodha*).

nonreturner (*anāgāmin*). One who has attained the third of four stages of religious development that culminate in arhatship (e.g., stream enterer, once returner, nonreturner, arhat). Such a person will have no additional rebirths as a human; he will attain awakening after being reborn in one of the higher heavens.

once-returner (*sakṛtāgāmin*). One who has attained the second of four stages of religious development that culminate in arhatship (e.g., stream enterer, once returner, nonreturner, arhat). Such a person will attain awakening in his next rebirth.

perfectly awakened (*samyaksambuddha*). An epithet of a buddha. He is perfectly awakened, and hence his awakening is superior to the awakening of a disciple or solitary buddha.

piśāca. A kind of demon. According to Monier-Williams (1990), "possibly so called either from their fondness for flesh (*piśa* for *piśita*) or from their yellowish appearance."

Pūraṇa Kāśyapa. An influential teacher and a contemporary of the Buddha who espoused a doctrine of "non-action," denying the efficacy of karma.

quiescence (*śamatha*). See *tranquility*.

root of virtue (*kuśalamūla*). A "virtuous deed" (*kuśala*), or the merit accrued from such a deed, that functions as a "root" or "foundation" (*mūla*) for a request or aspiration.

Śakra. The chief of the Trāyastriṃśa heaven, who is said to be the leader of the gods (*devendra*).

saṃsāra. The repeating cycle of life, death, and rebirth, which is characterized by suffering. In short, existence as we know it.

Śāriputra. One of the Buddha's chief disciples, regarded as foremost in comprehending the dharma.

sense bases (*āyatana*). There are twelve: the six senses (i.e., eye, ear, nose, tongue, body, mind) and their corresponding objects (i.e., the visible, sound, odor, taste, tactile objects, mental objects).

seven factors of awakening (*saptabodhyaṅga*). The factors that lead one to awakening. These are the awakening factors of mindfulness (*smṛti*), dharma analysis (*dharmapravicaya*), strength (*vīrya*), joy (*prīti*), serenity (*praśrabdhi*), concentration (*samādhi*), and equanimity (*upekṣā*).

single guardian [which is mindfulness] (*ekārakṣa*). According to Pali sources, the third of ten noble dispositions (*ariyavāsa*). The *Dīgha-nikāya* (iii 269) explains that the single guardian is, in fact, mindfulness.

six [good] qualities (*ṣaḍaṅga*). According to Pali sources, the second of ten noble dispositions (*ariyavāsa*). The *Dīgha-nikāya* (iii 269) explains that one who is endowed with these qualities remains equanimous and mindful in six instances: upon seeing a sight, hearing a sound, smelling a smell, tasting a flavor, touching a tactile object, and cognizing a mental object with the mind.

six perfections (*ṣaṭpāramitā*). These are virtues that are to be practiced and perfected by the bodhisattva. They are the perfection of generosity (*dānapāramitā*), the perfection of morality (*śīlapāramitā*), the perfection of tolerance (*kṣāntipāramitā*), the perfection of strength (*vīryapāramitā*), the perfection of meditation (*dhyānapāramitā*), and the perfection of wisdom (*prajñāpāramitā*).

solitary buddha (*pratyekabuddha*). One who attains awakening on his own, as would a buddha, but who does not found a community.

special knowledges (*vidyā*). There are three: the knowledge of remembering past lives (*pūrvanivāsānusmṛtijñāna*), the knowledge of the passing away and arising [of beings] (*cyutyupapādajñāna*), and the knowledge of the destruction of the corruptions (*āsravakṣayajñāna*). Following *Saṅghabhedavastu* ii 249–50. See also *Dīgha-nikāya* i 81–85.

stream enterer (*srotāpanna*). One who has attained the first of four stages of religious development that culminate in arhatship (e.g., stream enterer, once returner, nonreturner, arhat). Such a person will attain awakening within seven rebirths.

suffering (*duḥkha*). The Buddhist diagnosis that existence in *saṃsāra* is fundamentally unsatisfactory.

sugata. An epithet of a buddha. Often said to mean "one who has attained bliss" or "one who is fully realized."

superhuman faculties (*abhijñā*). Powers and abilities possessed by arhats. These are clairvoyance (*divyacakṣu*), clairaudience (*divyaśrotra*), telepathy (*paracittajñāna*), remembrance of past lives (*pūrvanivāsānusmṛti*), and magical powers (*ṛddhi*)—for specifics, see *magical powers*. Sometimes included as a sixth faculty is the knowledge of the destruction of the corruptions (*āsravakṣayajñāna*).

tamāla. *Cinnamomum tamala*. The *tamālapatra* is a tree in the Lauraceae family that, as its name indicates, is prized for its leaves (*pātra*). The leaves are aromatic and used for both culinary and medicinal purposes. They are sometimes called "Indian bay leaves," although the common bay leaf, which comes from the bay laurel (*Laurus nobilis*), is of a different genus, appearance, and aroma.

tathāgata. An epithet of a buddha. This term has a variety of interpretations (e.g., "Thus come," "Thus gone," "Thus not gone") but is used only in reference to a buddha. Often it is used by Śākyamuni Buddha to refer to himself. For a more complete exegesis of the term, see Bodhi 1978, 331–44.

ten powers (*daśabala*). Powers by which a buddha exercises his influence. They are the power from knowing what is possible and impossible (*sthānāsthānajñānabalam*); the power from knowing the results of actions (*karmavipākajñānabalam*); the power from knowing various inclinations [of living beings] (*nānādhimuktijñānabalam*); the power from knowing [the world with its] various elements (*nānādhātujñānabalam*); the power from knowing the superiority and inferiority of the faculties [of living beings] (*indriyavarāvarajñānabalam*); the power from knowing courses of conduct that lead to all destinations (*sarvatragāmanīpratipattijñānabalam*); the power from knowing the defilement, cleansing, and emergence of contemplations, liberations, meditative concentrations, and attainments (*sarvadhyānavimokṣasamādhisamāpattisaṅkleśavyavadānavyutthānajñānabalam*); the power from remembering past lives (*pūrvanivāsānusmṛtijñānabalam*); the power from knowing the passing away and rebirth [of living beings] (*cyutyutpattijñānabalam*); the power of the destruction of the corruptions (*āśravakṣayabalam*). For a slightly different list, with helpful glosses, see *Majjhima-nikāya* i 69–70; trans. in Ñāṇamoli and Bodhi 1995, 166.

terrible realms of existence (*apāyagati*). The realms of hell beings, hungry ghosts, and animals.

thirty-two marks of a great man (*dvātriṃśat mahāpuruṣalakṣaṇa*). The primary characteristics of a great man. According to the *Lakkaṇa-sutta* in the *Dīgha-nikāya* (iii 143–45; following trans. in Walshe 1995, 441–42), these are:

[1] He has feet with level tread. This is one of the marks of a great man. [2] On the soles of his feet are wheels with a thousand spokes, complete with felloe and hub. [3] He has projecting heels. [4] He has long fingers and toes. [5] He has soft and tender hands and feet. [6] His hands and feet are net-like. [7] He has high-raised ankles. [8] His legs are like an antelope's. [9] Standing and without bending, he can touch and rub his knees with either hand. [10] His male organs are enclosed in a sheath. [11] His complexion is bright, the color of gold. [12] His skin is delicate and so smooth that no dust can adhere to his body. [13] His body-hairs are separate, one to each pore. [14] His body-hairs grow upward, each one bluish-black like collyrium, curling in rings to the right. [15] His body is divinely straight. [16] He has the seven convex surfaces. [17] The front part of his body is like a lion's. [18] There is no hollow between his shoulders. [19] He is proportioned like a banyan-tree: the height of his body is the same as the span of his outstretched arms, and conversely. [20] His bust is evenly rounded. [21] He has a perfect sense of taste. [22] He has jaws like a lion's. [23] He has forty teeth. [24] His teeth are even. [25] There are no spaces between his teeth. [26] His canine teeth are very bright. [27] His tongue is very long. [28] He has a Brahmā-like voice, like that of the *karavīka*-bird. [29] His eyes are deep blue. [30] He has eyelashes like a cow's. [31] The hair between his eyes is white and soft like cotton-down. [32] His head is like a royal turban.

three objects for self-control (*tridamathavastu*). Presumably these are body, speech, and mind.

three realms (*traidhātuka*). See *three worlds*.

three worlds (*triloka*). The three levels of existence in a world system such as our own. These are the realms of desire (*kāma*), form (*rūpa*), and formlessness (*ārūpya*). The Buddha is said to be the teacher of the three worlds.

tranquility (*śamatha*). A type of meditation that aims at the development of perfect and effortless concentration and leads to the attainment of magical powers.

Trāyastriṃśa. The heaven of the thirty-three gods, located atop Mount Meru and ruled by Śakra.

truth. See *four noble truths*.

unsurpassed perfect awakening (*anuttarasamyaksambodhi*). The complete awakening of a buddha.

Vaiśravaṇa. See *four world protectors* and *yakṣa*.

view of individuality (*satkāyadṛṣṭi*). The false belief that an individual really exists. For more, see Collins 1982, 93–94 and 132–33.

wheel-turning king (*cakravartin*). One who uses the seven treasures to conquer the four corners of the earth and rule an entire world system.

yakṣa. Minor deities who possess magical powers and are associated with forests. Kubera (= Vaiśravaṇa, Dhanada), one of the four world protectors, is their lord.

Notes

1 Brontë 2000, 370.

2 LaFleur 1989, 273. There is an unmistakable parallel between Western dismissals of hungry ghosts and of Indian art more generally. Just consider the title of Partha Mitter's history of European reactions to Indian art, *Much Maligned Monsters* (1977), which would make a fitting title for a history of Western scholarship on hungry ghosts.

3 For more on the Mūlasarvāstivādin affiliation of the *Avadānaśataka*, see Przyluski 1918, 486; Waldschmidt 1948, 255; Vaudeville 1964, 85–86; Hartmann 1985; Hahn 1992; Meisig 2004, 33–42, 57–65, 74, 77–79, and 128–54; Schopen 2004, 122–69; Demoto 2006; Dhammadinnā 2015, 491; and Muldoon-Hules 2017, 187–90. Note too that the Tibetan translation of the Sanskrit recension, which was produced by Jinamitra and Devacandra in the beginning of the ninth century, was also carried out in a Mūlasarvāstivādin mileu and agrees quite closely with the Sanskrit original (Demoto 2006, 1–2, and Dhammadinnā 2015, 496n26).

4 As Dhammadinnā (2015, 506) notes, "The textual history of the *Avadānaśataka* recensions—(a) Sanskrit (Nepalese)/Tibetan 'mainstream' manuscript tradition, (b) the versions attested in the Schøyen fragments, (c) the abridged Central Asian summary in the Turfan collection, and (d) the received Chinese translation (T 200)—is quite intricate and debated." The Chinese translation, for example, which was produced between the second half of the fifth and the end of the sixth centuries CE—and which may also have different layers (Meisig 2004 and Demoto 2006, 6–7)—does not closely correspond with Sanskrit text in its present form. "On the contrary," Demoto (2006, 4) observes, "a close comparison of both texts has revealed that the latter is the result of a revision done probably by the Mūlasarvāstivādins." For more on the dating and connection of these recensions, see Formigatti 2016, 105–14, and Muldoon-Hules 2017, 179–86.

5 Stories 36, 37, 38, 40, 46, 54, 78, 86, and 100 in the *Avadānaśataka* have close parallels in the *Mūlasarvāstivāda-vinaya*. For a survey of the scholarly literature, see Muldoon-Hules 2017, 187–90.

6 The easy assumption is that a Mūlasarvāstivādin monk revised an earlier recension of the *Avadānaśataka* to make it more like the *Mūlasarvāstivāda-vinaya*—that is, more like the legal code by which the monk himself was bound—which is why there are so

many Mūlasarvāstivādin expressions and formulae in the present Sanskrit text. See, for example, Hahn 1992, 171; Schopen 2000, 151nII.36; Schopen 2004, 125–26; and Schopen 2014, 362. It is also possible, however, that some of these stories were revised and incorporated into the *Mūlasarvāstivāda-vinaya,* suggesting that these stories were not only revised to be more "legal" but were recognized as legal exempla worth adopting. Yamagiwa (1992) suggests as much for story 46—which is part of the present translation—noting that the story is far more intelligible, and a far better fit, in the *Avadānaśataka* than in the *Mūlasarvāstivāda-vinaya* (Yamagiwa 2001, §4.2). See too note 245. For more on the latter on these "two possible and opposing ideas," see Kishino 2016, 256–61, citation from 259n61.

7 While I agree with Muldoon-Hules (2017, 15) that "the *Avadanaśataka* should be thought of, first and foremost, as a work written by monks for the consumption of monks"—like story 48, presumably—it is quite likely that stories from the collection were also used to instruct laypeople. Seven of the ten hungry ghost stories in the text, for example, feature laypeople and demonstrate the importance of lay offerings to monastics and the disastrous consequences of being mean—just the kind of message a monk or nun might want to pass on to a potential lay donor. For a similar argument about the *Divyāvadāna,* another anthology likely associated with the Mūlasarvāstivādins, see Rotman 2008, 23–30. As Dhammadinnā (2016, 80) notes, "In general, the proximity of avadāna and Vinaya transmission is explained by the shared didactic function of their narratives. Vinaya narrative serves teaching purposes in the context of the saṅgha's moral and legal education. Jātaka and avadāna tales are put to the service of the same teaching purposes, not limited to the laity as their target audience, but also for the legal training of the saṅgha, as is shown by the incorporation of jātakas and avadānas in Vinaya texts." See too Anālayo 2017, 134–41.

8 For more on these two decades, see Appleton 2015. As she notes, "All the stories of the second decade involve acts of devotion towards buddhas of the past, while those in the fourth decade instead have no past buddhas, and the Bodhisattva acting more independently," and this "offers us a window into some of the generic conventions of both jātaka and avadāna" (Appleton 2015, 19). For more on the various decades in the text, see Feer 1891, xiv–xvi.

9 In early Brahmanical materials, it was thought that after a human dies, he then abides in a liminal state between this life and the next as a kind of ghost (*preta*). If his relatives perform for him the requisite rituals—which are elaborated in enormous detail in the Dharmaśāstras (Kane 1953, 334–51)—he leaves behind this dangerous and impure state and becomes an "ancestor" (*pitṛ*), joining his forefathers. In standard Buddhist cosmology, which appears to be an adaption of this system, pretas are no longer liminal beings; instead, they are the inhabitants of one of five (sometimes six) realms of existence—gods, humans, animals, hungry ghosts, and hell beings—and to physically transform from a being in one realm to a being in another, one must die and be reborn there. Buddhists, it seems, accepted the idea that one can die and become a preta, but they transformed the category, from a state of existence into a realm of existence, and imagined the inhabitants as uniformly hungry and tormented. For more on the relation between these Brahmanical and Buddhist systems, see Scherman 1892, 65n1; Gombrich 1971; Knipe 1977; Holt 1981; White 1986; Krishan 1997, 337–43; Olivelle 2011; and Sayers 2013, 86–99.

10 Avś i 244.14.

11 Perhaps there is a different explanation. All the characters in these stories die in the human realm and are then reborn as hungry ghosts, suggesting a continuity with the Brahmanical system discussed in note 9. Hence a hungry ghost in these stories might very well remember his or her last existence, for there wouldn't be a sharp separation between one's ghost incarnation and one's preceding human one. And perhaps this Brahmanical precedent (and varying Buddhist needs for differentiation) helps explain why the *Petavatthu* (a collection of hungry ghost stories included in the Pali canon) and the *Petavatthu-aṭṭhakathā* (Dhammapāla's later commentary on the collection) have such different existential understandings of being a *peta*. In the former, according to James Egge (2002, 94), "*peta* maintains its etymological sense of a being that has 'departed' from human existence." In the latter, "*peta*s constitute a distinct *gati* [realm of existence], the *petayoni*. Consequently, birth as a *peta* need not follow a human birth, but in several stories follows birth in a hell (Pv-a 14, 21, 178, 263, 284)." Note too that in the *Pettavatthu*, which is much less systematized than its commentary, there are also stories that "seem to confuse birth as a ghost, a yakṣa, or a deity" (Egge 2002, 79), so perhaps the text itself is confused or perhaps it simply demonstrates a more fluid and less hierarchical understanding of these various forms of identity. Regardless, Buddhists were engaged in reworking ideas and practices regarding deceased ancestors, whose fate had been (and continues to be) a pressing concern (Shastri 1963 and Parry 1994), and they arrived at diverse conclusions at different times and in different texts.

12 Hungry ghosts are often described and represented as having giant stomachs and tiny mouths, symbolizing their craving and its insatiability, but this imagery is absent in the *Petavatthu*, and it came to the Pali tradition quite late. As Steven Collins observed in some summary remarks about hungry ghosts (H-Buddhism, September 15, 2008), "the big belly / small mouth petas in SE Asia are derived from Sanskritic, North Indian tradition(s), not the Pali tradition as mediated through Sri Lanka." Cf. Stede 1914, 26.

13 Avś i 245.7, i 248.10, i 255.11–12, i 260.10, and i 273.12–13. Cf. Avś i 266.4.

14 *Divyāvadāna* 302.1–5 (cf. trans. Rotman 2017, 99).

15 For possible etymologies, see Rhys Davids and Stede 1986 and Trenckner et al. 1924, s.v. *kaṭukañcukatā*. As Ñāṇamoli (1979, 478n69) notes, "It is impossible to render into English this 'portmanteau' etymology, e.g., *kucchita-kata—kukata, kukutatā* . . . *kukkucca,* which depends mostly on a fortuitous parallelism of meaning and verbal forms in the Pali. While useless to strict modern etymologists, it has a definite semantic and mnemonic use."

16 Following Rhys David and Stede 1986, s.v. *macchariya*. There are, however, dissenting voices in the Pali materials about what precisely causes rebirth in the realm of hungry ghosts, such as committing one of the ten courses of evil action or not honoring one's parents, or even killing someone by depriving them of water or inappropriately following ascetic vows (*dhutaṅga*). See Holt 1981, 9, and *Milindapañha* 303 and 357 (trans. Horner 1969, ii 135 and ii 217).

17 *Visuddhimagga* 470 (cf. trans. Ñāṇamoli 1979, 478). Nearly the same definition occurs in Buddhaghosa's *Atthasālinī* (257–58; trans. Tin and Rhys Davids 1920, 343), where it is followed by a definition of "close-fistedness" (*kaṭukañcukatā*), attesting to the interconnectedness of these terms.

18 For instances of their pairing, for example, see the *Abhidharmakośa* (Pradhan 1975, 312 and 314), *Dharmasamuccaya* (Caube 1993, 1.15), *Kāśyapaparivarta* (Staël-Holstein 1926, 7), and *Ṣaḍgatikārikā* (Mus 1939, 244, v. 40). See, too, the *Mahābhārata* (Sukthankar et al. 1933–59, iii 247.16; trans. van Buitenen 1975, 704). And for more on their conjoining as *saṃyojana,* a term that is frequently translated as "fetters," see the *Sakkapañha Sutta* (*Dīgha-nikāya* ii 276; trans. Walshe 1995, 328). See too Edgerton (BHSD, s.v. *saṃyojana*); Rhys Davids and Stede 1986, s.v. *saṃyojana*; Rotman 2017, 456–57; and Barua 2018.

19 *Visuddhimagga* 470 (cf. trans. Ñāṇamoli 1979, 478).

20 Avś i 277.9.

21 *Atthasālinī* 376 (cf. trans. Tin and Rhys Davids 1920, 483). In the same passage, Buddhaghosa directly equates the two terms: "meanness is said to be close-fistedness" (*maccheraṃ kaṭukañcakatā ti vuttam*).

22 Avś i 278.1.

23 According to the Buddha's explanation in the story, the first wife is reborn as a hungry ghost because *īrṣyā* led her to commit murder, but the particular torment of bearing five children every day and being forced to eat them is the result of lying while taking an oath. While the other stories in this decade end with the Buddha urging one to rid oneself of mātsarya, here the Buddha encourages one only to rid oneself of misdeeds of speech (Avś i 278.3) and makes no mention of *īrṣyā.*

24 See, for example, *Dīgha-nikāya* iii 234 (trans. Walshe 1995, 495); *Aṅguttara-nikāya* iii 272 (trans. Bodhi 2012, 839); *Dhammasaṅgaṇi* 199 (trans. Rhys Davids 1900, 299–300; trans. Kyaw Khine 1996, 588–89); and *Visuddhimagga* 683 (trans. Ñāṇamoli 1979, 713).

25 *Aṅguttara-nikāya* iii 139 (cf. trans. Bodhi 2012, 738). Notice that here possessing *macchariya* leads to a rebirth in hell (*niraya*) and not in the realm of hungry ghosts.

26 *Manorathapūraṇī* ii 282–83 (closely following trans. Bodhi 2012, 1736n1123). For a more extensive explanation, see Buddhaghosa's commentary on the above-cited list in the *Dhammasaṅgaṇi* (199), which is found in the *Atthasālinī* (375; trans. Tin and Rhys Davids 1920, 482–83).

27 The Venerable Yifa (2002, 301n6) notes that the Buddhist monastic codes in China instruct monks to snap their fingers before going to the toilet, either to purify the area or to alarm the spirits. According to the *Zhengfa nianchu jin*, "those who, as a result of their avaricious and spiteful nature"—an excellent description of mātsarya—"give unclean food to Buddhist monastics or Brahmans (non-Buddhist priests) will be reborn in the realm of the hungry ghosts who eat excrement." She then shares this anecdote from the *Za piyu jing*: "A monk once entered the toilet without snapping his fingers. Without the customary warning, the hungry ghost that dwelled inside the latrine had his face soiled. The ghost was furious but was prevented from killing the discourteous monk by his impervious virtue, for he was a monk who diligently upheld the precepts." In other words, hungry ghosts want to be fed, not shit on, and it is thus the responsibility of a defecating monk to alert any hungry ghosts who might be residing at that toilet.

28 Avś i 286.4, *atīvāvāsamatsarī.*

29 Avś i 286.4–5.

30 Cf. *Aṅguttara-nikāya* iii 181 (trans. Bodhi 2012, 770) and its commentary at *Manorathapūraṇī* ii 195.

31 Owing to mātsarya, humans in these stories "berate" begging mendicants, calling them "hungry ghosts," as does a young woman in "Food," five hundred merchants in "Maudgalyāyana," and Uttara's mother in "Uttara" (Avś i 248.8, i 257.6, and i 262.5). Conversely, the Buddha "berates" a hungry ghost in "The Merchant," and the monk Uttara does the same in "Uttara." (Avś i 272.10 and i 266.1). Apparently "berating" is an effective way of reasoning with hungry ghosts, giving them, as it were, a taste of their own medicine. There appears to be a similar connection in Pali materials between possessing *macchariya* and "berating others" or "being abusive" (*paribhāsaka*). See, for example, the *Petavatthu* (8, 10, 20, 29, 61, 65) and the *Aṅguttara-nikāya* (iv 80–81; trans. Bodhi 2012, 1054–56), where a stock description is repeated of "one without faith who is mean, miserly, and abusive" (*assaddho maccharī kadariyo paribhāsako*).

32 Avś i 270.3 and i 278.3, respectively.

33 For more on confession and forgiveness, see Hiraoka 1991, Derrett 1997, and Attwood 2008.

34 In high Hindi, the two words are sometimes compounded, *dravyalābha*, to create a word meaning "money" or "lucre."

35 "Organizational identification is defined as a perceived oneness with an organization and the experience of the organization's successes and failures as one's own" (Mael and Ashforth 1992, 103). Workers who identify as such tend to choose courses of action that best promote the apparent interests of the organization, even to their own detriment. One example of trying to create such an identification comes from my home institution, Smith College, which initiated an "I am Smith" campaign, designed in part to diminish the distinction between the college and its students, and feelings of alienation that students and alumnae might have toward the organization. See www.smith.edu/topics/i-am-smith.

36 According to Buddhaghosa's commentary in the *Atthasālinī* (375; cf. trans. Tin and Rhys Davids 1920, 482), "As a result of possessing *macchariya* with regard to material gains, one is reborn in the shit-hell." The text also explains that if one possesses *macchariya* for monastic property and then makes use of it as if it were one's personal property, one is reborn as a yakkha, a hungry ghost, or a giant snake.

37 Cf. Avś ii 71.6. And for numerous references to the Pali equivalent, see Trenckner et al. 1924, s.v. *ariyadhamma*. See too Hiltebeitel 2011, 184. And for more on the usage of dharma in the plural in Buddhist materials, see Hiltebeitel 2010, 44–49.

38 Wijeratne and Gethin 2002, 60.

39 Sayadaw 2016, 423–24.

40 Sayadaw 2016, 221.

41 "Stinginess [*macchariya*] is the kind of stinginess or avarice that is so strong that one cannot bear the thought of or approve of another person possessing one's belongings" (Sayadaw 2016, 221).

42 Nyi 2010, 48. The venerable Janakābhivamsa (Nyi 2010, 241, s.v. *macchariya*) also notes the close connection between *macchariya* and *issā* in his definition of the former: "Stinginess, avarice (usually combined with *issā* as *issāmacchariya*)."

43 This wish is almost like an inversion or even perversion of a "fervent aspiration" (*praṇidhāna*). Cf. Avś i 287.6. See too *Divyāvadāna* 14.19 (trans. Rotman 2008, 56),

where a woman makes an "improper fervent aspiration" (*mithyāpraṇidhāna*), and as a result is reborn as "a hungry ghost with great power" (*pretamaharddhikā*).

44 Speaking more technically than euphemistically, Aaron James (2012, 4–5) defines an "asshole" as someone who "allows himself to enjoy special advantages in social relations out of an entrenched sense of entitlement that immunizes him against the complaints of other people." Here I use the term more loosely, although mātsarya can be thought to generate a kind of entitlement, however deluded.

45 Avś i 248.8, i 251.1–2, and i 271.15.

46 Avś i 245.7–8, i 248.10–11, i 255.12, i 260.10, i 266.4–5, i 273.13, and i 278.4.

47 See Rotman 2003 and Rotman 2009, 129–48.

48 Gethin 1998, 121.

49 Gethin 1998, 122–23.

50 For more on the mental worlds of hungry ghosts, see Sonam Kachru's provocative analysis of Vasubandhu's *Viṃśikā* (*A Work in Twenty Verses*). According to Vasubandhu, Kachru (2015, 172) notes, "We are all prone to error, all of us, for much of our lives, and periodically dream, but we are, at the present time, not privy except by acts of the imagination to what *it is like to* experience the world as a *preta*."

51 Avś i 173.6–12. Cf. *Divyāvadāna* 290.20–291.4 (trans. Rotman 2017, 84). See too parallel passages in the *Itivuttaka* (18–19; trans. Masefield 2000, 14) and the *Ekottarikāgama* (Tripāṭhī 1995, 18.21–23).

52 In the *Aṅguttara-nikāya* (iii 287; cf. trans. Bodhi 2012, 864), there is a telling description of the "recollection of generosity," which is one of the six subjects of recollection. It advises that "a noble disciple recollects his own generosity with this thought: 'It is truly my good fortune and my gain that in a world of people overwhelmed by the stain of *macchariya*, I live at home with a mind free from the stain of *macchariya*, freely generous, openhanded, delighting in relinquishment, devoted to charity, delighting in giving and sharing." For a commentary on this passage, see *Visuddhimagga* 223–24 (trans. Ñāṇamoli 1979, 220–21).

53 In "Uttara," for example, the eponymous hero encounters a hungry ghost who, in her previous life, was his own mother (Avś i 262–64).

54 For a poignant example of hungry ghosts lamenting their plight, especially the fact that "because they are unable to perform meritorious deeds they gain nothing at all" (*kiṃ punar akṛtapuṇyāto yena kiṃcit na labhanti*), see *Mahāvastu* i 27–29 (cf. trans. Jones 1949–56, i 22–24). On the grammar of *akṛtapuṇyāto*, see Edgerton 1993, i 53, §8.51.

55 This has similarities with early Christian ideas about the inhabitants of purgatory. As Jacques Le Goff (1984, 11) notes, "Purgatory is an intermediary other world in which the trial to be endured by the dead may be abridged by the intercessory prayers, the 'suffrages,' of the living."

56 See Avś i 259.7–8, i 282.1–2.

57 See Avś i 273.1–6.

58 See Avś i 264.15–265.3.

59 See Avś i 272.11–12.

60 Nevertheless, in the *Milindapañha*, in a section on the efficacy of making offerings and dedicating them to the deceased (294–97; trans. Horner 1969, ii 123–24), it is said that only some hungry ghosts receive benefits from such offerings, while others

do not; those who feed on vomit (*vantāsika*), those who are tormented by hunger and thirst (*khuppipāsina*), and those who are consumed by thirst (*nijjhāmataṇhika*) don't benefit, while those who live on the gifts of others (*paradattūpajīvina*) do. These subdivisions of hungry ghosts, however, are not present in the *Avadānaśataka*, nor is there any indication that some hungry ghosts are "beyond reach" and unable to receive merit assigned to them.

61 This is nicely illustrated in "The Story of Koṭikarṇa," which occurs in similar form in the *Mūlasarvāstivāda-vinaya* (Dutt 1984, iii 4, 176.7–9) and in the *Divyāvadāna* (12.25–28; trans. Rotman 2008, 54). The character Śroṇa Koṭikarṇa stumbles upon some hungry ghosts, who then beg him for food, but when he tries to feed them, his offerings transform into something inedible, as per the karma of each hungry ghost. "Śroṇa tossed some food to one of the hungry ghosts, and it turned into dung beetles. He tossed some to another, and when that hungry ghost began to eat it, it turned into balls of iron. He tossed some to another, and when that hungry ghost began to eat it, it turned into the hungry ghost's own flesh. Then he tossed some to yet another, and it turned into pus and blood." Scenes of Śroṇa Koṭikarṇa encountering these hungry ghosts are found in Xinjiang, China, in Kizil cave 212 (ca. 513–637 CE) (Waldschmidt 1967). See plate 1.

62 Elsewhere, however, the situation is more confusing. "In the case of offerings to deceased ancestors," Rita Langer (2007, 168) notes, "there are no unambiguous passages in which *dakkhiṇā* can only be understood as merit [as opposed to food], but there are passages that suggest that actual food is given to the *petas* either directly or indirectly (by way of monks as mediators)." For more on the intricacies of this transference of merit (and sometimes food), see Gombrich 1971, Holt 1981, and Schmithausen 1986. And for more on hungry ghost festivals that have proliferated across Asia, at which time family members invite their ancestors back to the human realm for a feast, see Teiser 1988, Ladwig 2012, and Davis 2016.

63 Edgerton (BHSD, s.v. *chandaka*). Cf. Schopen 2005, 151n113.

64 Avś i 257.7–10.

65 A "general collection of alms" (*chandakabhikṣaṇa*), in terms of etymology, designates an offering of "alms" (*bhikṣaṇa*) given according to the donor's "free will" or "desire" (*chandaka*)—a voluntary gift rather than a coerced payment. In "Cloth" (no. 55) and "Muktā" (no. 77) in the *Avadānaśataka*, laypeople make a "general collection of alms" for the Buddha and monastic community, gathering primarily jewelry, gold, and cash at people's homes and on city streets. No mention is made of food or other monastic provisions being collected, so presumably these donations were to be cashed in for more appropriate offerings.

Monastics can also initiate (and terminate) a "general collection of alms," although some of what they do seems at odds with monastic rules and conventions. In "Maudgalyāyana," for example, some hungry ghosts request the venerable Maudgalyāyana to make "a general collection of alms" from the homes of their relatives. He does so and then uses the alms to prepare a meal and feed the community of monks led by the Buddha, who then assigns the resultant merit to those hungry ghosts. Peculiar here is the fact that the venerable Maudgalyāyana is shown collecting alms and then preparing a meal "all by himself" (*svayam eva* | Avś i 257.14). Usually such a meal would be prepared by a householder at his own home with his own food, not prepared by a monk at a monastery with provisions he had acquired through begging.

In the early years of the monastic community, monks were generally not supposed to cook; the food they consumed was to be prepared by the unordained (Wijayaratne 1990, 64–66). And in "Blind from Birth," a young woman goes forth as a nun and takes up residence in a nunnery that her relatives built for her and which they provide with regular offerings of food. But when the nun is expelled from the nunnery for bad behavior, she suspends the "general collection of alms," ending the offerings that her relatives (and benefactors) had been making. The relatives had apparently agreed to make donations at specified intervals, turning a donation given according to one's "desire" (*chandaka*) into a kind of subscription. Edgerton (BHSD, s.v. *chandaka*) hints at this meaning in his definition, but it isn't one of the attested meanings in Rhys Davids and Stede's *Pāli-English Dictionary* or Cone's *A Dictionary of Pāli.* And there is no reference to *chandaka* as a donation or offering of any kind in the various Sanskrit dictionaries I consulted, for the term—whatever exactly it means—is apparently and peculiarly Buddhist.

Nevertheless, *candā* meaning "subscription" does occur in a wide variety of South Asian materials. The term is something of a "false friend" of *chandaka*, apparently coming from the Persian—as a nominalized form of *cand*, meaning "some" or "a few"—and entering Urdu and Hindi, where it is quite common, although the etymology is mostly forgotten. Among the Persian dictionaries I consulted, however, *candā* appears only in those published in South Asia, not in those published outside the subcontinent. It seems that both *chandaka* and *candā* have their origins in South Asia, with both terms being neologisms for a kind of subscription model of donation, suggesting the prevalence of the idea and the paucity of the available terms to describe it—or maybe just the need for some kind of differentiation. My thanks to Mahesh Deokar and Amina Steinfels for their advice on this note.

66 The poor woman's observation is quite cutting: "If this householder is so rich, wealthy, and prosperous, and can even see hoards of treasure buried underground, why does he wander around begging from other families" (Avś i 314.10–315.1)? Cf. Schopen 2000, 192nXV.1.

67 Avś i 315.2–3.

68 According to Malalasekera (1995, s.v. *Anāthapiṇḍika*), "He fed one hundred monks in his house daily in addition to meals provided for guests, people of the village, invalids, etc. Five hundred seats were always ready in his house for any guests who might come. He fed 1,000 monks daily . . ."

69 Avś i 242.8, i 246.10–11, and i 274.12–13.

70 Avś i 274.12–14. Cf. Avś i 242.8–9 and i 246.11.

71 Once again "The Story of Koṭikarṇa" is instructive. Koṭikarṇa makes a visit to the realm of hungry ghosts, where he witnesses individuals undergoing unique and terrible torments. The same scenario plays out repeatedly: He asks, "What deed led you to be reborn here?" And he receives this reply: "The people of Jambudvīpa (i.e., the Indian subcontinent) are difficult to convince. You won't believe me/us." To which he responds, "I can see what's before my eyes. Why wouldn't I believe you?" (Dutt 1984, iii 4, 159.4–193.20 and *Divyāvadāna* 1–23; trans. Rotman 2008, 39–70). The message here is that eyewitnesses are to be trusted; seeing is believing. And the Buddha has

seen it all. His words, as they say, are gospel. For more on this story and its connection to belief, see Rotman 2009, 23–64.

72 See, for example, "The Master Weaver" (chapter 1, story 9), which is preserved with commentary in the *Petavatthu-aṭṭhakathā* (42–46; trans. Ba Kyaw and Masefield 1980, 46–50). A master weaver's wife, we are told, was "mean and miserly" (*maccharinī kadariyā*), so she cursed and berated Buddhist monks and was therefore reborn as a hungry ghost who ate only "excrement and urine, pus and blood." Noteworthy is that Dhammapāla, in his commentary on this story, explains *kadariya* as a more developed form of *macchariya*: "at first she was 'mean' because her character was filthy with meanness, and then after practicing this meanness again and again she became 'extremely mean' (*thaddhamaccharinī*), and thus she was 'miserly.'" Dhammapāla likewise defines *kadariya* as "extremely mean" (*thaddhamaccharī*) later in his commentary (*Petavatthu-aṭṭhakathā* 102, 251; cf. trans. Ba Kyaw and Masefield 1980, 109, 259).

73 Robert DeCaroli (2004, 96), in his work on early Buddhism's relationship to spirit religions, reads the *Petavatthu* less as a set of cautionary tales than as a "means" to get people to donate to the monastic community: "The text does not seek to be a field guide to the supernatural; rather, it provides cause-and-effect lessons on the karmic consequence of bad behavior. This text, which was produced at some point prior to the fifth century CE and is related to second-century CE prototypes, identifies the *saṃgha* as the supreme field of merit. It is represented as the ideal institution through which to create positive karma for oneself or by which to transfer positive merit to a deceased loved one. The ghost stories are simply a means to that end." Appleton (2014b, 56) suggests that "the *Petavatthu* is in a broader sense a manual for dealing with death and the recently deceased . . . ," which could be taken as either a counter or complement to DeCaroli's assessment.

74 Avś i 242.5, i 246.7–8, i 249.8, i 253.1, i 256.9, and i 267.11.

75 As Appleton (2014b, 55) notes, "Although [in the *Petavatthu*] the *preta* realm is clearly a place of suffering, many *preta*s also enjoy divine rewards in some limited way. For example, in *Petavatthu* 1, 3 we meet a *preta* that has a beautiful golden body but a putrid mouth full of worms; this, we learn, is the result of that being having been a monk who practiced austerities but also slandered other people . . . A further *preta* who used to be a hunter by day but very pious by night lives in a divine mansion by night but spends each day being devoured by dogs (3, 7)." Cf. *Petavatthu-aṭṭhakathā* 12–16 and 204–7; trans. Ba Kyaw and Masefield 1980, 16–20 and 214–17. "The Story of Koṭikarna," as it is preserved in both the *Mūlasarvāstivāda-vinaya* (Dutt 1984, iii 4, 168.4–180.3) and the *Divyāvadāna* (7.13–15.7; trans. Rotman 2008, 47–57), likewise features hungry ghosts who experience divine pleasures by night and horrific miseries by day and vice versa.

76 The phrase occurs more than forty times in the *Avadānaśataka*, although only twice in the decade of stories about hungry ghosts (Avś i 245.8–9 and i 269.13–14).

77 Shirkey 2008, 341. Incidentally, although the documentary film *Scared Straight!* (1978) was a critical success, prompting many states to initiate "scared straight" programs to rehabilitate young delinquents, the programs themselves have not been particularly successful; some research even indicates that they lead to increased rates of offense and recidivism (Robinson and Slowikowski 2011). While there is recognition

within Buddhist soteriology that fear can be beneficial, it can also be an impediment to spiritual growth, generating suffering and misery (Giustarini 2012).

78 Avś i 285.14.

79 For more on the complicated relationship between wealth and merit, see Payutto 1994, especially chapter 4.

80 Valeri 1991, 42–45.

81 See, for example, the Buddha's critique in the *Saṃyutta-nikāya* (i 89–91; trans. Bodhi 2000, 182–83) of a wealthy merchant who was a "lowly man" (*asappurisa*) and hoarded his wealth, only to die without an heir.

82 Avś i 286.4, *pṛthagjanaḥ*.

83 Avś i 286.4, *naivāsikaḥ*, which in what follows is used interchangeably with *āvāsikaḥ*. For more on these terms, see Silk 2008, 147–58.

84 Peter Masefield (1986, 1–36) considers the distinction between "ordinary folks" (*puthujjana*) and "noble disciples" (*ariyasāvaka*) in Pali materials and argues that this bifurcation, rather than "monastic" and "lay," was the main spiritual division of the early Buddhist world. He concludes that the former refers to "one who has not heard the Dhamma, one who is unable to discern who are ariyans, one who is not guided in the Dhamma of the ariyans, one who is unable to discern who are sappurisas ["worthy men"], one who is unconversant with the Dhamma of the sappurisas, and one who is not guided in the Dhamma of the sappurisas" (Masefield 1986, 3; asterisks omitted). In short, one who doesn't know Buddhist teachings and was separate from the Buddhist path. For commentaries on this position, see Harrison 1987 and Hallisey 1988.

85 *Visuddhimagga* 573 (cf. trans. Ñāṇamoli 1979, 595).

86 Brahmanical texts, especially the Dharmaśāstras, are preoccupied with issues of purity, especially recovering one's lost purity, which is essential for maintaining one's spiritual well-being (Olivelle 1998). But there are certain vile deeds, like "consuming human urine and excrement" (*Āpastamba Dharmasūtra* 1.21.16; trans. Olivelle 1999, 32) that some believed led to a permanent loss of purity or even a loss of caste. For such individuals, contemplating a life as a hungry ghost "whose only food was pus-filled blood and shit" (Avś 279.7–8) would surely have been horrific.

87 See note 7.

88 There is a lot of material on the connection between monks and merchants in early Buddhist India. See, for example, the exemplary work of Gregory Schopen (2004, 2005, 2014), as well as Heitzman 2009, Rotman 2009, Neelis 2011, and many others.

89 Sircar 1966, 317. See too Fišer 1954 and Rotman 2017, 352n43.

90 Avś i 244.3–4, i 261.6–7, i 271.6–7, and i 275.14–15.

91 As Collett (2006, 166) notes, "The formula describes a *gṛhapati* [householder] in stories 26, 51, 82, 83, 95, 96, 97 and 98, but it is also used to describe the wealth of a brahmin (in stories 1, 74 and 94) or a city merchant (*śreṣṭhin*) as in stories 3, 6, 20, 37, 41, 46, 48, 49, 71, 77, 92 and 93. On two occasions (36 and 85), it describes traders (*sārthavāha*)." In addition, a variant of the trope, once again used to describe a *śreṣṭhin*, occurs in story 25.

92 Lüders (1912), in his list of Brāhmī inscriptions, cites twenty-four attestations of *śreṣṭhin* or one of its close variants. Cf. Neelis 2011, 25n71.

93 For more on intention and giving in Buddhist narratives, see Strong 1979 and Rotman 2009, 66–112.

94 As a point of comparison, consider Patrick Olivelle's (2012, 177) observations about the audience for King Aśoka's inscriptions:

> There are indications that the implicit audience of these texts consists of well-to-do or middle-class householders or others holding positions of authority. The elements of Aśoka's Dharma I have outlined here include three significant aspects: Giving gifts to various groups including Brahmins and religious mendicants, spending and hoarding little, and treating slaves and servants with kindness . . . That his message would be directed at the leaders of communities and families, especially the more affluent ones, seems appropriate, given his civil religion, like the similar one in an equally sprawling land like America that was brought into a political unity only recently, was aimed at securing the loyalty of diverse populations that had no historical or emotional ties to the rulers . . .

95 "Maudgalyāyana" features five hundred mātsarya-filled merchants, and "The Merchant" tells the story of a merchant who became a mātsarya-filled monastic, apparently not ready to leave behind the world of commerce and clinging.

96 The term *śrāddha* occurs five times in the *Avadānaśataka* as a description of a woman, but the term doesn't occur at all in the decade of stories about hungry ghosts. For more on issues of gender in the *Avadānaśataka*, see Green 2007, Finnegan 2009, Dhammadinnā 2015, and Muldoon Hules 2017.

97 This wariness of "the commoners among us"—or, more alliteratively, the mediocre mortals in our midst—might strike some as a kind of scapegoating, as with the Ethiopian officials, in Ryszard Kapuscinski's (1983, 113 and 139) telling, who blamed the demise of Haile Selassie's empire on those of middling wealth and (purportedly) middling intellect:

> Who destroyed our Empire? Who reduced it to ruin? Neither those who had too much, nor those who had nothing, but those who had a bit. Yes, one should always beware of those who have a bit, because they are the worst, they are the greediest, it is they who push upward . . . Mediocrity is dangerous: when it feels itself threatened it becomes ruthless . . . Fear and hatred blind them, and the basest forces prod them into action: meanness, fierce egotism, fear of losing their privileges and being condemned. Dialogue with such people is impossible, senseless.

98 For more on Buddhist rules regarding monastic property, see Schopen 1995, 473–87. For more on Buddhist bowls and robes, see Clough 2015.

99 *Saṃyutta-nikāya* iii 140 (cf. trans. Bodhi 2000, 950). There is also a category of "blind ordinary people" (*andha-puthujjana*), which Buddhaghosa explains as those who have not "studied, interrogated, learned, memorized, or reviewed the teaching on the aggregates, elements, sense bases, etc." (*Sumaṅgala-vilāsanī* i 59; cf. trans. Bodhi 1978, 111).

100 *Dhammapada,* verse 174 (cf. trans. Carter and Palihawadana 1987, 43).

101 I take inspiration here from Raimundo Panikkar's (1982) notion of "diatopical

hermeneutics," for I don't want to treat mātsarya as a universal, even if it is treated that way in various Buddhist texts. As Boaventura de Sousa Santos (2002, 48) explains, "A diatopical hermeneutics is based on the idea that the *topoi* of an individual culture, no matter how strong they may be, are as incomplete as the culture itself... The objective of a diatopical hermeneutics is, therefore, not to achieve completeness—that being an unachievable goal—but, on the contrary, to raise the consciousness of reciprocal incompleteness to its possible maximum by engaging in a dialogue, as it were, with one foot in one culture and the other in another, accounting for its diatopical character." My thanks to Tarinee Awasthi for this reference.

102 Helpful perhaps is Julia Kristeva's (1982, 71) contention that "excrement and its equivalents (decay, infection, disease, corpse, etc.) stand for the danger to identity that comes from without: the ego threatened by the nonego, society threatened by its outside, life by death." But even if one doesn't want to read excrement symbolically or ponder its relationship to abjection in Buddhist materials, one still might find it productive to contemplate Milan Kundera's (1984, 246) observation that "shit is a more onerous theological problem than is evil."

103 Francis Clooney (2003, 110), while writing about justifications of violence in Brahmanical materials, observes that "intending harm is always condemned, but causing pain can and indeed must occur in certain situations. Thus 'nonviolence' (*ahiṃsā*) is both 'not causing pain' and also 'not intending harm.'" As defined above, however, "meanness" involves both causing pain and intending harm. For more about early Buddhist attitudes toward violence and nonviolence, see Gethin 2008.

104 Consider the Dalai Lama's *A Call for Revolution* (2018), which calls for a "revolution of compassion," building on his earlier call for "spiritual revolution" (Dalai Lama 1999, 17). Consider, too, Pierre Bourdieu's (1962, 134, and 150) insights into Algeria's colonization by France and what might prompt the need for such a revolution: "The colonial situation thus creates the 'contemptible' person at the same time that it creates the contemptuous attitude; but it creates in turn a spirit of revolt against this contempt... [and] the first demand of the members of the dominated society is that they be treated with respect and dignity."

105 O'Connor 1955, 21–22.

106 For example, in "The Story of Svāgata" in the *Divyāvadāna* (186.2–6; trans. Rotman 2017, 313), the venerable Svāgata enters into a state of loving kindness to subdue a fierce nāga, and as a result the latter's fearsome weapons turn into divine flowers and fall harmlessly upon him. For more, see Schmithausen 1997 and Gethin 2004, 185–87.

107 Philips and Taylor 2010, 9.

108 Philips and Taylor 2010, 12.

109 Philips and Taylor 2010, 64.

110 Mark Shields, "... And Boesky," *Washington Post*, June 2, 1987.

111 Like the film's director, Oliver Stone, Michael Lewis crafted an exposé of Wall Street in the mid-1980s—*Liar's Poker: Rising Through the Wreckage on Wall Street*—and returned to it twenty-odd years later for a reassessment, noting that apparent aberrations had become norms. In the afterword to the twenty-fifth-anniversary edition of the book, Lewis (2010, 312–13) observes: "The events I'd taken in 1989 for absurdities of the moment... wound up being long-term trends. They led directly into a

world-historic financial crisis, and far deeper dysfunction inside the financial sector than anything I'd witnessed while working in it." Unlike Gekko, however, he seems to think that Wall Street executives know what they're doing is wrong. They're just deceitful: "Wall Street has gone from being the loud guy who organizes bus tours to strip clubs for his pals but still loves his wife and kids, to the quiet guy who fakes a pious devotion to his family while secretly cheating on his wife every chance he gets."

112 *Webster's Revised Unabridged Dictionary of the English Language* (1913).

113 In legal materials, "bad faith" is generally a gloss on the ways that individuals deceive others, especially in contracts and negotiations (Summers 1968). For more on "the duty to bargain in good faith," see Cox 1958.

114 Panthaka is a self-proclaimed "fool, absolute fool, idiot, complete idiot," and the Buddha and the monastic community agree. Once Panthaka's bad karma is destroyed, however, he attains arhatship and becomes a brilliant teacher: foremost among the Buddha's disciples in skillfully transforming the minds of others. The Buddha explains that Panthaka had seemed like a fool as the karmic consequence of deeds done in previous lives. As a monk during the time of the Buddha Kāśyapa, he cultivated mātsarya with regard to the dharma. This resulted in his being reborn as a pork dealer, at which time he mimicked the meditation practices of solitary buddhas but could only produce a low level of consciousness. This, in turn, led him in his present life to seem stupid. See *Divyāvadāna* 504.25–505.29 (cf. trans. Rotman 2017, 227–28, especially 408n716).

115 *Divyāvadāna* 494.13–18 (cf. trans. Rotman 2017, 215). The Tibetan suggests that he lowered the seat of great honor to its proper place. Cf. Rotman 2017, 402n634. Elevated seats are for elevated teachers, and although Panthaka is an arhat and fully deserving the lofty position, he nevertheless moves the seat, likely trying to mitigate the karmic consequences for the nuns' harmful deed.

116 A "lion throne" (*siṃhāsana*) is a seat of honor, for kings or spiritual masters, and it is closely associated with the Buddha. Elsewhere in the *Divyāvadāna*, a wealthy merchant named Jyotiṣka is said to possess one in his palatial home (*Divyāvadāna* 279.14).

117 For more on this formula as well as the obligations and compulsions of faith, see Rotman 2009, 75–82.

118 *Divyāvadāna* 495.25–26 (cf. trans. Rotman 2017, 217).

119 *Divyāvadāna* 493.24 (cf. trans. Rotman 2017, 214)

120 *Divyāvadāna* 493.6–7, 493.13 (cf. trans. Rotman 2017, 213)

121 See Schopen 2004, 219–59.

122 The characters who cultivate mātsarya did so "long ago" (*bhūtapūrvam*) during the times of an unnamed solitary buddha ("Sugar Mill" and "A Pot of Shit"), the Buddha Kāśyapa ("Food," "Drinking Water," and "Blind from Birth"), and the Buddha Krakucchanda ("Jāmbāla"), or more recently during the time of the Buddha Śākyamuni ("Uttara," "The Merchant," and maybe—although the text isn't clear—"Maudgalyāyana"). The one character who cultivates *īrṣyā* did so during the time of the Buddha Krakucchanda ("Jāmbāla").

123 The term *śrāddha* occurs frequently in the text—see note 96—but *aśrāddha* occurs only three times (Avś i 83.7–8, i 205.5, and i 369.3–4), each time explicitly contrasting "believers" and "unbelievers," or perhaps "disbelievers." In "The Miracle," which appears in the second decade of stories, it is said that after Ajātaśatru murdered his father, King Bimbisāra, who was a just and righteous king, and usurped the throne,

"disbelief became strong and belief became weak." And then a senior minister "who had no belief [in the noble dharma]" (*aśrāddhaḥ*) and who despised the teachings of the Blessed One began to commission sacrifices from brahmans. The notion here is that as people began to lose belief in Buddhism, they started to follow other dharmas—replacing, as it were, one religion with another religion.

124 Mātsaryans and Meanists seem to practice something like the "ethical egoism" advocated by Ayn Rand (1996, 1075): "Man—every man—is an end in himself, not a means to the ends of others; he must live for his own sake, neither sacrificing himself to others nor sacrificing others to himself; he must work for his rational self-interest, with the achievement of his own happiness as the highest moral purpose of his life."

125 For more on Buddhist descriptions of the ways that "faith" (*prasāda*) can be instilled, see Rotman 2003.

126 Unlike Freud, who explains self-deception through repression, Sartre (1966, 89) maintains, in *Being and Nothingness*, that when I deceive myself, "I must know in my capacity as deceiver the truth which is hidden from me in my capacity as the one deceived. Better yet I must know the truth very exactly *in order* to conceal it more carefully—and this not at two different moments, which at a pinch would allow us to reestablish a semblance of duality—but in the unitary structure of a single project." For more on the relationship between self-deception and bad faith, see Wood 1988.

127 Catalano 1990, 687 and 692–93. See too Gordon 1995, for an argument that racism is a form of bad faith.

128 Sartre 1966, 68.

129 Sartre 1966, 65.

130 Sartre 1966, 67.

131 Avś i 244.1, i 247.13, i 248.6, i 249.11, i 250.8, etc.

132 Nyi 2010, 49.

133 Cited, famously, by Francis Bacon (1996, 357), the English Renaissance philosopher and statesman, in his essay "On Envy": "We will add this in general, touching the affection of envy; that of all other affections it is the most importune and continual. For of other affections there is occasion given but now and then; and therefore it was well said, *Invidia festos dies non agit*: for it is ever working upon some or other."

134 See www.angry.net/people/w/welfare_recipients.htm.

135 For more on the ways that markets function as "intensely moralized, and moralizing, entities," see Fourcade and Healy 2007, 2. And for more on the thoroughgoing commoditization associated with neoliberalism, see Harvey 2005, 165–72.

136 Kuttner 1999.

137 Steven Collins (2016, 6) makes this observation about the *Vessantara Jātaka*, which is a central text for Buddhists across Asia, in part because it prompts laypeople and monastics to think hard about charity and its moral dilemmas. The hungry ghost stories in the *Avadānaśataka* likely did the same.

138 Donald Trump Jr., October 31, 2017, 3:53 PM (twitter.com/DonaldJTrumpJr/status/925495970032443392)

139 Hermit Hwarang, October 31, 2017, 4:25 PM (twitter.com/hermit_hwarang/status/925504107514699776); Elite Bear Agents, October 31, 2017, 4:25 PM (twitter.com/Bearpigman/status/925506848358305792); and Matt Blackwell, October 31, 2017, 4:26 PM (twitter.com/matt_blackwell/status/925504306626908160).

140 Pulitzer Prize–winning legal journalist Linda Greenhouse offers a pithy assessment of the Trump administration and its policies that inadvertently links together the likes of Donald Trump Jr. and hungry ghosts. As she notes, "at the heart of this tale is meanness." See Linda Greenhouse, "Four Years of the Trump Administration in Court. One Word Stuck in My Head," The New York Times, Nov. 19, 2020.

141 Avś i 80.6, i 85.12, i 100.3, i 104.10, etc.

142 Avś i 65.10, i 69.04, i 120.1–2, i 134.9–10, etc.

143 Zin 2014, 277–78.

144 One notable exception is the "wheel of existence" (*saṃsāracakra, bhāvacakra*) painted outside of cave 17 at Ajanta (fifth century). Although damaged, it still contains a small portion of the hungry ghost realm (Zin and Schlingloff 2007, 89–91, and Zin 2014, 278–80). There are also some early representations of Avalokiteśvara bestowing mercy upon a kneeling and skinny hungry ghost (Mukhopadhyay 1981).

145 For more on the visual imagery of hungry ghosts in East Asia, see, for example, LaFleur 1989 and Tsai 2015, 45–89.

146 Wu Hung 1992, 137 and 145.

147 See, for example, Rotman 2009, 177–95.

148 Ginzburg 1989, 35.

149 For a helpful assessment of Pinney's book and project, see Sinha 2007.

150 Pinney 2004, 8.

151 LaFleur 1989, 274.

152 LaFleur 1989, 286–87.

153 The text (*Saṃyutta Nikāya* iv 19; trans. Bodhi 2000, 1143) asks rhetorically, "And what, bhikkhus, is the all that is burning?" And then it explains, "The eye is burning, forms are burning, eye-consciousness is burning, eye-contact is burning, and whatever feeling arises with eye-contact as condition—whether pleasant or painful or neither-painful-nor-pleasant—that too is burning. Burning with what? Burning with the fire of lust, with the fire of hatred, with the fire of delusion; burning with birth, aging, and death; with sorrow, lamentation, pain, displeasure, and despair, I say." And the same applies to the other sense bases. This text is also the inspiration for the third section of T. S. Eliot's *The Waste Land*, called "The Fire Sermon," which ends, famously,

> Burning burning burning burning
> O Lord Thou pluckest me out
> O Lord Thou pluckest
>
> burning

154 LaFleur 1989, 278.

155 According to the *Abhidharmakośa* (Pradhan 1975, 165), the "primary dwelling place" of hungry ghosts is five hundred leagues below the surface of the earth, where Yama, "the king of the hungry ghosts," has an enormous palace. But very often "pretas themselves disperse from that palace" (Huntington 2019, 40) and coexist with humans. As such, the *Saddharmasmṛtyupasthāna(sūtra)* (150–400 CE) recognizes "two different types of hungry ghost: those that can be seen at night in the human realm, and those that dwell exclusively in the realm of hungry ghosts" (Stuart 2012, 50).

156 Srivastava 1997, 10.

157 LaFleur 1989, 278.

158 Khurana, Ojha, and Singh 2009. For more on manual scavengers and their plight, see Singh 2009 and Human Rights Watch 2014.

159 LaFleur 1989, 294.

160 Hungry ghosts are said to look like "burned-out tree stumps." This could be a description of extremely dry and cracked skin, which is a symptom of severe dehydration.

161 LaFleur 1989, 297.

162 B. R. Ambedkar (1891–1956), Indian lawyer, scholar, and activist, famously argued against this kind of karmic calculus in *The Buddha and His Dhamma*, claiming that this formulation "was calculated to sap the spirit of revolt completely. No one was responsible for the suffering of man except he himself. Revolt could not alter the state of suffering; for suffering was fixed by his past Karma as his lot in this life" (Ambedkar 1957, i.v.iii.40). As someone born into one of the lowest castes, Ambedkar recognized the danger of any doctrine designed "to suppress and exploit the weak and to keep them in a state of complete subjugation" (Ambedkar 1957, i.v.iii.39).

163 In many Buddhist traditions, Susanne Mrozik (2006, 22) notes, "body and morality are so closely related that a description of a person's features may serve as commentary on his or her moral character."

164 Writing about the *Mahāvaṃsa*, a fifth-century poetic chronicle of Sri Lanka, Kristin Scheible (2016, 156) demonstrates the various ways that "the text's purpose is to generate first *saṃvega*, anxious thrill, and then the resulting *pasāda*, serene satisfaction." And Trent Walker (2018, 276) contends that "the evocation of *saṃvega* and *pasāda* is central to the contemporary performance of Cambodian Dharma songs." Especially noteworthy is the song "Hungry Ghosts' Lament," which poignantly describes the suffering of abandoned hungry ghosts (Walker 2018, 288–89). For more on *prasāda* as a practice, see Rotman 2009, 65–148.

165 *Buddhacarita* 3.4 (cf. trans. Olivelle 2008, 61). The conceit here is that there is a correlation between the degree of care with which the afflicted are sent away—i.e., "with supreme gentleness (*pareṇa sāmnā*)—and the degree of beauty that the royal highway now possesses—i.e., it is "supremely beautiful" (*śobhāṃ parām*). For the Buddha, such a conceit is not only mistaken but also dangerous.

166 *Divyāvadāna* 296.12–13, *kāyikī dharmadeśanā na vācikī*. See too *Divyāvadāna* 133.7 and 313.12; *Mūlasarvāstivāda-vinaya* (Dutt 1984, iii 1, 232.5–6 and 252.3–4); and *Saṅghabhedavastu* ii 46.

167 The connection between hungry ghosts and ancestors, which I discussed previously (see notes 9, 11, and 62), is also apparent in Aśvaghoṣa's *Buddhacarita*. The text seems to confuse (or equate) "the realm of hungry ghosts" (*pretaloka*) with "the realm of ancestors" (*pitṛloka*), recognizing the features of the former but attributing them to the latter. According to the text (*Buddhacarita* 14.27–28), "those whose minds are overwhelmed with mātsarya are reborn in the pitch-dark realm of ancestors where they experience their reward in misery. They have mouths as tiny as a needle's eye and stomachs as gigantic as a mountain. They are tormented with the sufferings of hunger and thirst. Suffering is their lot in life." Aśvaghoṣa seems to imagine hungry ghosts living deep below the earth's surface near Yama's palace where it would presumably be "pitch dark" (*nirāloka*).

168 Merton 1948, 82–83.

169 James Madison, Federalist Paper no. 54; cited in Delbanco 2018, 87.

170 As Judith Butler (2020, 56) notes, "Grievability governs the way in which living creatures are managed, and it proves to be an integral dimension of biopolitics and of ways of thinking about equality among the living."

171 Huntington 2021, forthcoming.

172 Avś i 280.4, *paramabībhatsaḥ*. This description seems quite deliberate, indicating that Jāmbāla engendered disgust in those who saw him. Bībhatsa is one of the eight (or nine) *rasa*s in traditional Indian aesthetics. Bharata, in his famous *Nāṭyaśāstra* (*Treatise on Drama*) explains, "The macabre [*bībhatsa*] can be pure or impure: the former is disturbing, and is brought about by the sight of blood and the like; the latter is disgusting, and is brought about by the sight of excrement, maggots, and so on" (Pollock 2016, 53).

173 In the story, the heretical teacher Pūraṇa Kāśyapa thinks Jāmbāla a holy man and initiates him, but either he offers Jāmbāla no instruction or the latter rejects it. Pūraṇa Kāśyapa is infamous for his belief in the inefficacy of action (*akiriya-vāda*), whereby volitional acts have no consequence and moral judgments are rejected. As he explains in the *Sāmaññaphala Sutta*, "If one were to go along the north bank of the Ganges giving gifts and inducing others to give gifts, making offerings and inducing others to make offerings, by doing so there would be no merit or outcome of merit. By giving, self-control, restraint, and truthful speech there is no merit or outcome of merit" (*Dīgha Nikāya* i 52–53; trans. Bodhi 1989, 19, cf. trans. Walshe 1995, 93–94). After his initiation, Jāmbāla immediately wanders off "doing good deeds," the very existence or benefit of which Pūraṇa Kāśyapa would not recognize. To be sure, Jāmbāla follows a different dharma.

174 *Divyāvadāna* 490.19–23; trans. Rotman 2017, 209–10.

175 In the story, no one in the great city would admit that the emperor's new clothes were no clothes at all, for it was said that the clothes were invisible to anyone who was unfit for their office or unusually stupid. Everyone was cowed into willful blindness until the young child proclaimed, "But he hasn't got anything on." Then the whole city acknowledged the truth. But not the emperor. "The Emperor shivered, for he suspected they were right. But he thought, 'This procession has got to go on.' So he walked more proudly than ever, as his noblemen held high the train that wasn't there at all." Sometimes seeing the truth isn't enough; fear and pride are formidable impediments. See andersen.sdu.dk/vaerk/hersholt/TheEmperorsNewClothes_e.html.

176 *Divyāvadāna* 7.13–15.7; trans. Rotman 2008, 47–57. Cf. *Mūlasarvāstivāda-vinaya* (Dutt 1984, iii 4, 168.4–180.2).

177 My thanks to Lilla Russell-Smith, curator of the Museum für Asiatische Kunst, for permission to use this image and for her insightful comments.

178 Kitsudō Kōichi and Arakawa Shintarō (2018) have identified the component parts in this mural based on a single sheet of printed paper (X-2538, The State Hermitage Museum) that was excavated at the ruins of Khara-khoto in the Inner Mongolia Autonomous Region and which depicts the same compositional structure as the mural. Both, it seems, build on Zunshi's schematic of the ten realms found in his *Yuandun Guanxin Shifajietu* (*Illustration of the Ten Realms of Mind Contemplation in the Perfect and Immediate Teaching*).

179 As Lilla Russell-Smith (2005, 109–10) notes, "The mural in Bezeklik Cave 18 is an excellent example of a compositional type that evolved from many different sources,

and is a proof of the close links of Uygur art with the Tanguts and the Liao, and through them with the development of later Chinese art. It is also an example of shared iconography and interaction between Bezeklik and Dunhuang." For an image of the full wall painting, see Raschmann 2020, 213 and fig. 8.2. For more on cave 18 at Bezeklık, see Russell-Smith 2005, 104–10, and Moriyasu 2008.

180 My thanks to Phillip Bloom and Takashi Midori for helping me gain access to this image and to Venerable Mano, abbot of Shin Chion-in, Shiga Prefecture, Japan, for allowing me to reproduce it. And thanks to Phillip Bloom and Daniel Stevenson for their thorough explanations and incredible patience.

181 Stevenson 2001, 59. For more on this ritual, see Stevenson 2001.

182 Also helpful are *shuilu* ritual manuals, such as *Ritual Manual for Performing the Retreat of the Grand Assembly of All Saintly and Mundane Beings of Water and Land in This Dharma-Realm* (*Fajie shengfan shuilu shenghui xiuzhai yigui*), which was compiled by Zhipan (ca. 1220–75) and revised by Zhuhong (1535–1615). See *Shinsan Dai Nihon Zokuzōkyō*, vol. 74, no. 1497 (Tokyo: Kokusho Kankōkai, 1975–89; CBETA edition, cbetaonline.dila.edu.tw). The text, which was likely written near Ningbo in the thirteenth century, enumerates twenty-four classes of beings and names ten exemplars of each class. In its description of hungry ghosts, it follows Zunshi's classification, organizing hungry ghosts into three classes and nine categories, and in total it recognizes thirty-six types of hungry ghosts. As a point of comparison, the *Saddharmasmṛtyupasthāna(sūtra)* likewise envisions thirty-six types of hungry ghost (Stuart 2012, 50–53, and Moretti 2017).

183 "On the Visualizations [That Accompany a] Charitable Bestowal of Food [on Hungry Ghosts], in Reply to Questions of the Official Cui Yucai" (*Shishi guanxiang da Cui [Yucai] zhifang suo wen*). The tract is contained in a collection of Zunshi's short tracts entitled *Jinyuan ji* (*Golden Garden Collection*), CBETA, X57, no. 950, p. 12, a20–b14 // Z 2:6, p. 120, a15–b15 // R101, p. 239, a15–b15. All translations from Zunshi, here and in what follows, are by Daniel Stevenson.

184 According to Daniel Stevenson (personal communication), "Elsewhere Zunshi notes that these ghosts tend, as a result, to linger around ritual sites and events where such discarded offerings might be obtained. More powerful ghosts, he notes, are able to produce disturbances and extraordinary signs that are often mistaken as indications of the presence of powerful gods and spirits. Hoodwinked by these poltergeists, ignorant people enshrine and venerate these ghosts as gods—a claim regarding vernacular Chinese religion that is strikingly parallel to representations and attitudes toward vernacular gods and spirits of local mediums that appear in early religious Daoist treatises of the second century CE."

185 In the *Yuqie yankou* (Yoga Rite of Flaming Mouth), which is discussed in the following description of the *Flaming-Mouth Ghost King* (plate 4), Ānanda is taught a ritual to feed both hungry ghosts and brahman seers, so this could account for the latter's appearance here. See Lye 2003, 420.

186 My thanks to Phillip Bloom and Takashi Midori for helping me gain access to this image, and to Phillip Bloom and Daniel Stevenson for their insights about this image and the ritual world that it inhabits.

187 See Orzech 1996; Lye 2003, 417–25; and Stevenson 2004.

188 For more on this ritual of feeding hungry ghosts, see Stevenson 1999, 347–57 and 363–79; Lye 2003; and Stevenson 2015, 407–29.

189 Some contemporary Taiwanese Buddhists identify the vegetables as water spinach—known in Chinese as the "empty heart/mind vegetable," owing to its hollow stem. Supposedly, once the hungry ghosts eat the vegetable, their minds become empty (of delusion?) so that they can be reborn in the Pure Land.

190 My thanks to Monika Zin for helping me find the image; the State Museum of Ethnology in Munich for allowing me to use it; and Eric Huntington, Jinah Kim, Simona Lazzerini, Todd Lewis, Sara McClintock, and Adeana McNicholl for helping me make sense of it.

191 As Jinah Kim (personal correspondence) notes, "Stylistically, the painting follows mostly Tibetan visual idioms, and I think it's emulating a copy that was popular in more 'Tibetan' Buddhist spheres (especially in Central and Eastern Tibet and also in Mongolia). It is, in fact, quite close to some known examples from Mongolia, as there is a very interesting connection between Nepal and Mongolia (and all the way to Buryatia in Russia) through Baudhanath. The painting may be a copy of an image similar to the one in the Rubin Museum of Art, if not the very image (acc.# P1994.3.6). Of course, it is also possible there is an ur-image that both paintings copied." See www.himalayanart.org/items/78.

192 Hārītī is said to have had five hundred sons, and she is frequently depicted with a baby in her arms and several more children by her knees. She is also identified, in at least some sources, as "the queen of the pretas" (Waddell 1895, 99), although there are other contenders for that title, such as "Flaming Mouth" (Tib., Kha 'bar ma; Skt., Jvālāmukhī) (Nebesky-Wojkowitz 1996, 308; Karmay 1998, 102, no. 61; Mimaki 2000, 113n41; and Donaldson 2001 i 353). For more on the cult of Hārītī, which has received a lot of scholarly attention, see Peri 1917; Misra 1981, 73–80; Cohen 1998, 380–91; Ohnuma 2007; Langenberg 2013; and many others.

193 This figure is tricky to identify. Yama often bears a skeleton club, and he is said to be the king of hungry ghosts, living in a palatial home in the hungry ghost realm. See too Merh 1996; Siklós 1996; and Cuevas 2008, 44–54. Nevertheless, the figure could also be Hārītī's consort, Pāñcika (aka Jambhala, Kubera, Vaiśravaṇa), as the two are often pictured together, although Pāñcika is generally represented not with a staff made from a spinal column but with signs of great wealth (Dhirasekera 1976; Rowan 2002; and Brancaccio 2011, 177–79). Perhaps the artist wanted to portray a king and queen of hungry ghosts, or simply "royalty among the ghosts" (Teiser 2006, 7), and these figures are hybrids. As Eric Huntington (personal communication) notes, "It seems fairly common for the preta realm to have a singular male figure depicted in a building, sometimes even when there is no female holding children. These figures can differ greatly, but there are iconographic and textual reasons to think that some of them can be associated with Yama, understood as the king of pretas."

194 For more on the skeleton club, see Beer 1999, 292–94.

195 For images of the "six buddhas of the six realms," see www.himalayanart.org/search/set.cfm?setID=1881. See too Herrmann-Pfandt 2018; i, sections 1.6 and 2.1.5.

196 My thanks to Peter Skilling for helping me secure this image. And many thanks to Trent Walker for his help in deciphering it.

197 The first page of the *Phra Malai Klon Suat* is framed by the present image on the

left and an image of hell beings suffering various torments on the right. The textual description that accords with the present image appears a few pages later. The manuscript itself, as confirmed by the colophon, contains a few short excerpts from Pali texts before the *Phra Malai Klon Suat* begins. For more about the colophon, see Pakdeekham 2563 (2020), 45.

198 Unlike more encyclopedic accounts of the realms of hell and hungry ghosts, the text "names only one hell, Lohakumbhī [Iron Cauldron, where beings are submerged in molten metal], and does not even differentiate the various hell realms or distinguish them from the *peta* realms" (Brereton 1995, 115).

199 Brereton 1995, 115. The text offers a detailed explanation of the suffering this condition entails: "There was another type of suffering ghost who was in great torment. He had testicles that were as huge as water jugs. They hung way down to the ground like a yam shoulder bag. Rotten and putrid, bloated and stinking, they were like slimy snails. Whenever he wanted to go somewhere, he'd fling them over his shoulder, stagger under their weight, and reel from side to side. When he wanted to sit down, they'd get pinched between his legs, and he'd have to stand up, and then sit down on top of them. When he wanted to sit down, he was bent over with pain. He'd slowly straighten up, get up, 'ouch,' fling them over his shoulder, and stagger on his way under their weight, 'ouch, ouch,' getting weaker all the time" (Brereton 1995, 115). For an image of a hungry ghost suffering a similar affliction, see Anderson 2012, 72, image 28.

200 Phatsakon 2455 (1912), 17. My thanks to Trent Walker for all the references to the *Phra Malai Klon Suat*. For another illustration from a nineteenth-century Thai manuscript containing the Phra Malai story and excerpts from Pali texts, and which does contain a headless figure, see May and Igunma 2018, fig. 5.17.

201 Phatsakon 2455 (1912), 15.

202 For a detailed description of this torment, see Brereton 1995, 112–13.

203 Phatsakon 2455 (1912), 19.

204 The image is from the author's personal collection. For more about these prints, see Pinney 2018. For an example of a Jain compendium of such images, along with moral instruction, see the wonderfully graphic *Nārakī Citrāvalī* (*Pictures of Hell*) (Vijayajinendrasūrīśvarajī and Trivedī 1984).

205 My thanks to Matthew Meyer for permission to use this image and for his insights into his own creative process. For more, see Meyer 2015, s.v. *gaki* and yokai.com.

206 Personal communication, July 29, 2020.

207 For more details about the manuscripts, see Avś ii c–cvii. Demoto (2006, 2) offers this convenient description:

> B: Add. 1611 of the Cambridge University Library; written in Newarī script; dated 1645 A.D.; this is the common source of D, P and C below.
>
> D: The Hodgson mss. in the India Office Library; entitled *Śatakāvadāna*; written in Newarī script; dated 1792 A.D.; this is the oldest of 3 copies of B.
>
> P: D. 122; the Hodgson mss. in the Bibliothèque Nationale at Paris; written in Devanāgarī; no date, before 1837; it consists of two volumes; Feer's translation is chiefly based on it.
>
> C: Add. 1386 of the Cambridge University Library; written in Newarī script; a very bad copy which abounds in blunders.

F: Add. 1680 II of the Cambridge University Library; Palm-leaf ms. of 14–15th century; written in Newarī script; incomplete; it contains fragments of some *avadānas* of the fourth and fifth decades; it is the only ms. source independent from B.

208 Avś ii c–ci
209 Avś ii cvii..
210 See gretil.sub.uni-goettingen.de/gretil.htm.
211 For more details, see notes 3 and 6.
212 Rotman 2017, xxi–xxii.
213 For an interesting parallel between this decade of stories and an avadāna anthology discovered in Merv, Turkmenistan, see Karashima and Vorobyova-Desyatovskaya 2015, 220n295 and 489–505.
214 The corresponding Tibetan can be found at D 343 *mdo sde, aṃ*, 117a4–119a6. See too *Kalpadrumāvadānamālā*, no. 5.
215 Avś i 241.5, *jñāto mahāpuṇyo*. The Sanskrit and the corresponding Tibetan (117a6) present these terms as two separate characterizations of the Buddha, although one might infer that he is "renowned" (*jñāta*) as "one who possesses great merit" (*mahāpuṇya*). And perhaps this is what inspires others to provide him with monastic requisites, for gifts given to a great "field of merit" (*puṇyakṣetra*) earn extra merit for the donor. In this way, "worshiped" (*abhyarcita*) might be glossed as "honored with offerings." Cf. Avś i 32.6, i 36.9, etc. The term *mahāpuṇya* seems to shift in meaning between "one who possesses great merit" and "one who possesses great wealth," for the former generally entails the latter in Buddhist material. For example, in "The Story of Meṇḍhaka" in the *Mūlasarvāstivāda-vinaya* (Dutt 1984, iii 1, 241 / Vira and Chandra 1995, 228r6–9; cf. *Divyāvadāna* 123–24; trans. Rotman 2008, 223–24), it is said that once in the city of Bhadraṅkara there lived six people "who were renowned and possessed great merit" (*ṣaḍ jñātā mahāpuṇyāḥ*): the householder Meṇḍhaka and his wife, son, daughter-in-law, servant, and maid. Each had the proverbial Midas touch. So when the servant ploughed a single furrow, seven furrows would be plowed, and when the maid looked after one of anything, it would become sevenfold. Merit, the text makes clear, creates wealth, even if, as a servant or maid, it isn't yours to keep. Schopen (2000, 139nI.8, 101) observes that "a monk who was *mahāpuṇya* was a monk who had or received large amounts of material possessions"—in other words, "a circumlocution or euphemism for 'rich'"—and translates *jñāto mahāpuṇyaḥ* as "famous and of great fortune." Similarly Collett (2006, 160) translates them as "of great merit and fortune." See also Dhammadinnā 2015, 497n29.
216 Following Speyer (Avś i 241n3), Feer (1891, 162n3), and the Tibetan (117b2), read *śrutvā*. Avś i 241.11, "seen" (*dṛṣṭvā*).
217 Following Speyer's suggestion (Avś i 241n3), Avś i 243.4, and the Tibetan (117b2), read *cārikāyā āgatya*. Avś i 241.11, *tān āgatya*.
218 Avś i 241.11–242.1, *tatas tau tad adhiṣṭhānaṃ tathāvidhāṃ dharmadeśanāṃ kurutaḥ*. In this formulaic expression, the locution *tad adhiṣṭhānaṃ* is a bit peculiar, both in terms of meaning and grammar. As for meaning, I follow Edgerton (BHSD, s.v. *adhiṣṭhāna* 1); also possible would be "based on this." Feer (1891, 162–63) offers this translation: "Puis, les deux (āyuṣmat) firent à ce sujet un exposé de la loi tel que..." The

grammar, however, is still odd. Avś i 91.1 reads *bhagavatā ca tad adhiṣṭhānaṃ* (ms., *adhiṣṭhānāṃ*) *devamanuṣyāṇāṃ tādṛśī caturāryasatyasaṃprativedhikī dharmadeśanā kṛtā*. Speyer (Avś i 91n1) also suggests *adhiṣṭhānā* as a possible emendation and then refers to his index (Avś ii 227, s.v. *tadadhiṣṭhānam*), where he compiles citations but offers no translation. Avś i 264.15 likewise reads *tad adhiṣṭhānaṃ*, while Avś i 259.3 and ii 136.2 read *tad adhiṣṭhānā tathāvidhā dharmadeśanā kṛtā*. The corresponding Tibetan (117b3) to the present passage reads *de nas de gnyis kyis de la bstan* (read: *bsten*) *nas de dang 'thun pa'i chos ston par byed de*. At Avś i 259.3 and i 264.15, where the subject is the Buddha, the corresponding Tibetan (125a1, 127b2) reads *de nas bcom ldan 'das kyis gzhi de las brten nas de dang 'thun pa'i chos bstan te* and . . . *gzhi de las brten nas yi dags ma de dang skye bo mang po la de dang 'thun pa'i chos bstan te*. Speyer also cites an instance in the *Divyāvadāna* (577.29; cf. trans. Rotman 2017, 334) where an enterprising individual negotiates with the citizens of a town: "I have a deal for all of you" (*tad adhiṣṭhānaṃ vijñāpayāmi*). My thanks to Sara McClintock for her insights here.

219 Avś i 242.2, *dharmaśravaṇakathāyāś ca bhājanībhavanti*. Following the Tibetan (117b3), Feer (1891, 163) offers this translation: "et devinrent des vases du discours et de l'audition de la loi." In other words, they became vessels for hearing and telling the dharma (i.e., conduits for an oral narrative tradition of the dharma). Cf. *Divyāvadāna* 235.27 (trans. Rotman 2017, 11).

220 Avś i 242.3–4, *parvatakūṭaprakhyaṃ* (following ms. F). Ms. B adds an interlinear *ma*, *kūṭapra(ma)khyam*, and Speyer hypothesizes that other copyists may have taken the *ma* as a *mu*; hence, mss. CP, *kūṭapramukhyaṃ*, and ms. D, *kūṭamukhaṃ*. The text does not explain what part of the hungry ghost is being compared to a mountaintop, but here the copyists seem to have snuck in the idea that it is the hungry ghost's "face" (*mukha*). Feer (1891, 163) translates likewise. Omitted in the Tibetan (117b4). See too Avś i 243.5, where a description of this hungry ghost is repeated, and the text reads *parvatopamakukṣiṃ* instead of *parvatakūṭaprakhyaṃ samudradṛśakukṣiṃ*. This same reading also occurs at Avś i 247.3, i 249.7, i 250.5, i 252.10–11, etc.

221 The logic seems to be that hungry ghosts are engineers of their own misery, causing themselves to combust in an ongoing auto-cremation that never incinerates the body; it only causes excruciating pain. For more on self-cremations, see Ānalayo 2012.

222 Avś i 243.7, *pravṛddhaśailopamacañcitāśrayaḥ*. Cf. Avś i 247.5 and i 268.10. The simile here is a little obscure. The Tibetan (188a3–4), as Demoto (2006, 23–24n101) notes, "reads *lus chen ri bo mthon po 'dra ba la* '(whose) big body looks like a high mountain.' The Tibetan translators obviously understood *cañcita* as 'great' (*chen*)." Speyer (Avś ii 209), following Kern, suggests *-carvitāśrayaḥ*—"the receptacle of the chewed (food)"—and Vaidya (Avś-V 118.28) emends likewise. But this emendation seems unjustified; see Demoto (2006, 23–24n101) and Edgerton (BHSD, s.v. *cañcitāśraya*). How then to make sense of *pravṛddha-*? Perhaps the image being conjured is of someone shaky and unstable, either like an old, crumbling mountain, or maybe like a towering mountain (prone to landslides?). Feer (1891, 164) reads it quite differently: "se dressant comme un roc, ne sachant où se réfugier."

223 Avś i 243.10, *kapālapāṇir ghoraś ca*. Cf. Demoto 2006, 25. Feer (1891, 164 and 164n2), following the Tibetan, offers this translation: "(meurtrissant) son crâne (avec) sa main (d'une manière) horrible."

224 Avś i 244.15, *āha re* (ms., *āhara*). Vaidya (Avś-V 108.26) emends to *ahāra*. That is, "bring your bowl here and give it to me." The Tibetan (118b6) doesn't support Vaidya's emendation; it remains silent. Feer (1891, 165) offers this translation: "Allons, Bhixu, donne ton vase, je te donnerai du jus."

225 In other words, the solitary buddha would have to focus his attention in order to discern the workman's thinking, but he does not. For more on "focusing the attention" (*samanvāhara*), see Edgerton (BHSD, s.v. *samanvāharati*). For more on this trope, see Rotman 2008, 408n304, and Rotman 2017, 430n1003.

226 As an arhat, Maudgalyāyana has presumably eradicated meanness, so perhaps it is best to read the Buddha's instructions here as being addressed to a general audience.

227 Avś i 245.7–8, *yathā evaṃvidhā doṣā na syur ye pretasya* (mss., *syur yena pretasya*) *iti*. The idea seems to be that mātsarya gives rise to various "faults" (*doṣa*). The following story (no. 42) expresses nearly the same idea but with different wording: Avś i 248.10–11, *ete doṣā na bhaviṣyanti ye tasyāḥ pretyā iti*. Cf. Avś i 255.12, i 260.10, i 266.4–5, etc.

228 The corresponding Tibetan can be found at D 343 *mdo sde, aṃ*, 119a6–120b5. See too *Kalpadrumāvadānamālā*, no. 14.

229 Avś i 246.10, *anubhaviśyasīti*. As Speyer (Avś i 246n3) notes, the use of the future here "is somewhat strange. I think it is due to a mistake of some copyist. One expects . . . *anubhavasīti*."

230 Avś i 248.4, *cittaṃ pradūṣayati*. More literally, "she polluted her mind [with bad thoughts]," but here the idiom "hardening one's heart" seems to capture the meaning in English. Feer (1891, 165) translates likewise into French.

231 Avś i 248.8, *iyaṃ te bhikṣo satkriyā mā punar idaṃ gṛhaṃ pravekṣyasīti*. As Speyer (Avś i 248n3) notes, Feer (1891, 167) follows the Tibetan and reads *bhikṣo 'asatkriyā*—transforming *hospitality* into *inhospitality*—"but it is preferable to take the answer ironically."

232 The corresponding Tibetan can be found at D 343 *mdo sde, aṃ*, 120b5–122a2. See too *Ratnāvadānamālā* (Takahata 1954, no. 4) and *Dvāviṃśatyavadāna* (Okada 1993, no. 13).

233 Avś i 249.6–7, *dagdhastūṇāsadṛśīṃ*. This expression often appears in a phrase that contrasts a burned-out tree stump with a conscious body, with the suggestion that one should never cultivate bad thoughts toward the former, let alone the latter. My sense is that hungry ghosts are said to look like barely sensate objects—seemingly "dumb as stumps" but in many ways more conscious (and conscientious) than their previous, mātsarya-filled selves. Cf. *Divyāvadāna* 197.24 (trans. Rotman 2008, 331, 437n683) and 534.24 (trans. Rotman 2017, 267–68); *Saṅghabhedavastu* ii 252.27–28; *Śikṣāsamuccaya* 149.3–4 (trans. Bendall and Rouse 1971, 148); etc. See too note 159. My thanks to Peter Skilling for his thoughts on this expression.

234 The corresponding Tibetan can be found at D 343 *mdo sde, aṃ*, 122a2–123b3. See too *Ratnāvadānamālā* (Takahata 1954, no. 15).

235 Avś i 253.2, *tad api kṛcchreṇāsādayantīm*. Cf. Avś i 254.6, *tac ca duḥkhena labhyate*. Previously (Avś i 242.6), owing to context, I translated the same expression as "She made her way with difficulty." Feer (1891, 163 and 172–73) likewise offers varying translations: "c'est là qu'il allait, c'est là qu'il s'asseyait" and "et encore a-t-elle bien de la peine à se procurer cet (aliment)."

236 Following Vaidya (Avś-V 112.28) and other instances of this verse (Avś i 247.7, i 268.12, etc.), add *nagnā svakeśasaṃchannā asthiyantravaducchritā*. Avś i 254.4, *āha ca . . . ārtasvarā* (mss., *āha cāśu ārttasvarāṃ*). Speyer (Avś i 254n1) notes, "I suppose a half-śloka, at least, has perished, on account of the (1) abruptness of the metrical portion introduced by *āha ca*, (2) one half-śloka being wanted to complete the triad of ślokas to be expected here. Moreover mss. have also a superfluous syllable between *āha cā* (which I hold for a corrupted *āha ca*) and *ārtta-*. Some line like *nagnā svakeśaṃchannā* (cp. *supra* p. 247.7) seems to have dropped out." Likewise omitted in the Tibetan (125b1).

237 For a parallel, see Avś i 242.6. See too Feer 1891, 173n1.

238 Avś i 254.6, *varcaḥ pāsyāmi bhokṣye ca* (mss., *paśyāmi bhokṣe ca*). Speyer (Avś i 254n3) notes, "I have restored *pāsyāmi* in accordance with Feer (1891, 173n3) who rests his opinion on the Tibetan translation, and, consequently, I have emended likewise *bhokṣye*." The Tibetan (125b1) concurs.

239 The corresponding Tibetan can be found at D 343 *mdo sde, aṃ*, 123b3–125b5. For more on the connection between this story and the *Yulanpen Sūtra*, see Karashima 2013, especially 297–98. See too *Ratnāvadānatatva* (Takahata 1954, no. 4).

240 Avś i 257.1, *piṇḍāya prāvikṣat*. More literally, "he entered Rājagṛha for alms," but the five hundred hungry ghosts live outside the city.

241 Avś i 258.7, *karmavāyunā*. This is a technical term used to explain the force of karma, and it has been translated variously—action energy-winds, karmic energy, action motility, vital energy of past actions, etc.

242 Avś i 259.9, *paryuṣitaparivāsā*. Edgerton (BHSD, s.v. *paryuṣita*) offers this explanation: "*having completed residence* (in heaven; said of gods reborn there after having been lower beings previously; is divine existence regarded as a kind of *probation*? prob[ably] merely *change of residence*, sc. from earth." Referencing the present passage, he offers this translation: "It would not be proper that we should approach the Blessed One to see him after finishing our residence (probation?); let us, while it is still unfinished, (visit him)."

243 Avś i 260.6, *yat te . . . pretā deveṣu pratiṣṭhāpitāḥ*. Ms. B, *yattevamādaḥ pretāḥ*, but as Speyer (Avś i 260n3) notes, "the akṣaras *vamādaḥ* are cancelled with a reference to the upper margin, where we find the correction *prasāda*. [Ms.] C copied the prima manus, [ms.] P has *yattevaprasādaḥ*; [ms.] D *yattavaprasādaḥ*. I consider *prasāda* a bad correction and would rather suppose some word expressive of their number to be hidden under the corrupt *vamādaḥ*. The Tibetan version [125b2] has here *mang po dag* = *bahavaḥ* ["many"], as Mr. Thomas has told me."

244 According to Speyer (Avś i 260n4), "This sentence is wholly out of place here and looks like a clumsy repetition of the ordinary conclusion of the avadānas in this varga applied improperly." Vaidya (1958, 115n1) agrees. Feer (1891, 178) reads this sentence together with the one that follows it: "En conséquence, Maudgalyāyana, il te faut renoncer à l'égoïsme et faire de grands efforts pour ne pas commettre des fautes comme celles de ces Pretas."

245 The corresponding Tibetan can be found at D 343 *mdo sde, aṃ*, 125b5–128a3. See too *Ratnāvadānatatva* (Takahata 1954, no. 12).

246 This story has an unmistakable parallel in the *Pāṇḍulohitakavastu* of the *Mūlasarvāstivāda-vinaya*. Compare what follows with this portion of the text (Yamagiwa 2001, 66–67/§4.2; cf. trans. 158–59):

At one time Uttara came into the Blessed One's presence, and after seeing the Blessed One and listening to the true dharma, he developed faith in the Blessed One's order. Filled with faith, he was eager to go forth as a monk. He went before his mother and said, "Mother, grant me permission so that I may go forth as a monk according to the dharma and monastic discipline that have been so well expressed."

"You are my only son," she said. "As long as I'm still alive, don't go forth as a monk. When I die, you can do as you please."

"Mother," he said, "I won't go forth as a monk, but only if each and every day you prepare food for those monks specified by the monastic community."

"Son," she said, "I'll do just that."

Uttara would give all that he earned to his mother and say, "Mother, use this to make offerings to ascetics and brahmans."

But his mother was mean, miserly, and clung to her possessions. She couldn't even bring herself to offer something to a crow, let alone offer anything to ascetics and brahmans.

When ascetics and brahmans would come into her home in search of alms, she would berate and abuse them: "It's as though you were born as hungry ghosts, always begging for alms at people's homes!" And she would deceive her son: "Today I offered food to lots of monks and I gave alms to many ascetics and brahmans."

Since she practiced, developed, and cultivated this meanness, when she died she was reborn as a hungry ghost. After the loss of his mother, Uttara gave gifts, performed meritorious deeds, and then went forth as a monk according to the dharma and monastic discipline that have been so well expressed.

247 Speyer (Avś i 263n4) explains, "I have edited this part of the pretī's words as prose, though it is beyond doubt that her whole utterance must be a metrical one." Speyer goes on to suggest some minor edits to turn these lines into verse (in *triṣṭubh* meter). Vaidya (Avś-V 116.29–30), mostly following Speyer's suggested edits, prints these lines as verse:

> *saphalān vṛkṣān gacchāmi niṣphalā [me] bhavanti te* |
> *pūrṇāni sarāṃsi gacchāmi tāni śuṣkāṇi santi [me]* ||

248 Avś i 263.4–5, *sukhaṃ bhadantasya hi vṛkṣamūlaṃ bhajate śītalabhājana*| *kṛpāṃ janayitvā kṛpaṇāyai mahyaṃ dadasva toyaṃ tṛṣārtitāyai*. According to Speyer (Avś i 263n6–7), "one or more words are lost . . . In pāda C pronounce *janetvā*, in pāda d one short syllable is missing." Vaidya (1958, 117.1–2) emends, and sets it as verse:

> *sukhaṃ bhadantasya hi vṛkṣamūlaṃ [udakaṃ] bhajate śītala bhājanesmim* |
> *kṛpā janayitvā [janetvā] kṛpaṇāyai mahyaṃ dadasva toyaṃ tṛṣārtitāyai* ||

The Tibetan (127a2) likewise reads it as verse. Speyer (Avś i 263n6) offers this translation: "It is a quiet place near the Reverend's tree, there is also (fresh) cold water in thy waterpot. Well, show pity towards wretched me and give me water, for I am tormented by thirst."

249 Avś i 264.3, *dakṣiṇām ādeśaya deśanāṃ ca kāraya*. Following parallel passages in the text (e.g., Avś i 257.9 and i 264.11), one might expect *dakṣiṇādeśanāṃ ca kāraya*. The Tibetan (127a4) seems to concur.

250 Avś i 265.7, *yamalī*. According to Speyer (Avś i 265n6), "[ms.] B *yamalī*, both times *nī* is written above *malī*, [ms.] C has both times *yamalī*, but [ms.] D *yamanī*, [ms.] P has at first *yamanī*, afterward *yamanalī*. Perhaps both forms were in use, *yamalī* and *yamanī*." The Tibetan (127b6) reads *ras zung*. Feer (1891, 181), following the Tibetan, translates the term as "une paire de vètements en coton." In "The Story of Jyotiṣka" in the *Divyāvadāna* (276.5–278.22; trans. Rotman 2017, 64–68), the term *yamalī* refers to two identical lengths of unstitched, loom-woven cotton fabric, one of which gets used to cloak a deity and the other of which gets used as a fancy bathing garment. The pair are finely woven and expensive, although not everyone recognizes their worth. According to textile historian Rahul Jain (personal communication), "As pairs of unstitched fabric lengths (a lower and upper body drape) have been known as standard wear for both women and men in so many communities and regions of India, there is little reason to presume that this simplest form of covering the body would have changed significantly over the millennia. Two well-known modern examples are the *mundu-veshti* of Kerala and the *mekhela-chador* of Assam, both ensembles now worn with stitched underclothing that was likely unknown before the colonial period. The knee-length *dhoti* and *dupatta/angavastram* seem to have been worn forever, and in myriad styles, by men from various communities across India, as well as by the priestly class. At its briefest, the *dhoti* becomes a *langot*, a short unstitched length wound around the hip, likely the 'bathing garment' described in your Buddhist text. Many tribal communities across India continue to wear single or double-piece, unstitched lengths even today." Cf. Agrawala 1966, 74–75. Pairs of loom-woven fabric lengths have been used as unstitched garments in many parts of the Indian subcontinent throughout history.

251 Avś i 265.7, *krītā*. The Tibetan (127b6) likewise reads *nyos ba*. It is nonetheless unexpected to have a monk purchase an item from the monastic community. See, for example, Wiyajaratne 1990, 25–28.

252 Avś i 265.7, *mānavaka*. This term, as Edgerton (BHSD) notes, "is, or corruptly represents, a word meaning peg, post, or the like, for hanging clothes." The corresponding Tibetan (127b6) reads *gos kyi gdang la*.

253 The corresponding Tibetan can be found at D 343 *mdo sde, aṃ*, 128a3–129b7. See too *Karmaśataka* iii.6 (Jamspal and Fischer 2020: 3.241–256).

254 Following Speyer's suggestion (Avś i 267n2), the standard formula (Avś i 244.8, 252.6–7, etc.), and the Tibetan (128a6), add *piṇḍāya prāvikṣat śrāvastīṃ*. Avś i 267.6 (omitted).

255 Avś i 267.9, *śmaśānasadṛśīṃ*. More literally, "like a cremation ground." See *Ramāyaṇa* 5.26.26. But here the idea is likely that she is half burned not only like a "burned-out tree stump" but also like a corpse at a cremation ground. Feer (1891, 182) translates this as "semblable à (l'habitante d') un cimetière." See too *Saṅghabhedavastu* i 82.4.

256 Based on fragments in the Schøyen Collection, Demoto (2006, 23–26) has reedited the following portion of the text (= Avś i 268.3–271.10).

257 Demoto (2006, 25n109), following the standard formula (Avś i 246.15, i 250.1, etc.) and the corresponding Tibetan, adds *priyālāpina*. That is, "speak kindly." Avś i 268.3 (omitted).

258 Demoto (2006, 25n110), following the preceding parallel passage (Avś i 267.8) and the corresponding Tibetan, adds *jātyandhāṃ*. That is, "blind from birth." Avś i 268.6 (omitted).

259 Following Avś ii 337.14 and Demoto (2006, 25n111), read *viṃśativarṣasahasrāyuṣi*. Avś i 269.1, *viṃśatisahasrāyuṣi*; likewise, Avś i 237.10, i 250.11, i 334.16, ii 96.13, and ii 149.15. As Demoto (2006, 25n111) notes, "*varṣa* is missing in Speyer's text—probably due to inadvertency—although it occurs in his ms."

260 Demoto (2006, 25n112) adds *tathāgato 'rhan samyaksambuddho*. As she explains, "In the cliché of the appearance of a past Buddha these words are missing very often in Speyer's mss. Among more than 50 instances only 13 have kept them (Avś nos. 11–20, 24 and 86). They might have been omitted by the habit of a scribe who copied the phrase faithfully only up to the third decade."

261 Avś i 269.6, *bhikṣuṇīvarṣakaḥ*. Feer (1891, 183) translates this as "une habitation pour la saison des pluies, à l'usage des Bhixunīs." Similarly, Edgerton (BHSD) takes *varśaka* to be a "house, hut for the rainy season, for monks or nuns." Schopen (2008, 229), however, argues that the *varśaka* or *bhikṣuṇīvarṣaka* is a "nunnery" and that Indian Buddhist nunneries were "located, unlike male monasteries, inside towns or cities."

262 A portion of the text is missing here (Avś i 269.9). Speyer (Avś i 269n4) suggests *chinnāni*, *samucchinnāni*, "or some synonymous particle." Cf. Avś i 269.12, *samucchedaḥ kṛtaḥ*. Vaidya (Avś-V 119n1) suggests *ācchinnāni*. The corresponding Tibetan (129b1) reads *gcod du bcug*, which as Demoto (2006, 25n113) notes, "might point to *samuccheditāni*." Following the Tibetan, Feer (1891, 183) translates this as "Alors elle se mit à leur retrancher . . ."

263 Avś i 269.8, *dānapatigṛhebhyaḥ* (ms., *dānaprati-*). According to Demoto (2006, 25n113), "the Tibetans [129b1] seem to have read *dānapatigṛha**pati**bhyaḥ* (*sbyin bdag khyim* ***bdag*** *rnams*) in their Sanskrit original instead of *dānapatigṛhebhyaḥ* in Speyer's text. At present we cannot decide which is the better reading."

264 Following Speyer's suggestion (Avś i 269n6) and Demoto's suggestion (2006, 25v2), add *sṛgālaiś*. Avś i 269.12 (omitted).

265 Following the Schøyen fragments (Demoto 2006, 26n115) and the Tibetan (129b7), add *bhikṣava*. Avś i 270.2 (omitted).

266 The corresponding Tibetan can be found at D 343 *mdo sde, aṃ*, 130a1–131b3. For an English translation of this story, see Schopen 1995, 500–502. See too *Ratnāvadānatatva* (Takahata 1954, no. 19).

267 Here (=Avś i 271.10) ends the portion of text that, based on Schøyen fragments, was reedited by Demoto (2006, 23–26).

268 Avś i 271.13, *gṛhītapariṣkāro*. Perhaps read *gṛhīta-* in the sense of *āgṛhīta-*. That is, "he was stingy with those provisions." Cf. Avś i 248.3.

269 Avś i 272.1, *muṇḍikāṃ gaṇḍīṃ*. For more on the *muṇḍikā gaṇḍī*, see Hu-von Hinüber 1991, 751; Schopen 1992, 6; and Sobkovyak 2015, 707n89.

270 Schopen (1995, 488) maintains that in this instance the expression "bowl and robe" (*pātracīvaram*) "was a euphemism that covered a large variety of personal property." Perhaps the monk in the story was meant to be understood as hoarding numerous

monastic provisions, with "bowl and robe," the most iconic of these possessions, a synecdoche for monastic provisions in general.

271 Avś i 272.5, *śiṣyagaṇasyodvejanārtham*. The idea, as I mentioned previously (p. 23), is that the students will be "scared straight" by what the Buddha has them witness.

272 Avś i 272.9–10, *sajalajaladagambhīradundubhisvaraḥ* (mss., *-svarāḥ*). More literally, "in a voice like a kettle drum, deep, like a monsoon thundercloud." The idea is that his voice booms like a bass drum and thunders like a storm cloud. Cf. *Buddhacarita* 7.9.

273 Avś i 272.10, *tvayaivaitad ātmavadhāya pātracīvaraṃ samudānītam*. The Buddha "berates" (*paribhāṣitavān*) this hungry ghost, so his response here is pointed and personal. See note 31. Also possible, for different emphasis, "it was this bowl and robe, which you yourself procured, that led to your demise" or "it was you who collected this bowl and robe, and it was tantamount to suicide." Feer (1891, 185) offers this translation: "c'est pour ta propre ruine que tu acquérais vases et vêtements." According to Schopen (1995, 501): "this hoarding of bowl and robe by you is conducive to your own destruction." Cf. Avś i 291.7–8.

274 Avś i 273.7, *pūrvarātrāpararātraṃ jāgarikāyogam anuyuktā*. In the *Śrāvakabhūmi* (Deleanu 2006, i 25 §3.4.7), this is one of the thirteen requisites (*saṃbhāra*) for pursuing both the mundane and supramundane paths to spiritual awakening. See *Mahāvastu* i 284.1–2 (cf. trans. Jones 1949), where a seer likewise follows the practice and "masters the four meditations and the five superhuman faculties" (*catvāri dhyānāni utpāditāni paṃca ca abhijñā sākṣīkṛtā*). The Tibetan (131a6), as Feer (1891, 186n3) notes, simply reads "at dawn."

275 The corresponding Tibetan can be found at D 343 *mdo sde, aṃ*, 131b3–134a1. See too *Ratnāvadānatatva* (Takahata 1954, no. 11).

276 Avś i 276.2, *rājavidheyaṃ bhaviṣyatīti*. To be more technical, "it will revert by escheat to the king."

277 Avś i 276.3, *catvaradevatāḥ*. The term *catvara* generally refers to a "square." Here it could mean a "private quadrangle" or a "public square."

278 Avś i 277.1–2, *alpaṃ vā prabhūtaṃ vā*. Or perhaps, "both small and large." Feer (1891, 5) takes it to modify "when we are dead and gone": "qu'il se soit écoulé peu de temps ou qu'il s'en soit écoulé beaucoup."

279 The corresponding Tibetan can be found at D 343 *mdo sde, aṃ*, 134a1–138a7. Speyer (Avś i 280n3) notes that *Aśokāvadānamālā*, no. 17 (Cambridge Add. 1482, f 237a ff.) contains a "metrical paraphrase" of this story. For Pali parallels, see the *Dhammapada-aṭṭhakathā* ii 52–63 (trans. Burlingame 1921, ii 130–37); *Petavatthu*, no. 43: *Gūthakhādaka* (trans. Gehman 1974, 101–3); *Petavatthu-aṭṭhakathā*, 266–69 (trans. Ba Kyaw and Masefield 1980, 277–79); *Theragāthā*, vv. 283–86 (trans. Norman 1995, i 33); and *Theragāthā-aṭṭhakathā* ii 118–20. For more on these parallels, see Malalasekera 1995, s.v. *Jambuka Thera*. For a summary of the Chinese recension of this story, see Karashima and Vorobyova-Desyatovskaya 2015, 240–41. The authors observe that the Chinese recension, in comparison with the Sanskrit version, "seems to be more original."

280 Avś i 279.6, *nagaraparikhāyāṃ*. Moats are "commonly found around forts and *garh* sites especially in Vaishali" (Mandal 2010, 151). It is fitting that these hungry ghosts live in a moat that surrounds the city, for hungry ghosts are associated with liminal places (e.g., thresholds, crossroads, forests) and liminal times (e.g., dawn, dusk). As

Shirkey (2008, 87) notes with regard to the *Petavatthu*, "Peta-s, even though they inhabit their own plane of existence, their own 'world,' nonetheless seem to have one foot, so to speak, in the human world, too. They are neither fully 'there,' nor fully 'here.' Instead, they mingle with this world, living at its margins mostly—but not always—hidden from view."

281 Avś i 279.8, *āha ca*. More literally, "he said." As Speyer (Avś i 279n5) remarks, "The composition is here troubled. Perhaps *āha ca* is only employed as the usual introduction of a metrical portion of the same contents as the preceding prose." The Tibetan (134a6) reads *yang smras pa*.

282 Pūraṇa Kāśyapa seems to understand Jāmbāla's transgression of social conventions, especially norms around purity, as an indication of a kind of spiritual transcendence. For more on the behavior and customs of renouncers, see Olivelle 1992, 101–12. See too note 172.

283 Avś i 281.5, *kvacit prayojanena*. As Speyer (Avś i 285n4) notes, "Note the blunder of *kvacit* for *kenacit*, or can it be a clerical error?"

284 Avś i 282.6–7, *mandārakāṇāṃ* (mss. BC, *mandārakānāṃ*, mss. DP, *mandāravānāṃ*). As Speyer (Avś i 282n5) notes, "Perhaps the right reading is *mandārakā[dī]nāṃ*. That is, "coral-tree flowers, and more." Cf. Avś i 259.12.

285 Many of the following attributes of buddhas are explained in the glossary.

286 Cf. Avś i 17.2–3, which adds "And for whom, with sight fully obscured by the dark film of ignorance, shall I purify the eyes with the collyrium stick of knowledge?" Here (Avś i 283.11) and elsewhere in the text (Avś i 31.3, i 72.13, i 79.9, etc.), it is omitted.

287 Avś i 284.1, *vīthīm*. Often translated as "road," but see Avś i 134.6.

288 Following Speyer's suggestion (Avś i 284.4), read *labheya* or *labheyāhaṃ*. Avś i 284.5, *labheyaṃ*.

289 Avś i 284.7, *bhavyarūpaṃ viditvā*. Feer (1891, 192) offers this translation: "sachant parfaitement l'heureuse destinée de ce personnage." Or perhaps "who knew what was proper" or "who knew what was right to do." Cf Avś i 104.3, *bhavyarūpa iti viditvā rājñā prasenajitkauśalenānujñātaḥ*, which Naomi Appleton (2013, 27) translates as "Saying [more literally, *knowing*], 'It appears suitable,' King Prasenajit the Kośalan consented." King Prasenajit knows about propriety, not destiny; the Buddha, however, acts out of concern for destiny, not propriety.

290 This formulaic description usually begins with the words "head shaved, garbed in monastic robes" (e.g., *Divyāvadāna* 37.1, 48.20, 159.9, 281.24)—words that are repeated in the verse that follows—although these words are not included in the two instances when the formula occurs in the *Avadānaśataka* (Avś i 284.8 and i 347.10).

291 This formula generally reads ". . . hair and beard." Cf. Avś i 347.10.

292 Avś i 284.11, *tasyāvevaṃ sthito* (mss., *tasyau nevasthito*), following Speyer's conjecture. Cf. the Tibetan (136b2). As Speyer (Avś i 284n6) writes, "The tradition of the fourth pāda of this indravajrā is very depraved. Wheresoever this commonplace stanza occurs (e.g., *Divy*[*āvadāna*] 48.23, 159.11, 558.21) mss. afford either *naivasthitā* or *-to* or *nevasthito* as here, or *nepadhyasthito*, or an even still worse corrupted form (e.g., *Divy*[*āvadāna*] 463.36). I believe its original and genuine form cannot have been much different from what I have edited here." Edgerton (BHSD, s.v. *nepatthita*) maintains that "some such form (possibly with Prakritic v for p) must be read in *Divy*[*āvadāna*] 48.24, 49.16, 159.12, 342.4, 463.26, 558.22 . . . in all these the mss.

(followed by the edd.) are corrupt…" Likewise, Hiraoka (2009, 37), based on Tibetan and Chinese parallels, suggests reading "clothed" (*nepatthitaḥ*) for each instance of this trope in the *Divyāvadāna*. Nevertheless, consider this remark by Feer (1891, 192n3): "*Nepathya* désigne un costume riche et appartient à la langue du théâtre (!) en sorte qu'on pourrait entendre que le personnage en question 'jouait le *rôle* d'un Buddha.'"

293 Avś i 285.4, *lūhenābhiramate*. Feer (1891, 192) offers this translation: "il se plaisait dans les ordures."

294 Avś i 285.14, *kalpaśatair api*. As Speyer (Avś i 285n7) notes, "All mss. agree here in the depraved reading." Elsewhere (e.g., Avś i 80.13, i 90.11, i 117.8) the manuscripts read the same, but Speyer nevertheless emends to *kalpakoṭiśatair api*.

295 For more on this passage (Avś i 286.1–287.3; D 343 *mdo sde, aṃ*, 137a5–137b5), see Silk 2008, 191–92 and 265–66.

296 Avś i 286.4, *atīvāvāsamatsarī*. This seems to parallel the Pali *āvāsamaccharī*. Vaidya (Avś-V 126.25) nevertheless emends to *atīvātīvāmatsarī*. That is, "tremendously stingy."

297 Avś i 286.7, *vihārasvāmī*. For more on this term, see Schopen 2004, 219–59.

298 Avś i 286.8, *jentākasnātreṇa*. This reading is a conjecture. As Speyer (Avś i 286n6) notes, "The word is written here *jentākastrātreṇa* ([ms.] D, *jentakākaṣṭhā-*), further on *jentākastrātre* and *-traṃ*." It seems that the term was obscure to the text's scribes. For more on these steam baths, see *Vinayasūtra* (D 4117 *'dul ba, wu* 6a1 ff.). See too Boyer et al. 1920–29, 321. Writing about the Gāndhārī documents from the third–fourth centuries CE discovered in Niya, near the southern edge of the Taklamakan Desert, they note that the terms *śātra*, *jaṃdākaśātra*, and *śāpaka*, which are found in inscription 511, also occur in their Sanskrit forms in the *Avadānaśataka*. Meicun Lin (1996, 195) seems to have judged this to be an actual textual parallel, but I don't find this convincing. See also Iwamatsu (2001, 168) for other avadāna references in this connection. My thanks to Stefan Baums for his suggestions here.

299 Avś i 286.11, *āgantukasya bhikṣoḥ parikarma kurvāṇam*. Feer (1891, 193) translates this as "qui s'empresse autour du Bhixu de passage pour le servir," while Silk (2008, 191) renders this as "engaged in perfuming the visiting monk." Perhaps the owner of the monastery is playing the role of steam-bath attendant and applying scented oils or powders to the visiting monk's body. Cf. *Abhisamācārikā Dharmāḥ* 42.31.37B6–7 (Karashima and von Hinüber 2012 iii 57), *jentākavārikena tailaṃ śeṣaṃ bhavati praveśayitavyam* (ms. –*tavyaḥ*) | *cūrṇṇaṃ śeṣaṃ bhavati praveśayitavyaṃ*. In what follows, the resident monk utters harsh words, likewise invoking the image of a body being slathered, not with scented oils or powders, but with shit.

300 Avś i 287.13–14, *skandhakauśalaṃ dhātukauśalam āyatanakauśalaṃ pratītyasamutpādakauśalaṃ sthānāsthānakauśalaṃ ca kṛtam*. These are known as "the five benefits of great learning" (*pañcānuśaṃsā bāhuśrutye*) in the *Mūlasarvāstivāda-vinaya* (Dutt 1984, iii 1, 23.10–12; cf. Vogel and Wille 1996, 287–88). For a slightly different list, see *Divyāvadāna* 340.26–28 (trans. Rotman 2017, 150).

Bibliography

Agrawala, Vasudeva S. 1966. "Some Obscure Words in the Divyāvadāna." *Journal of the American Oriental Society* 86.2: 67–75.

Ambedkar, B. R. 1957. *The Buddha and His Dhamma*. Bombay: R. R. Bhole.

Anālayo. 2012. "Dabba's Self-cremation in the Saṃyukta-āgama." *Buddhist Studies Review* 29.2: 153–174.

———. 2017. *Vinaya Studies*. Dharma Drum Institute of Liberal Arts Research 7. Taipei: Dharma Drum Publishing Corporation.

Anderson, Benedict. 2012. *The Fate of Rural Hell: Asceticism and Desire in Rural Thailand.* Chicago: University of Chicago Press.

Appleton, Naomi. 2013. "The Second Decade of the *Avadānaśataka*." *Asian Literature and Translation* 1.7: 1–36.

———. 2014a. "The Fourth Decade of the *Avadānaśataka*." *Asian Literature and Translation* 2.5: 1–35.

———. 2014b. *Narrating Karma and Rebirth: Buddhist and Jain Multi-Life Stories*. Cambridge: Cambridge University Press.

———. 2015. "The 'Jātakāvadānas' of the *Avadānaśataka*: An Exploration of Indian Buddhist Narrative Genres." *Journal of the International Association of Buddhist Studies* 38: 9–31.

———. 2020. *Many Buddhas, One Buddha: A Study and Translation of* Avadānaśataka *1–40*. Sheffield, South Yorkshire: Equinox Publishing.

Atthasālinī of Buddhaghosa.
Edition. Müller 1897.
Translation. Tin and Rhys Davids 1920.

Attwood, Jayarava Michael. 2008. "Did King Ajātasattu Confess to the Buddha, and Did the Buddha Forgive Him?" *Journal of Buddhist Ethics* 15: 278–307.

Avadānaśataka
Edition. See Speyer 1902–9 and Vaidya 1958.
Translation. See Feer 1891.
Translation of Stories 1–40. See Appleton 2020.

Ba Kyaw, U, and Peter Masefield, trans. 1980. *Elucidation of the Intrinsic Meaning, So Named the Commentary on the Peta Stories (Paramatthadīpanī nāma Petavatthu-aṭṭhakathā) by Dhammapāla*. London: Pali Text Society.

Bacon, Francis. 1996. *Francis Bacon: The Major Works*. Edited with an introduction and notes by Brian Vickers. New York: Oxford University Press.

Barua, Dipen. 2018. *The Notion of Fetter in Early Buddhism*. New Delhi: Aditya Prakashan.

Beer, Robert. 1999. *The Encyclopedia of Tibetan Symbols and Motifs*. Boston: Shambhala Publications.

Bendall, Cecil, ed. 1897–1902. *Śikṣāsamuccaya*. Biblioteca Buddhica 1. St. Petersburg: Académie impériale des sciences.

Bendall, Cecil, and W. H. D. Rouse, trans. 1971 (1922). *Śikṣāsamuccaya: A Compendium of Buddhist Doctrine*. Delhi: Motilal Banarsidass.

Bloom, Philip. 2013. "Descent of the Deities: The Water-Land Retreat and the Transformation of the Visual Culture of Song-Dynasty (960–1279) Buddhism." PhD dissertation, Harvard University.

Bodhi, Bhikkhu, trans. 1978. *The Discourse on the All-Embracing Net of View: The Brahmajāla Sutta and Its Commentarial Exegesis*. Kandy, Sri Lanka: Buddhist Publication Society.

———, trans. 1989. *The Discourse on the Fruits of Recluseship: The Samaññaphala Sutta and Its Commentaries*. Kandy, Sri Lanka: Buddhist Publication Society.

———, trans. 2000. *The Connected Discourses of the Buddha: A Translation of the Saṃyutta Nikāya*. Boston: Wisdom Publications.

———, trans. 2012. *The Numerical Discourses of the Buddha: A Translation of the Aṅguttara Nikāya*. Boston: Wisdom Publications.

Bourdieu, Pierre. 1962. *The Algerians*. Translated by Alan C. M. Ross. Boston: Beacon Press.

Boyer, A. M, E. J. Rapson, É. Senart, and P. S. Noble. 1920–29. *Kharoṣṭhī Inscriptions Discovered by Sir Aurel Stein in Chinese Turkestan*. Oxford: Clarendon Press.

Brancaccio, Pia. 2011. *The Buddhist Caves at Aurangabad: Transformations in Art and Religion*. Leiden: Brill.

Brereton, Bonnie Pacala. 1995. *Thai Tellings of Phra Malai: Texts and Rituals Concerning a Popular Buddhist Saint.* Tempe: Arizona State University.

Bronte, Charlotte. 2000 (1847). *Jane Eyre.* Introduction by Sally Shuttleworth. New York: Oxford University Press.

Buddhacarita.

Edition and translation. See Olivelle 2008.

Burlingame, Eugene Watson, trans. 1921. *Buddhist Legends Translated from the Original Pali Text of the Dhammapada Commentary* (*Dhammapada-aṭṭhakathā*). 3 vols. Harvard Oriental Series 28–30. Cambridge: Harvard University Press.

Burnouf, Eugène. 1844. *Introduction a l'histoire du bouddhisme indien.* Paris: Imprimerie Royale. Translated as *Introduction to the History of Indian Buddhism* by Katia Buffetrille and Donald S. Lopez Jr. (Chicago: University of Chicago Press, 2010).

Butler, Judith. 2020. *The Force of Nonviolence: An Ethico-Political Bind.* New York: Verso Books.

Carter, James Ross, and Mahinda Palihawadana, eds. and trans. 1987. *The Dhammapada.* Oxford: Oxford University Press.

Catalano, Joseph S. 1990. "Successfully Lying to Oneself: A Sartrean Perspective." *Philosophy and Phenomenological Research* 50.4: 673–93.

Caube, Vijaya Sankara, ed. 1993. *Dharmasamuccaya.* Varanasi: Sampurnanda Sanskrit University.

Clooney, Francis. 2003. "Pain but Not Harm: Some Classical Resources Toward a Hindu Just War Theory." In *Just War in Comparative Perspective,* edited by Paul Robinson, 109–25. Burlington, VT: Ashgate Press.

Clough, Bradley. 2015. "Monastic Matters: Bowls, Robes, and the Middle Way in South Asian Theravāda Buddhism." In *Sacred Matters: Material Religion in South Asian Traditions,* edited by Tracy Pintchman and Corinne G. Dempsey, 173–94. Albany: State University of New York Press.

Cohen, Richard S. 1998. "Nāga, Yakṣiṇī, Buddha: Local Deities and Local Buddhism at Ajanta. *History of Religions* 37.4: 360–400.

Collett, Alice. 2006. "List-Based Formulae in the *Avadānaśataka.*" *Buddhist Studies Review* 23.2: 155–85.

Collins, Steven. 1982. *Selfless Persons: Imagery and Thought in Therāvāda Buddhism.* Cambridge: Cambridge University Press.

———. 2016. *Readings of the Vessantara Jātaka.* New York: Columbia University Press.

Cone, Margaret. 2010. *A Dictionary of Pāli: Part 2, g–n*. Bristol: The Pali Text Society.

Cowell, E. B., and R. A. Neil, eds. 1886. *Divyāvadāna*. Cambridge: University Press.

Cox, Archibald. 1958. "The Duty to Bargain in Good Faith." *Harvard Law Review* 71.8: 1401–42.

Cuevas, Bryan J. 2008. *Travels in the Netherworld: Buddhist Popular Narratives of Death and the Afterlife in Tibet*. New York: Oxford University Press.

Dalai Lama XIV. 1999. *Ethics for the New Millennium*. New York: Riverhead Books.

Dalai Lama XIV and Sofia Stril-Rever. 2018. *A Call to Revolution*. New York: William Morrow.

Davis, Erik. 2016. *Deathpower: Buddhism's Ritual Imagination in Cambodia*. New York: Columbia University Press.

DeCaroli, Robert. 2004. *Haunting the Buddha: Indian Popular Religions and the Formation of Buddhism*. Oxford: Oxford University Press.

Delbanco, Andrew. 2018. *The War Before the War: Fugitive Slaves and the Struggle for America's Soul from Revolution to the Civil War*. New York: Penguin Press.

Deleanu, Florin. 2006. *The Chapter on the Mundane Path (Laukikamārga) in the Śrāvakabhūmi: A Trilingual Edition (Sanskrit, Tibetan, Chinese), Annotated Translation, and Introductory Study*. 2 vols. Tokyo: The International Institute of Buddhist Studies.

Demoto, Mitsuyo. 2006. "Fragments of Avadānaśataka." In *Buddhist Manuscripts*, edited by Jens Braarvig, 3:207–44. Manuscripts in the Schøyen Collection. Oslo: Hermes Publishing.

Derrett, J. Duncan M. 1997. "Confession in Early Buddhism." In *Bauddhavidyāsudhākaraḥ: Studies in Honour of Heinz Bechert on the Occasion of his 65th birthday*, edited by Jens-Uwe Hartmann and Petra Kieffer-Pülz, 55–62. Swisttal-Odendorf: Indica et Tibetica Verlag.

Dhammadinnā, Bhikkhunī. 2015. "Predictions of Women to Buddhahood in Middle-Period Literature." *Journal of Buddhist Ethics* 22: 479–531.

———. 2016. "From a Liberated One to a Liberated One: An Avadāna Quotation in the Abhidharmakośopāyikā-ṭīkā." *Dharma Drum Journal of Buddhist Studies* 19: 63–91.

Dhammapada.

Edition and translation. See Carter and Palihawadana 1987.

Dhammapada-aṭṭhakathā.
Edition. See Norman 1906–14.
Translation. See Burlingame 1921.
Dhammasaṅganī.
Edition. See Müller 1885.
Translation. See Rhys Davids 1900 and Kyaw Khine 1996.
Dharmasamuccaya.
Edition. See Caube 1993.
Dhirasekera, J. D. 1976. "Hārītī and Pāñcika: An Early Buddhist Legend of Many Lands." In *Malalasekera Commemoration Volume*, edited by O. H. de A. Wijesekera, 61–70. Colombo: Malalasekera Commemoration Volume Committee.
Dīgha-nikāya.
Edition. See Rhys Davids and Carpenter 1890–1911.
Translation. See Walshe 1995.
Divyāvadāna.
Edition. See Cowell and Neil 1886.
Translation. See Rotman 2008 and 2017.
Donaldson, Thomas Eugene. 2001. *Iconography of the Buddhist Sculpture of Orissa*. 2 vols. New Delhi: Abhinav Publications.
Dutt, Nalinaksha, ed. 1984 (1950). *Gilgit Manuscripts*. 4 vols. Delhi: Sri Satguru Publications.
Edgerton, Franklin. 1993 (1953). *Buddhist Hybrid Sanskrit Grammar and Dictionary*. 2 vols. Delhi: Motilal Banarsidass Publishers.
Egge, James. 2002. *Religious Giving and the Invention of Karma in Theravada Buddhism*. Richmond: Curzon.
Feer, Léon, ed. 1884–98. *Saṃyutta-nikāya*. 5 vols. London: Pali Text Society.
———, trans. 1891. *Avadana-Çataka: Cent légendes (bouddhiques)*. Annales du Musée Guimet 18. Paris: E. Leroux.
Fišer, Ivo. 1954. "The Problem of the Seṭṭhi in the Buddhist Jātakas." *Archiv Orientalni* 22: 238–66.
Finnegan, Damchö Diana. 2009. "'For the Sake of Gender, Too': Ethics and Gender in the Narratives of the *Mūlasarvāstivāda Vinaya*." PhD dissertation, University of Wisconsin–Madison.
Formigatti, Camillo A. 2016. "Walking the Deckle Edge: Scribe or Author? Jayamuni and the Creation of the Nepalese *Avadānamālā* Literature." *Buddhist Studies Review* 33.1–2: 101–40.

Fourcade, Marion, and Kieran Healy. 2007. "Moral Views of Market Society." *Annual Review of Sociology* 33.14: 1–27.

Gehman, H. S., trans. 1974. "Petavatthu: Stories of the Departed." In *The Minor Anthologies of the Pali Canon, Part 4*. Also contains "Vimānavatthu: Stories of the Mansions," translated by I. B. Horner, assisted by N. A. Jayawickrama. London: Pali Text Society.

Gethin, Rupert. 1992. *The Buddhist Path to Awakening: A Study of the Bodhi-Pakkhiyā Dhammā*. Leiden: E. J. Brill.

——— 1998. *The Foundations of Buddhism*. New York: Oxford University Press.

———. 2004. "Can Killing a Living Being Ever Be an Act of Compassion? The Analysis of the Act of Killing the Abhidhamma and Pali Commentaries." *Journal of Buddhist Ethics* 11: 167–202.

———. 2008. "Buddhist Monks, Buddhist Kings, Buddhist Violence: On the Early Buddhist Attitudes to Violence." In *Religion and Violence in South Asia: Theory and Practice*, edited by John R. Hinnells and Richard King, 62–82. London and New York: Routledge.

Ginzburg, Carlo. 1989. "From Aby Warburg to E. H. Gombrich: A Problem of Method." In *Clues, Myths and the Historical Method*, translated by John and Anne C. Tedeschi, 17–59. Baltimore: Johns Hopkins University Press.

Giustarini, Giuliano. 2012. "The Role of Fear (Bhaya) in the Nikāyas and in the Abhidhamma." *Journal of Indian Philosophy* 40.5: 511–31.

Gnoli, Raniero, ed. 1977–78. *The Gilgit Manuscript of the Saṅghabhedavastu*. 2 vols. Rome: Istituto Italiano per il Medio ed Estremo Oriente.

Gombrich, Richard. 1971. "'Merit Transference' in Sinhalese Buddhism: A Case Study of the Interaction Between Doctrine and Practice." *History of Religions* 11: 203–19.

Gordon, Lewis R. 1995. *Bad Faith and Antiblack Racism*. Atlantic Highlands, NJ: Humanities Press.

Green, Philip Scott Ellis. 2007. "Female Imagery in the *Avadānaśataka*." MA thesis, University of Florida.

Griffiths, Paul J. 1994. *On Being Buddha: The Classical Doctrine of Buddhahood*. Delhi: Sri Satguru.

Grünwedel, Albert. 1920. *Alt-Kutscha: Archäologische und religionsgeschichtliche Forschungen an Tempera-Gemälden aus Buddhistischen Höhlen der ersten acht Jahrhunderte nach Christi Geburt*. Berlin: Otto Elsner, Veröffentlichungen der Preussischen Turfan-Expeditionen.

Hahn, Michael. 1992. "The Avadānaśataka and Its Affiliation." In *Proceedings of the XXXII International Congress for Asian and North African Studies, Hamburg 25th–30th August 1986*, edited by Albrecht Wezler and Ernst Hammerschmidt, 170–71. Zeitschrift der Deutschen Morgenländischen Gesellschaft 9. Stuttgart: F. Steiner.

Hallisey, Charles. 1988. "Review of *Divine Revelation in Pali Buddhism*, by Peter Masefield." *The Journal of the International Association of Buddhist Studies* 11.1: 173–75.

Hardy, Edmund, ed. 1894. *Dhammapāla's Paramatthadīpanī: Part 3, Being the Commentary on the Petavatthu.* London: Pali Text Society.

Harrison, Paul. 1987. "À propos Peter Masefield's 'Divine Revelation in Pali Buddhism' by Peter Masefield." *Numen* 34.2: 256–64.

Hartmann, Jens-Uwe. 1985. "Zur Frage der Schulzugehörigkeit des Avadānaśataka." *Zur Schulzugehörigkeit von Werken der Hīnayāna-Literatur*, edited Heinz Bechert, 1:219–24. Symposien zur Buddhismusforschung 3.1. Göttingen: Vandenhoeck and Ruprecht.

Harvey, David. 2005. *A Brief History of Neoliberalism.* New York: Oxford University Press.

Heitzman, James. 2009. "The Urban Context of Early Buddhist Monuments in South Asia." In *Buddhist Stūpas in South Asia: Recent Archaeological, Art-Historical, and Historical Perspectives,* edited by Jason Hawkes and Akira Shimada, 192–215. Delhi: Oxford University Press.

Herrmann-Pfandt, Adelheid. 2018. *The Copper-Coloured Palace: Iconography of the rÑiṅ ma School of Tibetan Buddhism.* 3 vols. Delhi: Agam Kala Prakashan.

Hiltebeitel, Alf. 2010. *Dharma.* Honolulu: University of Hawai'i Press.

———. 2011. *Dharma: Its Early History in Law, Religion, and Narrative.* Oxford: Oxford University Press.

Hiraoka, Satoshi. 1991. "The Idea of Confession in the *Divyāvadāna.*" *Journal of Indian and Buddhist Studies* 40.1: 507–12.

———. 2009. "Text Critical Remarks on the *Divyāvadāna* (1)." *Sōka Daigaku Kokusai Bukkyōgaku Kōtō Kenkyūjo Nenpō* (*Annual Report of the International Research Institute for Advanced Buddhology at Soka University*) 12: 29–72.

Holt, J. C. 1981. "Assisting the Dead by Venerating the Living: Merit Transfer in the Early Buddhist Tradition." *Numen* 28: 1–28.

Horner, I. B., trans. 1969 (1963). *Milinda's Questions* (*Milindapañha*). 2 vols. London: Pali Text Society.

Hu-von Hinüber, Haiyan. 1991. "Das Anschlagen der Gaṇḍī in buddhistischen Klöstern: Über einige einschlägige Vinaya-Termini." In *Papers in Honour of Prof. Dr. Ji Xianlin on the Occasion of His 80th Birthday*, edited by Li Zheng and Jiang Zhongxin, 2:737–68. Beijing: Peking University Press.

Human Rights Watch. 2014. *Cleaning Human Waste: "Manual Scavenging," Caste, and Discrimination in India*. Available at: www.hrw.org/report/2014/08/25/cleaning-human-waste/manual-scavenging-caste-and-discrimination-india.

Huntington, C. W., Jr. 2021. *What I Don't Know About Death: Reflections on Buddhism, Literature, and Philosophy*. Somerville, MA: Wisdom Publications.

Huntington, Eric. 2019. *Creating the Universe: Depictions of the Cosmos in Himalayan Buddhism*. Seattle: University of Washington Press.

Itivuttaka

Edition. See Windisch 1975.

Translation. See Masefield 2000.

Iwamatsu, Asao. 2001. "Karōshutī bunjo daiban 511 ni tsuite (1)" (On Text 511 of the Kharoṣṭhī Inscriptions, Part 1). *Jinbun-Ronshū* (*Studies in the Humanities*) 13: 157–91.

James, Aaron. 2012. *Assholes: A Theory*. New York: Doubleday.

Jamspal, Lozang, and Kaia Tara Fischer, trans. 2020. *The Hundred Deeds* (*Karmaśataka*). See read.84000.co/translation/toh340.html.

Jayawickrama, N. A., ed. 1977. *Vimānavatthu and Petavatthu*. London: Pali Text Society.

Jones, J. J. 1949–56. *The Mahāvastu*. 3 vols. London: Luzac and Company.

Kachru, Sonam. 2015. "Minds and Worlds: A Philosophical Commentary on the Twenty Verses of Vasubandhu." PhD dissertation, University of Chicago.

Kane, Pandurang Vaman. 1953. *History of Dharmaśāstra*, vol. 4. Poona: Bhandarkar Oriental Research Institute.

Kapuscinski, Ryszard. 1983. *The Emperor: Downfall of an Autocrat*. Translated by Willam R. Brand and Katarzyna Mroczkowska-Brand. San Diego: Harcourt Brace Jovanovich.

Karashima, Seishi. 2013. "The Meaning of *Yulanpen*—'Rice Bowl' on *Pravāraṇā* Day." *Annual Report of The International Research Institute of Advanced Buddhology at Soka University* 16: 289–305.

Karashima, Seishi, and Margarita I. Vorobyova-Desyatovskaya. 2015. "The Avadāna Anthology from Merv, Turkmenistan." In *Buddhist Manuscripts from Central Asia: The St. Petersburg Sanskrit Fragments*, 1:145–524. Tokyo: The Institute of Oriental Manuscripts of the Russian Academy of Sciences & The International Research Institute for Advanced Buddhology, Soka University.

Karashima, Seishi, and Oskar von Hinüber. 2012. *Die Abhisamācārikā Dharmāḥ: Verhaltensregeln für buddhistische Mönche der Mahāsāṃghika-Lokottaravādins*. 3 vols. Tokyo: International Research Institute for Advanced Buddhology, Soka University.

Karmay, Gyeltsen. 1998. *The Little Luminous Boy: The Oral Tradition from the Land of Zhangzhung Depicted on Two Tibetan Paintings*. Bangkok: Orchid Press.

Khurana, Indira, Toolika Ojha, and Bhasha Singh. 2009. *Burden of Inheritance: Can We Stop Manual Scavenging? Yes, But First We Need to Accept It Exists*. New Delhi: WaterAid India.

Kishino, Ryōji. 2016. "Further Study of the *Muktaka* of the Mūlasarvāstivāda-vinaya: A Table of Contents and Parallels." *Bulletin of the Association of Buddhist Studies* (Bukkyō University) 21: 227–83.

Kitsudō, Kōichi, and Arakawa Shintarō. 2018. "Kanjin jippōkai zu o meguru shin kenkyū: Seika to Uiguru no jirei o chūshin ni" [New Research on the *Guanxin Shifajietu* (Illustration of the Ten Realms of Mind Contemplation): The Case of the Xixia and Uyghur Kingdoms]. *Kokka* 477: 5–20.

Knipe, David. 1977. "Sapiṇḍīkaraṇa: The Hindu Rite of Entry into Heaven." In *Religious Encounters with Death*, edited by F. E. Reynolds and E. H. Waugh, 111–24. University Park: The Pennsylvania State University Press.

Krishan, Yuvraj. 1997. *The Doctrine of Karma: Its Origin and Development in Brāhmaṇical, Buddhist and Jaina Traditions*. Delhi: Motilal Banarsidass.

Kristeva, Julia. 1982. *Powers of Horror: An Essay on Abjection*. Translated by Leon S. Roudiez. New York: Columbia University Press.

Kundera, Milan. 1984. *The Unbearable Lightness of Being*. Translated by Michael Henry Heim. New York: Harper and Row.

Kuttner, Robert. 1999. *Everything for Sale: The Virtues and Limits of Markets*. Chicago: University of Chicago Press.

Kyaw Khine, U. 1999. *The Dhammasaṅganī: Enumeration of the Ultimate Realities*. 2 vols. Delhi: Sri Satguru Publications.

Ladwig, Patrice. 2012. "Feeding the Dead: Ghosts, Materiality and Merit in a Lao Buddhist Festival for the Deceased." In *Buddhist Funeral Cultures of Southeast Asia and China*, edited by Paul Williams and Patrice Ladwig, 119–41. Cambridge: Cambridge University Press.

LaFleur, William. R. 1989. "Hungry Ghosts and Hungry People: Somaticity and Rationality in Medieval Japan." In *Fragments for a History of the Human Body*, edited by Michael Feher, 270–303. New York: Zone Publications.

Langenberg, Amy Paris. 2013. "Pregnant Words: South Asian Buddhist Tales of Fertility and Child Protection." *History of Religions* 52.4: 340–69.

Langer, Rita. 2007. *Buddhist Rituals of Death and Rebirth: Contemporary Sri Lankan Practice and Its Origins*. New York: Routledge.

Le Goff, Jacques. 1984. *The Birth of Purgatory*. Translated by Arthur Goldhammer. Chicago: University of Chicago Press.

Lewis, Michael. 2010 (1986). *Liar's Poker: Rising Through the Wreckage on Wall Street*. 25th Anniversary Edition. New York: W. W. Norton and Company.

Lin, Meicun. 1996. "Kharoṣṭhī Bibliography: The Collections from China (1897–1993)." *Central Asiatic Journal* 40.2: 188–220.

Lüders, Heinrich. 1912. *List of Brahmi Inscriptions from the Earliest Times to about A.D. 400 with the Exception of Those of Aśoka*. Edited by Sten Konow. Appendix to Epigraphia Indica 10. Calcutta: Superintendent Government Printing.

Lye, Hun Yeow. 2003. "Feeding Ghosts: A Study of the *Yuqie Yankou* Rite." PhD dissertation, University of Virginia.

Mael, Fred, and Blake E. Ashforth. 1992. "Alumni and the Alma Mater: A Partial Test of the Reformulated Model of Organizational Identification." *Journal of Organizational Behavior* 13: 103–23.

Mahāvastu.

Edition. See Senart 1977.

Translation. See Jones 1949–56.

Malalasekera, G. P. 1995 (1938). *Dictionary of Pali Proper Names*. 2 vols. New Delhi: Munshiram Manoharlal Publishers.

Mandal, Ram Bahadur. 2010. *Wetlands Management in North Bihar*. New Delhi: Concept Publishing Company.

Masefield, Peter. 1986. *Divine Revelation in Pali Buddhism*. London: George Allen and Unwin, 1986.

———, trans. 2000. *The Itivuttaka*. Oxford: Pali Text Society.

May, San San, and Jana Igunma. 2018. *Buddhism Illuminated: Manuscript Art from South-East Asia*. Seattle: University of Washington Press.

Meisig, Marion. 2004. *Ursprünge buddhistischer Heiligenlegenden: Untersuchungen zur Redaktionsgeschichte des Chuan tsih pêh yuän king*. Forschungen zur Anthropologie und Religionsgeschichte 38. Münster: Ugarit-Verlag.

Merh, Kusum P. 1996. *Yama: The Glorious Lord of the Other World*. Reconstructing Indian History and Culture 12. New Delhi: D. K. Printworld.

Merriam-Webster's Collegiate Dictionary. 2003. 11th ed. Springfield, MA: Merriam-Webster, Inc.

Merton, Thomas. 1948. *The Seven Story Mountain*. New York: Harcourt Brace.

Meyer, Matthew. 2015. *The House of Evil Spirits: An Encylopedia of Mononoke and Magic*. Self-published.

Milindapañha.

Edition. See Trenckner 1880.

Translation. See Horner 1969.

Mimaki, Katsumi 2000. "A Preliminary Comparison of Bonpo and Buddhist Cosmology." In *New Horizons in Bon Studies*, edited by Samten G. Karmay and Yasuhiko Nagano, 89–115. Bon Studies 2. Osaka: National Museum of Ethnology.

Misra, Ram Nath. 1981. *Yaksha Cult and Iconography*. New Delhi: Munshiram Manoharlal.

Mitter, Partha. 1977. *Much Maligned Monsters: A History of European Reactions to Indian Art*. Oxford: Clarendon Press.

Monier-Williams, Monier. 1990 (1899). *A Sanskrit-English Dictionary*. Delhi: Motilal Banarsidass Publishers.

Moretti, Constantino. 2017. "The Thirty-Six Categories of 'Hungry Ghosts' Described in the *Sūtra of the Foundations of Mindfulness of the True Law*." In *Fantômes dans l'Extrême-Orient d'hier et d'aujourd'hui*, edited by Marie Laureillard and Vincent Durand-Dastès, 1:43–69. Paris: Inalco.

Moriyasu, Takao. 2008. "Chronology of West Uighur Buddhism: Re-examination of the Dating of the Wall-Paintings in Grünwedel's Cave No. 8 (New: No. 18), Bezeklik." In *Aspects of Research into Central Asian Buddhism: In Memoriam Kōgi Kudara*, edited by Peter Zieme, 191–227. Turnhout: Brepols.

Mrozik, Susanne. 2006. "Materializations of Virtue: Buddhist Discourses on Bodies." In *Bodily Citations: Religion and Judith Butler*, edited by Ellen T. Armour and Susan M. St. Ville, 15–47. New York: Columbia University Press.

Mukhopadhyay, S. 1981. "Sucimukha, the Needle-Mouthed Denizen." *Journal of the Asiatic Society* 23: 57–62.

Muldoon-Hules, Karen. 2017. *Brides of the Buddha: Nuns' Stories from the* Avadānaśataka. Lanham, MD: Lexington Books.

Müller, Edward, ed. 1885. *The Dhammasaṅgaṇī*. London: H. Frowde (for the Pali Text Society).

———, ed. 1897. *The Atthasālinī: Buddhaghosa's Commentary on the Dhammasaṅgaṇī*. London: Pali Text Society.

Mus, P. 1939. *La Lumière sur les Six Voies: Tableau de la transmigration bouddhique d'après des sources sanskrites, pāli, tibétaines et chinoises en majeure partie inédites*. Paris: Institut d'Ethnologie.

Ñāṇamoli, Bhikkhu, trans. 1979. *The Path of Purification* (*Visuddhimagga*). Kandy, Sri Lanka: Buddhist Publication Society.

Ñāṇamoli, Bhikkhu, and Bhikkhu Bodhi, trans. 1995. *The Middle-Length Discourses of the Buddha: A New Translation of the Majjhima Nikāya*. Boston: Wisdom Publications.

Nebesky-Wojkowitz, Réne de. 1996 (1956). *Oracles and Demons of Tibet: The Cult and Iconography of Tibetan Protective Deities*. Kathmandu: Book Faith India.

Neelis, Jason. 2011. *Early Buddhist Transmission and Trade Networks Mobility and Exchange within and beyond the Northwestern Borderlands of South Asia*. Leiden: Brill.

Norman, H. C., ed. 1906–14. *Dhammapada-aṭṭhakathā*. London: Pali Text Society.

Norman, K. R., trans. 1995. *The Elder's Verses*. 2 vols. Oxford: Pali Text Society.

Nyi, U. 2010. *Practical Aspects of Buddhist Ideals: From Kokyint Abhidhamma in Myanmar by Ashin Janakābhivamsa of Mahagandhayon Monastery*. Central Milton Keynes, UK: AuthorHouse.

O'Connor, Flannery. 1955. *A Good Man Is Hard to Find and Other Stories*. New York: Harcourt, Brace and Company.

Ohnuma, Reiko. 2007. "Mother-Love and Mother-Grief: South Asian Buddhist Variations on a Theme." *Journal of Feminist Studies in Religion* 23.1: 95–116.

Okada, Mamiko. 1993. *Dvāviṃśatyavadānakathā: Ein mittelalterlicher buddhistische Text zur Spendenfrömmigkeit*. Indica et Tibetica 24. Bonn: Indica et Tibetica Verlag.

Oldenberg, H., and R. Pischel, eds. 1966. *Theragāthā* and *Therīgāthā*. 2nd ed. London: Pali Text Society.

Olivelle, Patrick. 1992. *Samnyasa Upanisads: Hindu Scriptures on Asceticism and Renunciation*. New York: Oxford University Press, 1992.

———. 1998. "Caste and Purity: A Study in the Language of the Dharma Literature." *Contributions to Indian Sociology* 32.2: 189–216.

———, trans. 1999. *Dharmasūtras: The Law Codes of Āpastamba, Gautama, Baudhāyana, and Vasiṣṭha*. New York: Oxford University Press.

———, ed. and trans. 2008. *The Life of Buddha by Aśvaghoṣa*. New York: New York University Press & JJC Foundation.

———. 2011. "The Living and the Dead: Ideology and Social Dynamics of Ancestral." In *The Anthropologist and the Native: Essays for Gananath Obeyesekere*, edited by H. L. Seneviratne, 65–73. London: Anthem Press.

———. 2012. "Aśoka's Inscriptions as Text and Ideology." In *Reimagining Aśoka: Memory and History*, edited by Patrick Olivelle, Janice Leoshko, and Himanshu Prabha Ray, 157–83. New Delhi: Oxford University Press.

Orzech, Charles D. 1996. "Saving the Burning-Mouth Hungry Ghost." In *Religions of China in Practice*, edited by Donald S. Lopez Jr., 278–83. Princeton: Princeton University Press.

Oxford English Dictionary. 1989. 2nd ed. 20 vols. Oxford: Oxford University Press.

Pakdeekham, Santi, ed. 2563 (2020). *Samut phra malai khamphi boran lae ekkasan boran wat mani sathit kapittharam phra aram luang amphoe mueang changwat uthai thani*. Bangkok: Fragile Palm Leaves Foundation and Amarin Publishing Services.

Panikkar, Raimundo. 1982. "Is the Notion of Human Rights a Western Concept?" *Diogenes* 30.20: 75–102.

Parry, Jonathan. 1994. *Death in Banaras*. Cambridge: Cambridge University Press.

Payutto, Phra Prayudh. 1994. *Buddhist Economics: A Middle Way for the Market Place*. 2nd ed., revised and enlarged. Bangkok: Buddhadhamma Foundation.

Peri, Noel. 1917. "Hāritī, la mère de démons." *Bulletin de l'École Française d'Extrême-Orient* 17.3: 1–102.

Petavatthu.

Edition. See Jayawickrama 1977.

Translation. See Gehman 1974 and Ba Kyaw and Masefield 1980.

Petavatthu-aṭṭhakathā

Edition. See Hardy 1894.

Translation. See Ba Kyaw and Masefield 1980.

Phatsakon. 2455 (1912). *Phra tham chet khamphi yo lae samut malai*. Bangkok: Rong phim pamrung nukun kit.

Philips, Adam, and Barbara Taylor. 2010. *On Kindness*. New York: Farrar, Strauss, and Giroux.

Pinney, Christopher. 2004. *"Photos of the Gods": The Printed Image and the Political Struggle in India*. London: Reaktion Books.

———. 2018. *Lessons from Hell: Printing and Punishment in India*. Mumbai: The Marg Foundation.

Pollock, Sheldon. 2016. *A Rasa Reader: Classical Indian Aesthetics*. New York: Columbia University Press.

Pradhan, Prahlad, ed. 1975. *Abhidharmakośabhāṣyam of Vasubandhu*. Rev. 2nd ed. Patna: K. P. Jayaswal Research Institute.

Przyluski, Jean. 1918. "Le parinirvāṇa et les funérailles du Buddha." *Journal Asiatique* 11: 485–526.

Ramāyaṇa. Critically edited by G. H. Bhatt et al. 7 vols. Baroda: Oriental Institute, University of Baroda, 1960–75.

Rand, Ayn. 1996 (1957). *Atlas Shrugged*. New York: Penguin Books.

Raschmann, Simone-Christiane. 2020. "Pilgrims in Old Uyghur Inscriptions: A Glimpse behind Their Records." In *Buddhism in Central Asia I: Patronage, Legitimation, Sacred Space, and Pilgrimage*, edited by Carmen Meinert and Henrik Sørensen, 204–29. Leiden: Brill.

Rhys Davids, C. A. F., trans. 1900. *A Buddhist Manual of Psychological Ethics*. London: Pali Text Society.

Rhys Davids, T. W., and J. E. Carpenter, eds. 1886. *The Sumaṅgala-vilāsanī, Buddhaghosa's Commentary on the Dīgha Nikāya*. 3 vols. London: Pali Text Society.

———, eds. 1890–1911. *Dīgha-nikāya*. 3 vols. London: Pali Text Society.

Rhys Davids, T. W., and Wilhelm Stede. 1986 (1921–25). *The Pali Text Society's Pali-English Dictionary*. London: Pali Text Society.

Rigzin, Tsepak. 1997. *The Tibetan-English Dictionary of Buddhist Terminology*. Revised and enlarged edition. Dharamsala: Library of Tibetan Works and Archives.

Robinson, Laurie O., and Jeff Slowikowsi. 2011. "Scary—and Ineffective." *Baltimore Sun*, January 11.

Rotman, Andy. 2003. "The Erotics of Practice: Objects and Agency in Buddhist Avadāna Literature." *Journal of the American Academy of Religion* 71.3: 555–78.

———, trans. 2008. *Divine Stories: The Divyāvadāna, part 1*. Classics of Indian Buddhism, inaugural volume. Boston: Wisdom Publications.

———. 2009. *Thus Have I Seen: Visualizing Faith in Early Indian Buddhism.* New York: Oxford University Press.

———, trans. 2017. *Divine Stories: The Divyāvadāna, part 2.* Classics of Indian Buddhism. Somerville, MA: Wisdom Publications.

Rowan, J. G. 2002. "Danger and Devotion: Hariti, Mother of Demons in the Stories and Stones of Gandhara: A Histography and Catalogue of Images." MA Thesis, University of Oregon.

Russell-Smith, Lilla. 2005. *Uygur Patronage in Dunhuang: Regional Art Centres on the Northern Silk Road in the Tenth and Eleventh Centuries.* Leiden and Boston: Brill.

Ṣaḍgatikārikā.
Edition and translation. See Mus 1939.

Saṃyutta-nikāya.
Edition. See Féer 1884–98.
Translation. See Bodhi 2000.

Saṅghabhedavastu.
Edition. See Gnoli 1977–78.

Santos, Boaventura de Sousa. 2002. "Toward a Multicultural Conception of Human Rights." In *Moral Imperialism: A Critical Anthology*, edited by Berta Esperanza Hernández-Truyol, 39–60. New York: New York University Press.

Sartre, Jean-Paul. 1966 (1949). *Being and Nothingness.* Translated by Hazel Barnes. New York: Pocket Books.

Sayadaw, Mahāsi. 2016. *Manual of Insight.* Translated by Vipassanā Mettā Foundation Translation Committee. Boston: Wisdom Publications.

Sayers, Matthew R. 2013. *Feeding the Dead: Ancestor Worship in Ancient India.* New York: Oxford University Press.

Scheible, Kristin. 2016. *Reading the* Mahāvaṃsa*: The Literary Aims of a Theravāda Buddhist History.* New York: Columbia University Press.

Scherman, Lucian. 1892. *Materialien zur Geschichte der Indischen Visionslitteratur.* Leipzig: Verlag von A. Twietmeyer.

Schmithausen, Lambert. 1986. "Critical Response." In *Karma and Rebirth: Post Classical Developments*, edited by Ronald W. Neufeldt, 203–30. Albany: State University of New York Press.

———. 1997. *Maitrī and Magic: Aspects of the Buddhist Attitude Toward the Dangerous in Nature.* Vienna: Österreichische Akademie der Wissenschaften.

Schopen, Gregory. 1992. "On Avoiding Ghosts and Social Censure: Monastic Funerals in the Mūlasarvāstivāda-Vinaya." *Journal of Indian Philosophy* 20: 1–39.

———. 1995. "Death, Funerals, and the Division of Property in a Monastic Code." In *Buddhism in Practice,* edited by Donald S. Lopez Jr., 473–502. Princeton: Princeton University Press. Reprinted in Schopen 2004, 91–121.

———. 2000. "Hierarchy and Housing in a Buddhist Monastic Code: A Translation of the Sanskrit Text of the *Śāyanavastu* of the *Mūlasarvāstivāda-Vinaya*—Part One [from the Sanskrit]." *Buddhist Literature* 2: 96–196.

———. 2004. *Buddhist Monks and Business Matters: Still More Papers on Monastic Buddhism in India.* Honolulu: University of Hawai'i Press.

———. 2005. *Figments and Fragments of Mahāyāna Buddhism in India.* Honolulu: University of Hawai'i Press.

———. 2009. "On Emptying Chamber Pots without Looking and the Urban Location of Buddhist Nunneries in Early India Again." *Journal Asiatique* 292.2: 229–56.

———. 2014. *Buddhist Nuns, Monks, and Other Worldly Matters: Recent Papers on Monastic Buddhism in India.* Honolulu: University of Hawai'i Press.

Senart, Emile, ed. 1977 (1882–97). *Le Mahāvastu: Texte sanscrit publié, pour la première fois et accompagné d'introductions et d'un commentaire.* 3 vols. Tokyo: Meicho-Fukyu-Kai.

Shastri, Dakshina Ranjan. 1963. *Origin and Development of the Rituals of Ancestor Worship in India.* Calcutta: Bookland.

Shirkey, Jeffrey C. 2008. "The Moral Economy of the Petavatthu: Hungry Ghosts and Theravāda Buddhist Cosmology." PhD dissertation, University of Chicago.

Siklós, Bulcsu. 1996. "The Evolution of the Buddhist Yama." In *The Buddhist Forum,* vol. 4, edited by Tadeusz Skorupski, 165–89. London: School of Oriental and African Studies.

Śikṣāsamuccaya of Śāntideva.
Edition. See Bendall 1897–1902.
Translation. See Bendall and Rouse 1971.

Silk, Jonathan. 2008. *Managing Monks: Administrators and Administrative Roles in Indian Buddhist Monasticism.* New York: Oxford University Press.

Singh, Rajeev Kumar. 2009. "Manual Scavenging as Social Exclusion: A Case Study." *Economic and Political Weekly* 44.26/27: 521–23.

Sinha, Ajay. 2007. "Visual Culture and the Politics of Locality in Modern India: A Review Essay." *Modern Asian Studies* 41.1: 187–220.

Sircar, Dineschandra. 1966. *Indian Epigraphical Glossary*. Delhi: Motilal Banarsidass.

Sobkovyak, Ekaterina. 2015. "Religious History of the Gaṇḍī Beam: Testimonies of Texts, Images and Ritual Practices." *Asiatische Studien—Études Asiatiques* 69.3: 685–722.

Speyer, J. S. 1902–9. *Avadānaśataka: A Century of Edifying Tales Belonging to the Hīnayāna*. 2 vols. Bibliotheca Buddhica 3. St. Petersbourg: Commissionnaires de l'Académie Impériale des Sciences.

Srivastava, B. N. 1997. *Manual Scavenging in India: A Disgrace to the Country*. New Delhi: Concept Publishing Company.

Staël-Holstein, Alexander von. 1926. *The Kāśyapaparivarta: A Mahāyānasūtra of the Ratnakūṭa Class Edited in the Original Sanskrit in Tibetan and in Chinese*. Shanghai: Commercial Press.

Stede, Wilhelm. 1914. *Die Gespenstergesgeschichten des Petavatthu: Untersuchungen, Ubersetzung und Pali-Glossar*. Leipzig: Otto Harrassowitz.

Strong, John S. 1979. "The Transforming Gift: An Analysis of Devotional Acts of Offering in Buddhist Avadāna Literature." *History of Religions* 18: 221–37.

Stevenson, Daniel. 1999. "Protocols of Power: Tz'u-yün Tsun-shih (964–1032) and T'ien-t'ai Lay Buddhist Ritual in the Sung." In *Buddhism in Sung Dynasty China,* edited by Peter N. Gregory and Daniel A. Getz Jr., 340–408. Honolulu: University of Hawai'i Press.

———. 2001. "Text, Image, and Transformation in the History of the *Shuilu fahui*, the Buddhist Rite for Deliverance of Creatures of Water and Land." In *Cultural Intersections in Later Chinese Buddhism*, edited by Marsha Weidner, 30–70. Honolulu: University of Hawai'i Press.

———. 2004. "Feeding Hungry Ghosts." In *Buddhist Scriptures*, edited by Donald S. Lopez Jr., 416–22. London: Penguin Books.

———. 2015. "Buddhist Ritual in the Song." In *Modern Chinese Religion I: Song-Liao-Jin-Yuan (960–1368 AD)*, edited by John Lagerwey and Pierre Marsone, 328–448. Leiden and Boston: Brill.

Stuart, Daniel Malinowski. 2012. "A Less Traveled Path: Meditation and Textual Practice in the *Saddharmasmṛtyupasthāna(sūtra)*." PhD dissertation, University of California–Berkeley.

Sukthankar, Vishnu S., et al., eds. 1933–59. *Mahābhārata*. 19 vols. Pune: Bhandarkar Institute.

Sumaṅgala-vilāsanī of Buddhaghosa.
Edition. See Rhys Davids and Carpenter 1886.
Translation. See Bodhi 1978.

Summers, Robert S. 1968. "'Good Faith' in General Contract Law and the Sales Provisions of the Uniform Commercial." *Virginia Law Review* 54.2: 195–267.

Takahata, Kanga. 1954. *Ratnamālāvadāna: A Garland of Precious Gems or a Collection of Edifying Tales, Told in a Metrical Form, Belonging to the Mahāyāna*. Tokyo: Toyo Bunko.

Teiser, Stephen F. 1988. *The Ghost Festival in Medieval China*. Princeton: Princeton University Press.

———. 2006. *Reinventing the Wheel: Paintings of Rebirth in Medieval Buddhist Temples*. Seattle: University of Washington Press.

Theragāthā.
Edition. See Oldenberg and Pischel 1966.
Translation. See Norman 1995.

Theragāthā-aṭṭhakathā [= *Paramatthadīpanī*, vol. 5].
Edition. See Woodward 1977.

Thurman, Robert, trans. 1983 (1976). *The Holy Teaching of Vimalakīrti: A Mahāyāna Scripture*. University Park and London: The Pennsylvania State University Press.

Tin, Maung, and C. A. F. Rhys Davids. 1920. *The Expositor (Atthasālinī): Buddhaghosa's Commentary on the Dhammasangani, the First Book of the Abhidhamma Piṭaka*. London: Pali Text Society.

Trenckner, Vilhelm, ed. 1880. *Milindapañha*. London: Pali Text Society.

Trenckner, Vilhelm, et al. 1924–. *A Critical Pali Dictionary*. Copenhagen, Commissioner: Munksgaard.

Tripāṭhī, Chandrabhāl, ed. 1995. *Ekottarāgama-Fragmente der Gilgit-Handschrift*. Reinbek: Verlag für Orientalistische Fachpublikationen.

Tsai, Chun-Yi Joyce. 2015. "Imagining the Supernatural Grotesque: Paintings of Zhong Kui and Demons in the Late Southern Song (1127–1279) and Yuan (1271–1368) Dynasties." PhD dissertation, Columbia University.

Vaidya, P. L., ed. 1958. *Avadānaśataka*. Buddhist Sanskrit Texts 19. Darbhanga: The Mithila Institute of Post-Graduate Studies and Research in Sanskrit Learning.

Valeri, Mark. 1991. "The Economic Thought of Jonathan Edwards." *Church History* 60.1: 37–54.

van Buitenen, J. A. B., trans. 1975. *The Mahābhārata*, vol. 2 (Book 2: The Book of Assembly; Book 3: The Book of the Forest). Chicago: University of Chicago Press.

Vaudeville, Charlotte. 1964. "La légende de Sundara et les funérailles du Buddha dans l'Avadānaśataka." *Bulletin de l'École française d'Extrême-Orient* 52.1: 73–91.

Vijayajinendrasūrīśvarajī and Prītamalāla Harilāla Trivedī. 1984. *Nārakī Citrāvalī* ["Pictures of Hell"]. Lākhābāvala-Śāntipurī, Saurāṣṭra: Śrī Harṣapuṣpāmṛta Jaina Granthamālā.

Vira, Raghu, and Lokesh Chandra. 1995. *Gilgit Buddhist Manuscripts*. Revised and enlarged compact facsmile edition. Biblica Indo-Buddhica Series 150–52. Delhi: Sri Satguru.

Visuddhimagga of Buddhaghosa.

Edition. See Warren 1950.

Translation. See Ñāṇamoli 1979.

Vogel, Claus, and Klaus Wille. 1996. "The Final Leaves of the Pravrajyāvastu Portion of the Vinayavastu Manuscript Found Near Gilgit: Part 1, Saṅgharakṣitāvadāna." In *Sanskrit-Texte aus dem buddhistischen Kanon: Neuentdeckungen und Neueditionen*, edited by G. Bongard-Levin et al., 3: 241–96. Göttingen: Vandenhoeck and Ruprecht.

Waddell, L. Austine. 1895. *The Buddhism of Tibet or Lamaism*. London: W. H. Allen & Co.

Waldschmidt, Ernst. 1948. *Die Überlieferung vom Lebensende des Buddha, Eine vergleichende Analyse des Mahāparinirvāṇasūtra und seiner Textentsprechungen*, vol. 2: *Vorgangsgruppe V–VI*. Abhandlungen der Akademie der Wissenschaften in Göttingen, Philosophisch-historische Klasse, Dritte Folge 30. Göttingen: Vandenhoeck and Ruprecht.

———. 1967. "Zur Śroṇakoṭikarṇa-Legende." In *Vom Ceylon bis Turfan: Schriften zur Geschichte, Literatur, Religion und Kunst des indischen Kulturraumes*, 203–25. Göttingen: Vandenhoek and Ruprecht.

Walker, Trent. 2018. "*Saṃvega* and *Pasāda*: Dharma Songs in Contemporary Cambodia." *Journal of the International Association of Buddhist Studies* 41: 271–325.

Walshe, Maurice, trans. 1995 (1987). *The Long Discourses of the Buddha: A Translation of the Dīgha Nikāya*. Boston: Wisdom Publications.

Warren, H. C., ed. 1950. *Visuddhimagga*. Revised by Dharmananda Kosambi. Cambridge, MA: Harvard University Press.

Webster's Revised Unabridged Dictionary of the English Language. 1913. Springfield, MA: G. & C. Merriam Company.

White, David Gordon. 1986. "'Dakkhiṇa' and 'Agnicayana': An Extended Application of Paul Mus's Typology." *History of Religions* 26.2: 188–213.

Wijayaratne, Mohan. 1990. *Buddhist Monastic Life: According to the Texts of the Theravāda Tradition*. Translated by Claude Grangier and Steven Collins. Cambridge: Cambridge University Press.

Wijeratne, R. P., and Rupert Gethin, trans. 2002. *Summary of the Topics* and *Exposition of the Topics of Abhidhamma*. Oxford: The Pali Text Society.

Windisch, E., ed. 1975 (1889). *Itivuttaka*. London: Pali Text Society.

Wood, Allen W. 1988. "Self-Deception and Bad Faith." In *Perspectives on Self-Deception*, edited by Brian P. McLaughlin and Amélie Oksenberg Rorty, 207–27. Berkeley: University of California Press.

Woodward, F. L., ed. 1977. *Paramatthadīpanī*. 5 vols. London: Pali Text Society.

Wu Hung. 1992. "What Is Bianxiang? On the Relationship between Dunhuang Art and Dunhuang Literature." *Harvard Journal of Asiatic Studies* 52.1: 111–92.

Yamagiwa, Nobuyuki. 1992. "Konpon setsuissaiubu Kendobu no kenkyū (3): Pāṇḍulohitakavastu to Avadānaśataka no kankei." *Journal of Indian and Buddhist Studies* (*Indogaku Bukkyōgaku Kenkyū*) 40.2: 950–55.

———. 2001. *Das Pāṇḍulohitakavastu: Über die verschiedenen Verfahrensweisen der Bestrafung in der buddhistischen Gemeinde, Neuausgabe der Sanskrit-Handschrift aus Gilgit, tibetischer Text und deutsche Übersetzung*. Indica et Tibetica 41. Marburg: Indica et Tibetica.

Yifa. 2002. *The Origins of Buddhist Monastic Codes in China: An Annotated Translation and Study of the Chanyuan qinggui*. Honolulu: University of Hawai'i Press.

Zin, Monika. 2014. "Imagery of Hell in South, South East and Central Asia." *Rocznik Orientalistyczny* 67: 269–96.

Zin, Monika, and Dieter Schlingloff. 2007. *Saṃsāracakra, Das Rad der Wiedergeburten in der indischen Überlieferung*. Düsseldorf: Haus der Japanischen Kultur.

Index

N

O

About the Author

Andy Rotman is a professor of Religion, Buddhism, and South Asian Studies at Smith College. His publications include *Divine Stories: Divyāvadāna, Part 1* and *Part 2* (Wisdom Publications, 2008 and 2017), *Thus Have I Seen: Visualizing Faith in Early Indian Buddhism* (Oxford University Press, 2009), and a coauthored volume, *Amar Akbar Anthony: Bollywood, Brotherhood, and the Nation* (Harvard University Press, 2015). He has been engaged in textual and ethnographic work on religious and social life in South Asia for more than twenty-five years.

What to Read Next from Wisdom Publications

Divine Stories
Divyāvadāna, Part 1
Andy Rotman

"These stories are to the Buddhist tradition what the *Arabian Nights* is to the Arabic, an ocean of stories from which Buddhist storytellers and artists throughout Asia drew their inspiration. The translation—precise, elegant, vernacular—flows clear as water in a mountain stream."—Wendy Doniger, Mircea Eliade Distinguished Service Professor of the History of Religions, University of Chicago

Divine Stories
Divyāvadāna, Part 2
Andy Rotman

"The Buddha was a skillful and inveterate storyteller who understood the enduring power of narrative to entertain, engage, and enlighten. In his beautiful translation, Andy Rotman ensures the transmission of these divine and very human stories to a new generation of readers."
—Ruth Ozeki, author of *A Tale for the Time Being*

Awakening from the Daydream

Reimagining the Buddha's Wheel of Life

David Nichtern

"A wonderful extension of the powerful Dharma teachings of Chögyam Trungpa Rinpoche. The transmission of these ancient lineages is intact in David's hands as he continues to update the traditional Buddhist teachings and make them ever more accessible to the contemporary audience."—Ram Dass, author of *Be Here Now*

Buddhism

One Teacher, Many Traditions

His Holiness the Dalai Lama and Thubten Chodron

"This book will reward those who study it carefully with a deep and wide understanding of the way these traditions have mapped their respective visions of the path to enlightenment."—Bhikkhu Bodhi, translator of *In the Buddha's Words*

Maya

A Novel

C. W. Huntington Jr.

"I've been waiting for someone to write a contemporary 'quest for enlightenment' novel, but I didn't expect it to be this good."
—David R. Loy, author of *A New Buddhist Path*

Science and Philosophy in the Indian Buddhist Classics
Volume 1: The Physical World
Volume 2: The Mind
Conceived and introduced by His Holiness the Dalai Lama
Edited by Thupten Jinpa

"*Science and Philosophy in the Indian Buddhist Classics* offers a rare gift of wisdom from the ancient world to the modern reader. The editors have curated a rich treasure of the philosophy and maps of the mind that have their origins in the early centuries of Indian thought, were preserved in translation for centuries in Tibet, and now are brought to all of us in this translation."—Daniel Goleman, author of *Emotional Intelligence*

About Wisdom Publications

Wisdom Publications is the leading publisher of classic and contemporary Buddhist books and practical works on mindfulness. To learn more about us or to explore our other books, please visit our website at wisdomexperience.org or contact us at the address below.

Wisdom Publications
199 Elm Street
Somerville, MA 02144 USA

We are a 501(c)(3) organization, and donations in support of our mission are tax deductible.

Wisdom Publications is affiliated with the Foundation for the Preservation of the Mahayana Tradition (FPMT).